More Praise for  ~ ~ ~ ~ Dying

"*The Art of Dying* offers a candid h... all must face: death. Each of us m... how much less lonely and frighter... accompanied by normalcy, under... written for us all."

—Jinny Tesik, nationally certified grief counselor and director of the Grief & Loss Center, Seattle, Washington

"[An] important resource for people facing death as well as for health-care providers helping them to cope with end-of-life issues. I recommend it highly."

—Michael D. Evans, M.D., Group Health Cooperative, Seattle, Washington

"As one who has faced life-threatening illnesses on several occasions, I find *The Art of Dying* both comforting and inspiring. Dr. Weenolsen has transformed personal death from a terrifying prospect to a more manageable experience practically, and to an extraordinarily positive experience spiritually. As a therapist, I will recommend this book to patients who face the dying of who they are. It will help them immeasurably."

—Nancy Logan, M.A., CMHC, therapist, Bellevue, Washington

"A thoughtful, compassionate and inspiring handbook from which each and every one of us can derive some benefit....Weenolsen's wise counsel pertains to intentional living, no matter where you are in your life span, as well as to making a graceful exit....Weenolsen's approach is pragmatic, generous, and gently witty....A commendable job."

—*Tacoma News Tribune/The News Tribune*

"[This book] is essential. It is a noteworthy gift. It will bring a significant new awareness to the experience of dying, and with it, lots of awareness for those who walk with the dying and the bereaved....You **must** read this book."

—The Rev. Richard B. Gilbert, MDiv., FAAGC, CPBC/*Connections*

"Weenolsen probes the questions that many may be afraid to ask... offers reassurances and comfort."

—*Newark Star-Ledger*

"A reassuring yet sensitive approach to difficult subjects."

—*Library Journal*

ALSO BY PATRICIA WEENOLSEN

Transcendence of Loss over the Life Span

PATRICIA WEENOLSEN, PH.D.

THE ART OF DYING

*How to Leave This World with
Dignity and Grace, at Peace with
Yourself and Your Loved Ones*

ST. MARTIN'S GRIFFIN ❀ NEW YORK

NOTE TO THE READER: The case histories in this book are true. Unless otherwise indicated, however, the names and certain identifying details have been changed. In these changes, I have attempted to preserve the "truth" of the person and the central course of his or her story. A few of the cases are composites.

Design by SONGHEE KIM

Library of Congress Cataloging-in-Publication Data

Weenolsen, Patricia.
    The art of dying : how to leave this world with dignity and grace, at peace with yourself and your loved ones / by Patricia Weenolsen : foreword by Bernie Siegel. — 1st St. Martin's ed.
        p.   cm.
    Includes bibliographical references and index.
    ISBN 0-312-16776-8
    1. Death—Psychological aspects.   2. Terminally ill—Psychology.   3. Death.   4. Loss (Psychology)   I. Title.
BF789.D4W34   1996
155.9'37—dc20   96-1952
                                                                            CIP

First St. Martin's Griffin Edition: October 1997
10 9 8 7 6 5 4 3 2 1

Dying, like aging, isn't for sissies! This book is dedicated to all of you courageously facing your own death and the deaths of others—those of you who have shared your struggles and triumphs with me, those I have yet to meet, those I will never know. . . .

CONTENTS

ACKNOWLEDGMENTS

To the following colleagues, I submitted for critique a "perfect" partial or complete manuscript (their choice) of The Art of Dying. They returned a generously flawed one! I am grateful for their suggestions, most of which I followed: Michael Evans, M.D., physician for the Group Health Cooperative, Seattle; Glenn Gillen, communications coordinator for the National Hospice Organization, Arlington, Virginia; Rabbi Harold Kushner, Temple Israel, Natick, Massachusetts; Nancy Logan, M.A., therapist, Bellevue, Washington; Margo McCaffery, R.N., M.S., FAAN, pain specialist and consultant, Los Angeles; Bernie Siegel, M.D., Woodbridge, Connecticut; M. Brewster Smith, Ph.D., psychology professor emeritus, University of California at Santa Cruz; Jinny Tesik, M.A., director of the Grief and Loss Center, Seattle; and Hannelore Wass, Ph.D., author and editor in the field of death and dying, and psychology professor emeritus, University of Florida, Gainesville.

I also acknowledge my appreciation to the following for the information and other assistance they provided: Harriet A. Fields, E.D.,

R.N., consultant to the National Citizens' Coalition for Nursing
Home Reform; Melissa Marott Sirovina, Xerox Corporation, Sacra-
mento and Seattle; Pamela Marott Wellman, R.D., CNSD, Long
Beach Community Medical Center, Long Beach, California.

A book isn't born until it's sold, edited, and published. For the
selling I express thanks to my agent, Ted Chichak, whose faith in the
project kept it on track. For the editing and publishing, special
praise to senior editor Barbara Anderson, who kept the book afloat
with both support and superb, meticulous critique, a delicate balanc-
ing act in any editor, wonderfully accomplished by this one. The
book and I are fortunate to have her. I thank assistant editor Joy
Chang for her wise counsel and many kindnesses. Also thanks to
Meg Drislane, Linda Elliot, Elizabeth MacNamara, Gary Cate, Joan
Higgins, Charles Rue Woods, Jose Condé, and everyone else at St.
Martin's.

In any writing endeavor, it is friends and family who make all the
difference. For long years of loving support, I am grateful to many,
but especially to Valerie Marott, Jennifer Marott, Anne and Dr.
Stephen Gray (and little Sean), Dr. Patricia Sullivan and Ray
Miller, April and Howard Roseman, Mary Sikkema, Roberta Kehle,
Debbie Smith, Frank Mihm, Ron (and Beau) Wilder, and always the
University of California, Santa Cruz.

When I think of dedicated service I think of librarians! I have
watched you help students research their high school papers; baptize
new users of the Internet and Infotrac; magically reveal resources on
buying cars, cooking, selling homes, getting jobs, wedding plans, and
other practical lifestyle questions; and find esoteric information for
scholars—all with a welcome that makes each person feel important.
My gratitude particularly to Rae Bass, Judy Evans, and everyone else
at the Henry Branch of the Seattle Public Library; to the reference
librarians of the downtown library, and last, but not least, to Nancy
Pearl, director of the Washington Center for the Book, and Chris
Higashi—I especially appreciate the opportunity to work in the
C. K. Poe Fratt Writers' Room. You all deserve the salaries of rock
stars and sports heroes! Surely your contributions in preserving and
passing on our civilization down through the ages are as worthy.

Finally, as this book goes to press, I have learned that Dr. Elisabeth Kübler-Ross has suffered a stroke and is recuperating in Arizona. Her center is closed, and she no longer teaches her workshops. Elisabeth Kübler-Ross has not reviewed this book, but it owes a debt, as do we all, to her superb pioneering work in the field of death and dying. Many millions of people suffering from bereavement or serious illness have read her books and attended her workshops; there they found the inspiration and courage to go on. Those of us in the field of death and dying are her "descendants." May I express heartfelt gratitude, love, and godspeed from all of us.

—Patricia Weenolsen, Ph.D.
Seattle, 1995

FOREWORD

This is a book about facing your death. I would like to remind you, however, that until you take your last breath, you are still living. As you know, I believe there may well be a part of us that continues living even beyond our last breath.

So, amazingly enough, "the art of dying" is really "the art of living." Think about it! Trish's suggestions for dying well—forgiving, doing what we love, overcoming loss, praying, connecting with the sacred, even making legal and medical preparations in a caring manner—all these are about living well! What is hard is *living*, not dying.

The art of dying is not about avoiding death. I want to caution you not to try and avoid dying. That is not living. Besides that, it doesn't work and you will be upset and angry when you find out. Concentrate on living and loving, on completing your life. In the process you may find you live a longer, healthier life because these attitudes are life enhancing. You should diet, exercise, love, pray, and meditate, not in order to avoid death, but because it feels right to live that way.

It is the *love* that makes all the difference. As Trish points out, the love is in the activities, creative spiritual relationships, and fulfilled longings with which we surround ourselves. To be immortal one must love.

So don't try to avoid dying, but don't rush it, either. Live in the moment. What Trish shows is that dying can be accomplished in ways that express love; ways that build bridges, restore broken relationships, create new links to the sacred; ways that fulfill all our longings for leaving the world with dignity and grace, at peace with ourselves and our loved ones. Her suggestions for activities and conversations both with self and with others can help you do so. When we live fully, the dying comes naturally. We are not denied permission by others, because it is our life!

We think of living and dying as two separate states. In reality they are one. As we die, we heal into wholeness and into another existence. I've seen so many instances of this, of people in this life having intimations of the next or experiencing contact with those who have died.

This practical and encouraging book shows how dying can heal us, and helps us make the final transition a time of love and new beginnings. All is one in the seamless flow from birth into death into rebirth. There are no endings, only beginnings.

Peace!

> —Bernie S. Siegel, M.D.
> Woodbridge, Connecticut
> September 1995

PREFACE

The Art of Dying is unique in its explicit primary audience—the dying person—for whom its topic is literally a life-and-death matter.

But all of us suffer from the incurable state of mortality. We are merely closer to or more distant from our own deaths, and can therefore benefit from the wise and respectful guidance that Dr. Weenolsen provides. From the perspective of the dying, what she writes should be particularly helpful to professionals and to friends and family who are participating in the death. Dr. Weenolsen's wealth of life experience, psychological knowledge, and involvement in death counseling show in her deft navigation of treacherous waters regarding divergent tough- and tender-minded approaches. She doesn't duck the tough questions. Neither does she impose her own answers to them: she goes a long way toward enabling the reader to find ways of coping that are right for him or her.

The Art of Dying is at once hope-inspiring and clear-headed. I regard it as a considerable contribution to the art of living.

—M. Brewster Smith, Ph.D.
Santa Cruz, California
September 1995

Death stands above me, whispering low
I know not what into my ear:
Of his strange language all I know
Is, there is not a word of fear

—WALTER SAVAGE LANDOR

INTRODUCTION

THE day you receive the diagnosis is the day everything catches up with you. It is indeed the first day of the rest of your life. Your entire self undergoes a continental shift, alternatives grind against each other, future years crumble into the ocean, and the earthquake fault that was always there suddenly gapes wide, a gash in the landscape of your life.

Never again will you be as you were. Even if by some miracle you heal, it will be only temporary.

A successful, hard-driving Chicago sales executive in his fifties, Bill was stunned. His wife had prodded him into the medical checkup for which he had no time. In the course of the examination, he happened to mention clumsiness in his hands and weakness in his arms, probably his imagination. "Old muscles turning to flab, Doc?" he'd joked. "Maybe I should join a gym?"

Now, numerous tests and specialists later, the diagnosis was in: Lou Gehrig's disease, amyotrophic lateral sclerosis (ALS), a motor neuron disorder. He would grow progressively weaker, his speech would slur, and his breathing muscles would one day become too weak to function. Estimated future lifespan: maybe two years. The physician appeared genuinely sorry.

As Bill left the medical center, myriad thoughts, questions, and feelings assailed him. He commented later how odd it was that one thought bobbed to the surface like a piece of driftwood from a sunken ship: he, Bill Schering, a model of strength and power in his family and his business, would die of weakness.

He went home that day and told no one.

Most of us go through a number of preliminary bouts before the main event. The lump is only a cyst, the pneumonia clears with antibiotics, fractured limbs knit, the blood test is negative, thanks to bypass surgery we are playing tennis again. During these rehearsals, we feared that this was "it." It wasn't.

Many others of us live in a country between health and illness: The lump was cancer, now cleared after surgery, radiology, and/or chemotherapy, but it may return. To be HIV positive is to be pre-AIDS, and no one can tell us if or when the transition will occur. We have inherited a predisposition to diabetes. That shaking hand may be Parkinson's or nonfatal benign essential tremor, but it is years too early to know.

Those of us who live with chronic illness, or under the sword of a specific disease, attest to major transformation. Both our selves and our lives are changed. We revise our priorities, placing walks down country lanes ahead of additional work that might lead to a promotion or raise. We take sensual pleasure in the here and now; we had no time yesterday. An inner softening opens us to new depths of love with mates, children, parents, friends, colleagues, even casual acquaintances. Although we would not have chosen our new suffering, we must admit to lessons positive, even joyous.

Yet no matter how long delayed, death will come, perhaps with unexpected suddenness. More often, it creeps up on us and is tapping us on the shoulder just as we had forgotten its existence.

When we learn of death's impending arrival, we may go through a transition period of trying to maintain our daily lives, suddenly more precious than ever, and of cramming in tests and treatments as if they were a hobby. A hobby is something you can give up if you don't have time for it. Gradually, our life veers, and for a while we are completely consumed with acquiring information about our illness, learning how to manage it, consulting other specialists. We're going to fight this thing. We're going to beat it. We become St. George out to slay the dragon, even as new symptoms appear.

During this period, we may begin those practical tasks of drawing up a will, if we haven't done so; delegating regular and/or durable power of attorney to a spouse or child who can then make business and/or treatment decisions if illness eventually incapacitates us; arranging care of any minor children; evaluating a medical directive and a "living will" to instruct our physician in end-stage treatment—more of it or less; perhaps investigating organ donorship if we were too queasy to do so before; checking our insurance coverage and reviewing our financial status in the new light of our threatened lives; planning our funeral or memorial.

These practical tasks distract us from the horrific thing that is happening to us. We can look neither into the sun nor death directly.

At first, as we handle these preliminary practical tasks, we are able to push our deepest fears to the back of our minds; many of us have done this all our lives. Practical matters become our defense, keeping our hands busy so we don't have to think.

It is when these projects are well under way that the *real* work—and, I would argue, the *hardest* work—begins. The day comes when the volcano, set off by the earthquake, erupts. The toughest questions bob to the surface of our consciousness, questions better answered earlier in our lives. Now time is running out, and in our often panicked, weakened, perhaps uncomfortable state, we must deal with them.

Those facing life-threatening illness are in the habit of keeping their psychological, emotional, and spiritual suffering to themselves. You may feel silly or ashamed. You may even fear that your most important questions are unanswerable, and brush them aside. Sometimes you can confide in a spouse or friend or religious counselor, especially further along in the dying process, except that you do not want to upset those you love. Mainly, you must work out answers for yourself. It is to help you deal with your deepest conflicts that I have written *The Art of Dying*.

Many years ago, I found myself in a hospital, standing by the bed of a dying woman. On one side sat her grief-stricken daughters. On the other stood the doctor and the nurse. I listened as the doctor and the relatives discussed the patient's progress *across* her body! No, she wasn't asleep or unconscious, and yes, she was still capable of thought and speech. Apparently, her treatment, preferences, values, individuality, past experiences, and concerns were none of her business! I think it was that moment that planted inside my breast the seeds of advocacy for these newly disenfranchised.

I am an ombudsman for those of you who have just received the dreaded diagnosis, although your death may be years away, as well as for those closer to your dying time. Caregivers have the support of relatives or medical colleagues, and so do the bereaved. But when we face our own death, we do not have fellow "die-ers" to see our point of view and take up our cause, or even joke in shockingly bad taste. Those tending us may do so wonderfully, but they are careful to separate themselves (or they might catch the dying from us!). They do this by making up stories about why we are dying and they are not (we ate too much, smoked, drank, took the elevator instead of the stairs, had bad genes, and the like). During our battle, they are turned from their own deaths to their own agendas regarding us.

Most books in the field of death and dying address either the caregivers or the bereaved. They ignore what *you* are experiencing now. In the justly esteemed AMA *Family Medical Guide*, the reader is addressed as "you" throughout eight hundred pages of various diseases. In the last section, however, the dying person is "him or her."[1] Recently I received a self-care book from an HMO. I looked up "Death" in the index. It said, "See *Grief*." Death happens only to survivors?

This book is for you. Here you will find information and logical reasoning, as well as commonsense psychological and spiritual guidance on such possible conflicts as:

- Am I living or dying? What do I have to gain and lose by thinking of myself as one or the other?

- Should I tell others that my illness is terminal, or should I keep it a secret?
- How much pain must I endure, and what methods of relief will be available to me?
- I'm terrified of losing control over the great and small decisions of my life. How do I retain it?
- How can I deal with the mutilation of my body that makes it unlovable?
- Are there ways to counteract the stigma of my disease so that people don't shy away?
- How can I come to terms with what I haven't accomplished?
- In the past, when I lost a lover, I still had my work, my friends, and the mountains. When I die, I face leaving everything I love. How can I possibly overcome these losses?
- I'm told I need to forgive, to reconcile myself with those from whom I am estranged. Must I go through a "deathbed forgiveness scene"? How can I forgive myself? God?
- What are the consequences of leaving someone out of my will?
- One minute I'm terrified, the next I'm furious, and the next I'm depressed. I've always handled my emotions well, but they're so much more intense these days. I'm on a roller coaster of highs and lows. Why is that? And how do I deal with it?
- What practical steps can I take to get through this stage of my life day by day? How have others done it?
- I want to maintain my identity, my sense of who I am. More than anything, I don't want my children to see me confused or out of my mind with pain, or as someone they don't recognize. Are there ways of preempting these possibilities?
- I need to feel that my life has had meaning, but sometimes it seems like such a waste. Is there any way, at this late date, to make my life more meaningful?
- What is dying like? What's going to happen to me when I die? There isn't any way of knowing, is there?
- Is there life after death? If my religion is not guidance enough for me, how do I know what to believe?
- I used to be the one who helped others, but increasingly I face dependence on them. I know I should be grateful, but I'm filled with resentment. What can I do about this?

- Is there any way of seeing death as positive rather than hideous and terrifying? Can the process of dying enhance my spiritual development rather than end it completely?
- I keep most of these questions secret, sometimes even from myself. I don't want to upset my husband (daughter, dad, partner, friend). The doctor has other patients, and the nurse says not to think this way. I get the feeling it's in bad taste to ask these questions. Where can I turn?

One place you can turn is this book, *The Art of Dying*.

These major conflicts are hardly new. In adolescence and at midlife we wrestle with issues of life meaning, identity, control, and feelings that much of life is a waste. We question whether we should make major changes in relationships, career, and lifestyle.

All our lives we struggle with dependence versus independence. As toddlers, we visited strange households and ran away from our mother's knee to explore, returning to familiarity and safety a short time later, and ranging a bit farther each time. As adolescents we rebelled against the security we needed. As husband and wife, we fight.

Near the end of our lives, however, many lifelong conflicts intensify or take new twists and turns. Some solutions that stood us in good stead at seventeen or thirty or fifty-five may help us now, but we must modify others and create new ones. For example, one coping strategy that has soothed our dissatisfaction with our accomplishments has been to look to—even plan—the future. When we are dying, that strategy changes.

Here you will learn to adapt old solutions and create new ones.

This brings us to a major point. You may think you have no experience with dying, that you're a "death virgin." You can rehearse giving speeches, changing diapers, mollifying the intractable boss, but you're doing death for the first time. However, it is likely that you've had other illnesses, so you've experienced the pokes and prods, the daunting machinery, the hospital system, the personnel who range from compassionate and professional to uncaring and inept. You may also have tended someone else who died, so you know the ugliness and the stench, as well as the unexpected spiritual strength and beauty. You've read death scenes in great literature, such as Tolstoy's *The Death of Ivan Ilych*. Indeed, you've read the morning papers!

You've had much experience in resolving previous forms of the major conflicts that intensify toward the end of life, such as life meaning, dependency, and control.

Finally, you are always you, unless you develop an illness like Alzheimer's (of which more later). You are the bridge between living and dying, your own bridge that you travel across. You may find that, on the dying side, you do more living, and that you were deader than you thought when you were more alive.

I have organized the chapters in *The Art of Dying* very roughly in the order that the conflicts I seek to help you resolve might arise, from early physical concerns to emotional to spiritual, from practical and psychological control to transformation. The first two chapters orient you to the positive aspects of living your life in the full awareness that you will die, and offer you the opportunity to test yourself on your feelings about death, thus "cutting death down to size." Chapters 3 to 7 offer psychospiritual assistance with the early practical decisions and problem management that you are likely to face. Coping with the psychological conflicts surrounding mutilation, shame, pain, emotional struggles, and hope are the focus of Chapters 8 to 12. They include twenty-seven rules for dying the "right way," and one rule for doing it *your* way. Chapters 13 to 16 stress more control over our dying, with decisions regarding aid-in-dying and identity. Chapters 17 to 22 assist you with specific spiritual problems such as forgiveness, transcending loss, letting go, coming to terms with what's left undone, creating life meaning from despair, and teaching others by how we die. The last five chapters address creating your own final rituals, evidence for and against the existence of an afterlife, enhancement of spiritual growth, and, finally, what happens when you die.

The substantial Notes and Resources section at the back of the book helps you explore any of these topics in more detail.

In *The Art of Dying*, you will learn the positive rewards of living in the full recognition that you will die. The surprising result is that the prospect of dying in the future may solve a lot of problems in the present.

In short, this book offers you "death insurance," an opportunity to learn what to expect and how to prepare, plan, control, rehearse, and gradually transform yourself from your physical life to a spiritual one. You will also gain solid information on resolving the major life-long psychological and spiritual conflicts that intensify and take new forms in the end-time. Most important, and with the help of a number of exercises, you will be able to integrate the positive gifts that death and dying bestow, thereby transforming whatever time you have remaining.

We began this chapter with the story of Bill. You'll recall how stunned he was at his doctor's verdict of ALS. We shall follow the course of his growth and development throughout the book, and we shall also have the chance to meet many others struggling through—and triumphing over—the difficult process of dying. They are an inspiration to us all.

In the mid-1970s, toward the end of the human potential movement, a book appeared entitled *If You Meet the Buddha on the Road, Kill Him!*[2] This maxim shocked me until I discovered what it meant. There are different interpretations, but one is that anyone who claims to have all the answers to the most important metaphysical and philosophical questions of our lives is either lying or deluded. No one is God except God.

While you read *The Art of Dying*, remember that no guru can tell everyone else how to die. But I *do* believe this book will help you bring to consciousness that which you already know. Ignore what feels wrong or contradicts your beliefs, and embrace only what works for you. I mean to bolster faith with information, reasoning, and intuitive truths, not to meddle with it.

As a psychologist with many years of experience in teaching death and dying courses, counseling the bereaved and the dying, leading seminars and workshops, speaking to various community groups and conventions, conducting research, and publishing work in the broader field of loss, I have found that religion is, indeed, a godsend for many people—although not for all.

Whatever resonates to the wisdom deep inside you, that is what you must follow.

ONE

PREPARING

FOR DEATH

CAN TRANSFORM

YOUR LIFE

HOW much time do I have?"

It's the first question we ask when we receive the dreaded news. Cryptic numbers on lab slips, vague shadows on X rays, reports from machines scanning and monitoring our bodies—all signal that our time is limited.

Physicians are the first to admit that prognosis is not an exact science. They answer questions in terms of likelihoods, probabilities, and statistics. Your doctor may respond, "With the medical treatment I propose, roughly 45 percent survive the five-year mark." That means roughly 55 percent don't. And you ask, "What kind of survival?"—vegetative or fully human?—even when you know he can't tell you. "Each patient is different," he says. Undoubtedly, he could tell you stories of patients at death's door who rallied inexplicably and lived ten years longer. (He could tell you stories of disaster as well, but he won't.)

So you don't know how much time you have left. Not with any certainty. But then, you never did, did you?

The fact is, you could have asked, "How much time do I have?" throughout your life. Perhaps you've filled out one of those questionnaires subtracting points for smoking and adding points for seat-belt use. On the basis of insurance statistics, they estimated your life span as twenty years beyond your present age.

The only answer to your question is that you used to have more time. Life has always been risky. War, AIDS, leukemia, car crashes, starvation, plague, drive-by shootings—all take their toll at any age. You're lucky you've survived this long.

It would have been logical to prepare for death earlier. And perhaps you have. Most of us would rather not acknowledge death's presence in our lives until we must. We'd rather approach death as we did the old swimming hole or the diving board when we were children. Teeter on the brink, close our eyes, hold our nose, and jump. Robert Browning wrote, "I would hate that death bandaged my eyes and forebore, and bade me creep past."[1] Many of us would choose precisely that. Hide me!

You won't get the definite answer you want, such as "You will die on Friday, November 17, at 6:22 A.M." So your next question is "How can I make the most of my remaining time?" For that there are abundant answers, depending on your physical capacities and how far along you are in the dying process.

Surprisingly, death, by its mere inescapable presence in our lives, has many gifts for us. Blessings, even. Carlos Castaneda's teacher, Don Juan, tells us death is a black crow, just on the edge of vision over our left shoulder, an adviser reminding us of its presence.[2] "You don't have eternity," it says, in effect. "Is this what you really want to do?" Death's presence guides our living in two ways:

1. It brings the gifts that the dying experience into our present lives. Why *wait* until the end-time?
2. It eases the dying passage itself.

When I set out to list all the ways in which preparing for death enriches our lives, even long before the final event, I was stunned to discover at least twenty-two. Twenty-two major gifts to the present from living within the context of future death! Here they are. Which would you do without?

1. Awareness of death makes us *less fearful* by desensitizing us to the idea. As a result, we grow bolder, take more risks. If you're going to die in a year or two, why not sign up for that rafting trip down the roiling Colorado River or the expedition through the Amazon jungle? What do you have to lose? Life becomes more exhilarating, an adventure, as death surely is.

2. Because there's less future, we live in the *here and now*, taking sensual pleasure in the small details of our lives. We delve deeper into the familiar, but we also appreciate the new: exotic people, foods, spices, smells, music, and art. We look and we *really see*. We listen and we *really hear*. Death's imminence warns us not to mortgage the present to the future.

3. We cut down on "musts" and "shoulds" and do more of what we *love*. It is not that we no longer do things for others, rather that we *choose* our sacrifices with more deliberation and wisdom. We have been taught that any behavior that doesn't benefit others is selfish, but if you play the piano for yourself alone, and you grow thereby, you take that happier, more fulfilled self out into the world.

4. We grow *closer* to friends and family, because we shall not always be together. Unexpectedly, we discover mutual thoughts and interests we never recognized. A soldier in a veteran's hospital told his roommate he regretted not learning more about birds, "Especially the mockingbird." "Me, too," his companion said. "I have an extra pair of binoculars. Let's go!"

5. The prospect of death encourages us to *create meaning* in our lives, that is, a sense of life's pattern, coherence, purpose, and significance. If we need to do something to make life more meaningful, we still have time.

6. Often we regret broken relationships, petty cruelties, things not done. When death is our adviser, we have the time and opportunity to *minimize regret*. Also, when our relationships deepen and we do more of what we love, we regret less.

7. Because we regret less, create more meaningful lives, do more of what we love, and draw closer to friends, we have a better sense of who we are, a more fulfilled *identity*. Identity is like one of those yellow animal balloons that street clowns blow up for kids. First the trunk expands, and then, one by one, all

those additional parts like ears, legs, and tail. Normally, the major part of your identity develops first, but other parts of you are ready to expand at the first opportunity.

8. Thus, oddly enough, the prospect of the future ending helps us *solve* many *present problems*, especially with people, work, and very specific personal longings.

9. We learn to *prioritize* our lives now, to delete the housecleaning and substitute throwing clay. Time becomes our ally, less of an enemy to beat, race, or even kill.

   Can you see how the shift from limitless horizons to life boundaries focuses us on what is worthwhile? Just as the blanket swaddles the newborn so she will not fling out in all directions—a "startle reflex"—time swaddles us.

   But there's more.

10. All our lives, we work to *transcend losses*—of physical abilities, loved ones, homes, jobs, but also of hopes and dreams. Transcendence is a two-stage process: first we overcome the loss, and then we re-create our lives and our selves. Our home burns to the ground, and we must first grieve it and then rebuild. But sometimes we get stuck in loss. We know we are stuck when the loss is as raw today as it was years ago, when it is a major part of our identity, when "I am a widow" is the first thing we tell people about ourselves.

    Death advises us, first, that nothing is ever ours forever and, second, that there are some losses, such as the death of a child, we will never get over. We must accept it as a new part of who we are. After we have done this, we can complete the third transcendence task, and that is to let the whole thing go, trusting that the person or thing we loved and lost is somewhere safe in the universe, or perhaps in the arms of God.

11. If there is someone we haven't forgiven yet, or who hasn't forgiven us, and if we believe that *forgiveness* will come on our deathbed (we may not), why not do it now? Then we will have all this precious time for joyful companionship.

    Besides, death is unpredictable. While we're mulling over that dramatic scene in our minds, the object of our wrathful affection has rolled over three times in a car on the interstate.

12. We've made horrible mistakes as parents, maligned a co-worker (she richly deserved it), and on occasion we've lied, cheated, or hurt someone's feelings, and on and on. We might as well *forgive ourselves* now rather than wait until the last minute. If we believe in a forgiving God, we've already prayed to Him, and He's forgiven us. Who are *we* to hold out?

13. There is more *peace* within us in our lives because we are forgiving, prioritizing, creating meaning, forgoing regret; we are less fearful, living in the here and now, doing what we love, becoming closer to others, and transcending loss.

14. We are more *helpful to others who are dying*, because we come from a more honest, more settled place of reflection on our own death. We're less likely to shy away from the dying and bereaved who need our compassion and support. We can handle it.

15. Because we are learning and developing now rather than later, we have a longer period to *teach* others, particularly our children (although, admittedly, they may be less receptive to us while we are still in full bloom).

16. As I show throughout this book, the prospect of death prods us to *resolve* such *conflicts* as dependence versus independence, intimacy versus solitude, and control or order versus chaos. Death presses final solutions upon us.

17. We know from experience that *rituals* such as baptism, bar mitzvah, and weddings help us through life passages. Why not a ritual for our final passing? Now is also a good time to select wake, memorial, and burial arrangements, as well as the many details of these, such as music, readings, and food.

18. Explore the pros and cons of near-death experiences and various religious teachings as evidence for or against an *afterlife*. If you're uncertain, take a position and stick with it, then plan accordingly.

19. Similarly, if you make decisions now about whether or not you want your life prolonged as much as possible, as well as *practical* arrangements concerning your will and the like, you will not have to do it later.

20. As we approach the end, many of us like to tell the story of

who we were and what we did with our lives. We may want to correct the stories others tell, particularly in families, some less than flattering, some untrue, a product of the tellers' agendas. We can begin that story or *myth* at any time, writing it down, taping it, or simply telling others.

21. Your *metaphor* is a very personal thing. It can be your image of yourself, or how an artist might paint you. It might be a stylization of your myth, or how your spirit might look if it were embodied, or you at your "best," your idealized self, perhaps. For example, you, who you are at your deepest level, might ride a horse with flying mane across the night sky, or breast the ocean in sunlight, or become motes of music throughout the universe. Or you may think of yourself as a soldier in life's wars. What image comes to mind? Working this out helps you live the rest of your life with deeper satisfaction.

22. All of the above assists you with your most important task, *spiritual development.*

These are all ways in which the prospect of death enhances our lives; they are death's gifts to us. Look them over again. Not a single gift is a minor one. Isn't it amazing? It might almost make death worth it—almost, but not quite. What's more, we can begin these preparatory tasks at any age, not just at the hour of our death. In fact, it's easier if we begin earlier rather than later. But make no mistake, as we approach death (until the final hours), tasks such as creating life meaning are crucial.

Let us turn to the ways in which early preparation for death can help us die. First, as we see from the above, we have already worked out a great deal, although the dying process itself adds a twist or two. However, preparation now eases our final passage.

1. We may have less *fear* of the process, although this may feel like splitting hairs. If you have ever had a phobia, you'll understand.

    Let us say you're terrified of flying and you need to take a plane to a wedding. Sleeplessness sets in a week before. The day of the flight you spring for a shuttle rather than drive your car under the influence of the sedative you took. In the plane, you pray for wine service as if you were an addict. The plane lifts off, the front of it canted toward the stratosphere, while you try to overcome your dizziness and breathlessness long enough to search with casual nonchalance for the barf bag. The wine arrives like the answer to a prayer; in fact, you have a brief image of the glass borne on two white wings. You swallow a few sips even though you know alcohol can intensify the effects of your medication, but you're more terrified of the plane dropping than of yourself dropping dead. Each time the plane shakes like a dog emerging from the water, you freak. Why did you agree to come? Why didn't you tell them you were ill—dead, even? (Once, while we were banking steeply before a landing in Amsterdam, my seatmate, a stranger, turned to me and asked quite out of the blue, "Does flying make you nervous?" I scanned her face in surprise. "How did you know?" Then I noticed that her arm was white beneath my clutching hand.)

The point is, if you have ever gradually overcome a phobia, you know the process by which your overwhelming terror faded to mere fear, which faded to dis-ease, which may by now have faded to boredom, because dis-ease can be very boring. You're not enjoying yourself. Preparing for death often fades the terror to fear.

On the other hand, some people report that they are not fearful of death at all. They fear more the treatment—the noisy metal machines, the smells, pokes, prods, and pricks. In fact, as one approaches death, the fear of death itself often eases.

2. We have imagined how we might die, and we are likely to die much as we imagine we will, although there are surprises. If we *visualize* death as awful, the pain and suffering intensify. If we visualize beautiful gardens, music, or a reunion with loved ones, we're going to expect them.

3. When we receive the final diagnosis (if this is how death comes to us), we are often in shock, filled with dread. It is difficult to concentrate on obtaining the information we need. But

if we have prepared, we have much of it already, with the exception of details about the specific illness itself—that being unpredictable. For example, we've learned about pain relief and hospice.

4. We have completed such *practical tasks* as making a will, arranging for a durable power of attorney or health-care proxy, planning finances, ascertaining the details of our health coverage, informing our physician of our treatment decisions, instructing our caregivers about final arrangements, and the like. We can relax.

5. We've made our ethical *decisions* regarding, for example, aid-in-dying.

6. We are able to impose *order* on chaos.

7. Our dying may be a bit more familiar and *predictable*—for example, we opt to die at home.

8. We can die more as we have lived, as the person we are, retaining our *identity* rather than turning ourselves over to someone else, even loving children and grandchildren.

9. Thus, we gain some *control* over the final dying process.

DYING WITH DIGNITY

The control we gain may include the opportunity to *die with dignity*. The phrase has been bandied about, and no one seems quite sure what it means. The image of the patient retreating down the corridor with his hospital gown open comes to mind. None of us thinks this is dignified. Some conceive of dignity in terms of negatives—*not* needing to go out screaming in pain and scare the children, or *not* looking so hideous they don't recognize you, or *not* mumbling inanities, or *not* losing control of body functions, or *not* pleading for life, or indeed other events too horrible for polite company.

Does loss of dignity mean no longer being able to keep up a front? Does it mean that such universal "secrets" as bleeding hemorrhoids and leaking bladders become public knowledge?

Others think of dignity in a more positive, even romantic, sense:

children gathered around the bed among the roses while you dispense wisdom that will descend to your great-great-grandchildren, the bloom of death upon your pallid cheek like a nineteenth-century consumptive (supposedly), hair flowing around your pillow, white dress suitable for rising.

What we probably mean by dignity is dying as ourselves and not as someone else, with someone else's hospital hairdo and agenda for proper or appropriate behavior.

We cannot predict it all. We can control more of what goes on inside us than what others do to us, but that takes practice as we shall see—a kind of psychospiritual rehearsal for the final event.

I think it is most important to ask, Who determines what is dignified and what is not? Who defines this? A woman has just given birth with her legs in the air—this is undignified? Maybe we should shape our own concept of "dignity."

As for me, I got through this life against some pretty terrific odds—and that's "dignity" enough!

When we look at these lists of death's gifts of transformation, which would we give up?

Suppose we lived forever? Forget for a minute that the world would be too populated to support us. All our memories would live on as well—our losses and our customary ways of responding to them, our quirks of temperament, our prejudices and preconceptions, and the blips on our mental screens. We would not learn the lessons I list above.

At the worst, death washes us clean of grief like the River Jordan, even if we know nothing afterward. It gives this world another chance with new people, new energies, new approaches to age-old problems, before they, too, pass these on to others.

Then again, death may be a rite of passage to a new existence, in a continuous evolutionary development of the universe. No one of us can logically or scientifically prove to another that this is or is not so. Belief is ours alone.

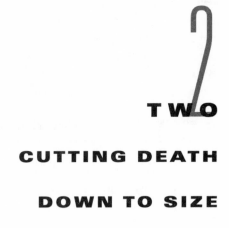

TWO

CUTTING DEATH

DOWN TO SIZE

FOR most of us, sex is a major motivating force of our lives. Even the vaguest prospect of sexual encounter prods us to include certain people in our circle, select college courses, workplaces, geographic locales to live in or visit, restaurants, new employees, and leisure activities. Advertising moguls know this and sexualize everything from cars to coffee. At any one moment, sex may dominate our minds or recede, but foreground or background, it is rarely absent from our thoughts altogether.

The same is true of death.

I wonder if this surprises you.

Death is another major motivating force in our lives. Age, that great yardstick by which we measure life lived, also measures life left. We try to appear to others, and to ourselves, as though we have more than we actually do. If we succeed, they'll collude with us in our deception, treating us as younger. Our jobs and sexual opportunities may depend on it. No one wants to be any nearer death than necessary, or any nearer to someone who is.

We measure our accomplishments by the same yardstick. The meter's running. A hallmark of the midlife transition around age forty is the realization that if we're unhappy with our jobs, opportunity is no longer endless; if our relationships aren't all we've dreamed, we must change while we still can; if life seems meaningless, we must dive into ourselves to discover what "meaningful" *means*.

The fact that we will die is a factor in our smaller decisions as well. We eat food that we believe promotes a healthy life (and long). We run up the stairs, take self-defense courses, and arm ourselves to save our lives.

Death shapes our political decisions. If health care becomes universal, there is more life for everyone. On the other hand, we subconsciously believe that what provides more life for others—money—in both quantity and quality provides less life for us. Each of us wants more life. Thus, death is the basic source of greed. We would not be so greedy if life had no end.

The fact of death influences our political choices concerning crime, drugs, war, the economy, education, and employment (to earn a *living*). It shapes our vote. If you and I disagree on the next election, it will be because you believe one candidate will bring more life to you and yours (lower taxes, perhaps), and I believe the other will.

So sex and death motivate us to select certain people and activities for our lives and to avoid others. Next time you have an important decision to make, try recasting it in these terms: Which alternative means death to you, and which means life? When you find yourself in conflict in your marriage, or with someone at work (most often it will be over sex and/or money—the two life-givers), try to recognize the conflict as, metaphorically, a life-and-death issue for each of you; it is this that lends it such intensity. Then try to figure out how both of you can live, rather than come to the decision that one of you must live on the death of the other.

For many of us, death is a huge, amorphous black blob of dread. One of the most helpful things we can do with this blob is to break it down into its essential components. Then we can seek to resolve those fears that, while scary, are smaller than the overarching terror. Already we are making progress!

The following questionnaire, "Cutting Death Down to Size," is designed to help you do exactly that. You will find that certain aspects of death feel overwhelming, while others leave you shrugging your shoulders. Further, anyone else completing this questionnaire may have different answers, different aspects they fear. We will explore the reasons for this.

This questionnaire simplifies the complex and is unscientific, but I believe it identifies most of the major aspects of death that people dread. Of course, your overall dread is greater than the sum of its parts. The questions, however, should help you raise to your consciousness what for you are the most terrifying dimensions of death. Overcoming them, even transforming them into a positive force for change, will be your next challenge.

THE "CUTTING DEATH DOWN TO SIZE" QUESTIONNAIRE

Instructions: Read the following questions and decide if each is "No problem" for you, a "Problem," or a "Major problem." Put a check mark under the one that pertains to you.

	No problem	Problem	Major problem
1. Do you dread the *process* of dying?	——	——	——
2. If you do, do you fear			
a. losing control	——	——	——
b. pain	——	——	——
c. disorder/chaos	——	——	——
d. being dependent	——	——	——
e. being a financial drain	——	——	——
f. being alive too long	——	——	——
g. medical technology	——	——	——
h. unpleasant/unwanted treatment	——	——	——
i. being alone/abandoned	——	——	——
j. mutilation, ugliness	——	——	——
k. stigma/shame	——	——	——
l. unpredictability	——	——	——
m. other _____	——	——	——
3. Do you fear or dread the loss of			
a. family/loved ones	——	——	——

	No problem	Problem	Major problem
b. looks	——	——	——
c. home	——	——	——
d. possessions	——	——	——
e. meaningful work/career/ vocation	——	——	——
f. political cause	——	——	——
g. physical abilities	——	——	——
h. creative abilities	——	——	——
i. value to others/prestige	——	——	——
j. faith	——	——	——
k. other _____	——	——	——

4. Do you worry that
   a. your death may be meaningless — —— —— ——
   b. your life may be meaningless — —— —— ——
   c. your life was wasted — —— —— ——
   d. you have not achieved — —— —— ——
   e. you are not forgiven — —— —— ——
   f. you cannot forgive others — —— —— ——
   g. you cannot forgive yourself — —— —— ——
   h. your dying will cause grief — —— —— ——
   i. you leave behind unsolved problems — —— —— ——
   j. other _____

5. Do you dread the *state* of being dead? —— —— ——

6. If so, what do you fear most?
   a. hell or other punishment — —— —— ——
   b. being buried alive — —— —— ——
   c. nothingness — —— —— ——
   d. reincarnation/karma — —— —— ——
   e. Judgment Day — —— —— ——
   f. decay of the body — —— —— ——

	No problem	Problem	Major problem
g. the unknown	——	——	——
h. other _____	——	——	——
7. Do you suffer from phobias?	——	——	——

Scoring: You want right answers? You want to know if you scored high? If you beat out your partner, or the average for test takers across the country? Does your score indicate genius, sports ability, physical irresistibility, or creative talent? Can you take these results to your boss and ask for that raise or promotion? Competitive, aren't you?

Okay. Score 0 for each "No problem," 1 for each "Problem," and 2 for each "Major problem." Add them all up, and then give yourself 100 for taking the test in the first place. A perfect score indicates that you are brave, thorough, detail-oriented, and gifted at test-taking. Also, you have a high need for achievement.

Now, place a check mark beside your "Major problems," and, if you like, beside your "Problems" as well. It is these you will work through as you read the book. By the way, if you want to go back and change any of your answers, you will not be expelled for cheating!

Our fear of death and dying is affected by a number of factors.

First, we *do* make the distinction between fear of death and fear of dying. Dying is the *process* of moving into the *state* of death. Dying still has movement, death is static. When we are dying, we are still alive, but when we are dead, life is past.

If you call for a show of hands in any group, and ask what they fear most, dying or death, you'll probably get an overwhelming vote for dying. In my classes, talks, and workshops, I always have. People fear the whole rigamarole of dying, with all its attendant and unpredictable problems as listed in the questionnaire. They fear it far more than they do the state of death or being dead. At worst, they figure they won't know they're dead, unless they believe in afterlife punishment.

Second, your age influences your fears.[1] As a rule, your age determines how far from death you are and how much longer you have to live. Intuitively, you would think that older people closer to death are more fearful. The opposite is true. Younger people are more fearful of death than older people (there are plenty of exceptions). Perhaps this is because older people have lived their lives, had their chances, fulfilled at least some of their potential, and have a longer opportunity to create life meaning. People who are "self-actualized," who have completed their "life projects," are also less fearful.[2] The eminent psychologist M. Brewster Smith points out that people who feel cheated about their lives are much more death-anxious than people who have fulfilled themselves.[3] So younger people would be, by definition, more anxious. Add to this the toll that AIDS is taking on our youth—as well as drive-by shootings—and we may see more anxiety among today's young people than yesteryear's.

When death comes to us *on time,* in our late seventies or beyond, there is a sense that it is less unfair, more fitting, and expected. Death seems more unfair when it hits *off time,* that is, when it cuts down the hemophiliac child, the young man in new bloom, even the fifty-year-old woman who, emancipated from family duties, is free to stretch herself and is, as she would tell you, "in my prime."

A third dimension influences fear of death, and that is spirituality. People who score higher on spirituality measures (not necessarily institutional religiosity) are less death-anxious.

Fourth, personality traits influence our fears.[4]

Nessa is a banker who manages her work and her children with equal attention to order: "A place for each thing, and each thing in its place." She cites the old maxim with a deprecatory laugh. Small wonder that one of her greatest fears surrounding death is the lack of order. She fears that she will die in the midst of chaos and then *into* chaos, into a black night of reeling stars and asteroids with no predictability.

Order is a major personality trait for Nessa because it keeps chaos—that is, death—at bay. When things are ordered and predictable, they are not chaotic. Nessa *binds,* or controls, her fear of death by creating order throughout her life. It seems unlikely that death will tap her on the shoulder next Tuesday when she has such a full day planned!

Our personality traits are our ways of dealing with death. They are adaptive. Some of these traits, such as extroversion, are *inborn*, a part of our genetic heritage. Extroversion shields us from death by turning our eyes to others who will protect us—in the tribal hunt or at work. Other traits we *learned* from our parents, who fought death with the same weapons. So it is only natural to fear that these weapons will be snatched from us or "neutralized" in our most difficult hours. If we use control of others to survive, we fear its loss through medical technology as well as illness. If we battled parents and spouse to become independent and fully alive, we fear diminishment by a return to dependence. If being with others is a major need, we fear abandonment in our last moments. If we have always won friends, love, approval, and even sex with our beauty, we fear mutilation, because the face of death is hideous. If we are highly gifted in any one area—physical prowess, intellectual abilities, mechanical acumen, creative talent—then we have taken much of our identity from these and we fear their loss.

And yet . . . and yet . . . it is by identifying precisely where our fears lie and how they are related to who we are, and then adapting them, that we can make death a positive force in our lives instead of a purely negative one.

How?

In the questionnaire above, you identified the aspects of death that terrify you most and, inadvertently, the personality characteristics that you use to ward off death. Now, experiment!

If it is *control* that you use against death and that you fear losing, try relinquishing it to someone else in so small a matter as a decision. During the 1960s, at the height of the human potential movement, there was something called a "trust exercise." People would gather in a swimming pool in various stages of undress and practice lying back on the extended arms of all other members, trusting that others would buoy them up. When you let go of control in your life, even in a single activity, even if only for a day, you trust that the universe will hold you up.

And it does!

If it is *order* or *predictability* you fear losing, try *unscheduling* your life for a time, even for a weekend—better, for your entire vacation. If you're organized out of existence and can tell me what you will be doing seventeen weeks from next Tuesday, try to incorporate what I call "float time" regularly into your life. Similarly, you can experiment with letting go of your needs for achievement, nurturance, independence, dominance, and aggression.

One reason we love travel is that it affords us this opportunity to practice letting go and surviving. Two years ago, I embarked on a year-long journey around the country. I, type A to the core (with the exception of hostility), stored my furniture and, with only the vaguest of plans, without even a calendar, set off on a great adventure.

Driving, hosteling, camping out, meeting people from all walks and from all over the world, I fell under the enchantment of an Australian accordionist who "played the sun down" on the California redwood coast; vibrated to a hummingbird's wings in Arizona as it thrummed up and down my body, and accepted the pronouncement of a New Mexican shaman that this was a blessing; listened for hours to a Cajun feminist in Louisiana, and pushed on to an eye-to-eye encounter with a pearly-white alligator, and tracked the footsteps of history along the Natchez Trace in Mississippi; celebrated sunset over sailing boats and among intense frangipani blossoms in Key West; stayed with a "mountain woman" who knew her copperheads along the Blue Ridge; lived the stories of a Mammoth Caves spelunker who told how the dank darkness here had housed nineteenth-century tuberculosis patients in hopes of cure. Yes, there was danger, too, such as in my encounter with a psychopath on the Appalachian Trail in the Great Smokies (his leg cramps gave me the opportunity to escape).

And that's for openers!

Letting go of so much for so long *did* indeed feel like a death to me. That journey was the most life-giving experience I've ever had.

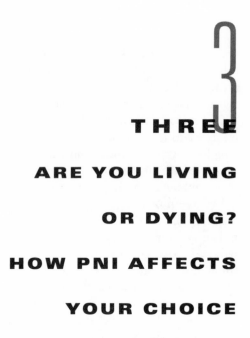

THREE

ARE YOU LIVING

OR DYING?

HOW PNI AFFECTS

YOUR CHOICE

MY friend Terri mulled over the news that her liver cancer was terminal.

"No more dental appointments!" she exclaimed finally. She'd been scheduled for a root canal and a crown.

Each year, 250,000 people learn that they have a terminal illness. The remainder of their lives depends, in part, on how they answer the question "Am I living or dying?"

What about you? Do you perceive yourself as living with your disease, or dying of it? Can your answer help promote healing? Can it ease the transition?

There are advantages and disadvantages to *both* perceptions. You must know these in order to make decisions best and truest to yourself. And yes, ultimately, your perception of whether you are living or dying is a *decision* you make, not a matter of fact.

First, let us look at a major scientific determinant of your choice.

THE MIND-BODY CONNECTION

Recent advances in the evolving science of psychoneuroimmunology, or PNI, show that the mind influences the onset and/or course of a great many illnesses, *for better or worse;* the body also influences the mind. PNI is the study of interrelationships among psychology, neurology, endocrinology, and immunology.[1]

For example, a *truly* optimistic outlook *and its consequent behaviors* can strengthen the body's immune system, its primary defense against disease.[2] Studies demonstrate that diabetes, cancer, heart disease, colds and other respiratory illnesses, infections, influenza, migraine, lupus, muscular sclerosis, arthritis, and possibly AIDS are just a few of the physical diseases apparently influenced by the mind. Indeed, we might better think of these as mind-body disorders, rather than simply physical. One researcher has discovered a kind of invisible wiring system whereby the body seems to talk to itself![3]

Supposedly physical causes of disease, such as being overweight, smoking, high cholesterol, and high blood pressure, have psychic components such as addiction or stress. If we think we're helpless to change these interactions, we are.[4] On the other hand, Alzheimer's disease, head trauma, plague, and many genetic disorders such as Huntington's chorea and sickle-cell anemia have physical causes for which any mental aspect or attribution seems unlikely. Diseases originally attributed to stress, such as peptic ulcer, are now recognized as having physical causes, in this case, a bacterium, treatable with antibiotics. But then again, a weakened immune system (because of stress or depression) would make the body more susceptible to bacteria or viruses, wouldn't it? In some studies, immunosuppression has actually been created in the laboratory by conditioning! As you can see, we're not dealing with a simple cause-effect system.

As to a more specific connection between *type* of stress or personality trait and a specific disease, there is a great deal of controversy. It is the observation of a number of psychologists, including Lawrence LeShan, that many cancer patients have difficulty expressing negative emotions such as rage and guilt (which depresses the immune system); they sacrifice themselves for the welfare of others rather than fulfilling their own needs.[5] Some researchers believe that although personality characteristics such as compliance, conformity, self-sacrifice, denial of hostility or anger, and inability to express emotions don't *cause* cancer and AIDS, it's possible they are fertile ground for immunosuppression.[6] Scientists have been able to give people personality tests and then predict with some accuracy who will develop cancer and who will not.

But we absolutely must not leap to the conclusion that everyone with cancer has these personality traits. Indeed, some researchers belive that the personality-disease link or "cancer personality" is a very weak one.[7] Genetic and other factors are strongly implicated. Further, personality traits result from a combination of inheritance and environment, as well as our own responses and actions. We must avoid blaming the illness on the patient. She has enough to contend with.

Contradictory evidence clouds another example of the mind-body connection, the type A personality—time-bound, competitive, impatient, and hostile. Some studies show a higher frequency of heart disease among these people; others do not. Free-floating hostility has been isolated as most damaging; indeed, one researcher recently found that anger doubles heart attack risk.[8] Both personality disposition and disease can be reversed with a low-fat, low-cholesterol diet, meditation, and exercise.[9] Heart disease also has a genetic component. Once again, the physical and the mental become tightly intertwined in a complex relationship by no means entirely understood.

Psychologists have shown that in addition to personality traits, stressful life events such as bereavement and marital separation, and even *positive* life changes like major achievements, vacations, and holidays, can predict illness in some people, but not in others who are especially "hardy." The more stress you experienced in the previous year, the more likely you are to become ill. Presumably, an event—even a positive one—seems threatening to you and is therefore stressful. You become angry or depressed or tense, all emotions proved to effect changes in the body, and these may result in disease.

One of the most stressful life events is major illness, for which you may go to the hospital. Ironically, a hospital is a very stressful place to be, even crazy-making.[10] Because patients are continually awakened, they do not get enough needed REM or dream sleep; extreme deprivation can cause psychotic experiences.

In addition, there may be rewards for becoming ill. Even so minor an ailment as a cold temporarily removes you from a stressful situation such as the office, allowing you to recuperate, recoup, and mobilize your defenses. Unfortunately, such rewards tend to make us repeat the act.

Thus, illness may result not only from stress, personality factors, depression, and consequent lowered immunity, but also from treatment, all of which can result in less cure and more illness—a vicious circle.

On the other hand, here again the evidence is contradictory.[11] Some researchers find *no* lowered immunity in depressed individuals; others find lowered immunity *but no increased illness*. One study shows that a rise in immune function did not lengthen the lives of patients with AIDS—counterintuitive results! Such antidepressants as exercise and an excellent social support system also counteract stress factors.

A warning here! If you accept PNI evidence that illness and health are partly dependent on stress, personality, and emotions, then you're saying, in effect, that we have partial control over our health status. Unfortunately, the next step is blaming others for their disease and feeling guilty over our own. If Uncle Harold weren't always blowing up at freeway drivers and line crashers, he wouldn't be in the ICU. (I'm relaxed, so I won't.)

As we have seen, the relationship is far more complex. Today we blame smokers for contributing to the national cancer and heart bills that we have to foot, and we penalize them with taxation and ostracism. Not only do we have statistics to back us up, but also many of us feel it is our right to breathe clean air. We penalize drinkers, too. But, to be fair, we should also place a tax on fatty, sugary, cholesterol-laden, and salty foods—everything except carrots. Then we should tax the overweight a dollar per pound a year. And then we should find some way to penalize the sedentary and all those who consult therapists for the depression that may be lowering their immune systems.

This blame-guilt cycle belies the underlying problem, which is the *denial that we will die*. Even if he takes anger management training and calms down, Uncle Harold will die of something (maybe the same thing)—probably later, that's all. As a matter of fact, the earth's resources will support him longer, and we'll support him through more diseases over his longer life.

We must strike a balance between responsibility and censure. The fact is that, no matter how virtuous we are, we could always exercise more, eat or drink less, and think happier thoughts. And we will all die eventually.

THE EXISTENTIAL CONNECTION

There are many spontaneous remissions in those with life-threatening illness; they are, by definition, unpredictable. In Dr. Bernie Siegel's experience, about 90 percent of them are preceded by what he calls an "existential shift," that is, a revolution in how the individual perceives himself and his relationship to others and the world.[12] This isn't a matter of saying *"mea culpa"* and paying lip service to the notion that he's somehow at fault for his disease, perhaps because he was too negative or didn't do what he loved. On the contrary, when one studies case histories, one sees that healing seems to come as a *by-product* of some radical spiritual vision or insight. Often, cure wasn't even the aim! The patient has been seduced away from such concerns by the spirit.

Marc Ian Barasch feels that, for many patients, their disease represents a "stuckness" of something once vital inside them. Healing a life may result in healing a disease.[13] Larry LeShan reminds us of W. H. Auden's observation that cancer may result from "a foiled creative fire." LeShan believes that many cancer patients have a "dream missing." To identify it, he suggests that patients imagine a fairy godmother who will help them live the life they want.[14] What would that be? What would make you live your life more zestfully?

In my own interviews with individuals concerning their "life dreams," I've found that most unfulfilled dreams were creative ones; the urge to create seems universal, and regret over not acting on the urge profound. In our society, it's hard to earn a living in creative pursuits, and they are less honored. Too, some of my interviewees felt incapable—parent, teacher, and peer opinion had cut off creative yearnings at the knees.

The theme of "life unlived" repeats itself in other views of disease; for example, that cancer is a kind of growth gone wild, living something of the life the patient would have, had that life not been re-pressed.[15] Kat Duff reminds us that the Iroquois believed illness was the result of desires of the soul that were ignored. "These desires of the soul are not the same as our usual conscious desires, they dwell deep within our hearts and reveal themselves only through dreams, which speak their language."[16] Audre Lord counsels, "Find some particular thing your soul craves for nourishment and do it."[17]

Siegel reminds us that the ancient Greeks believed disease had a purpose, to compel us to confront our disconnection from the gods. Illness could change a patient's spiritual relationship in a positive direction, partly helped by dreams.[18] Thus, illness may be an initiation into wisdom, and decay the beginning of transformation.[19] LeShan is convinced that life-extension therapies must emphasize not the negative but what's *right* with the patient and develop these.[20]

Thus, spiritual disconnection, foiled creative fire, and unlived dreams—all ways in which we die more than we live—may lead us into illness, which in turn can result in a radical existential shift, wisdom, and transformation. If you are dying to paint, perhaps you are!

Now, what does all of this mean to you, and how does it influence your decision that you are either living with your disease or dying of it?

THINK OF YOURSELF AS LIVING

The main advantage of seeing yourself as *living* is that you can very possibly extend your life.

If you believe you are dying, and if that depresses you, you may weaken your natural healing defenses.

"But," you say, "of course I'm depressed (or upset or angry or fearful). How can I change my feelings?"

We will deal with this problem at length in Chapter 12, when we look at emotions. For the present, it is important to point out that a positive outlook often results in positive body changes: if you think you can beat your disease, you are more likely to follow a health-promoting regimen for one thing.

Dr. Bernie Siegel describes case after case in which his "exceptional patients" *beat* cancer even though their goal was to *live* with it.[21] Who were these patients? What were they like? They did not take anyone's word for anything. They armed themselves with information. They made their own decisions about treatment. They fought, if they had to. They joined Dr. Siegel's Exceptional Patients groups. In addition to following their medical regimens as set out by their physicians and agreed upon by them, they emphasized living by engaging in such immuno-enhancing activities as visualization of healing forces overcoming their disease, hypnosis, group support, art therapy, play, laughter (Norman Cousins, author of *The Anatomy of an Illness*, watched old Marx brothers and *Candid Camera* films), exercise, nutrition suited to their disease, meditation, and religious or spiritual sustenance as appropriate.

To this list others add relaxation training, pet and music therapy, therapeutic touch (including massage), aromatherapy, herbs, vitamins, minerals, special diets prescribed by naturopaths, acupuncture, breathing exercises, and other alternative treatments. Recently, it is reported that approximately sixty thousand Americans use alternative medicine and rarely tell their doctors. To date, there is little or no objective scientific proof of cure or life extension resulting from many of these methods, but there is much anecdotal evidence.[22]

Unfortunately, quackery is alive and well, ready to scam desperate people seeking a cure, and aided and abetted by a slow FDA drug-approval system. "Sham shamans" are offering so-called AIDS or cancer cures that infuriate authentic medicine men.[23] The gradual opening, however, of traditional medicine to alternative treatments will offer increased protection.

The religious or spiritual element is especially important. The healing power of prayer is now actually documented.[24] Whatever connects you to your deeper self or a higher power—God, the Universe, Wisewoman, the Great Spirit—is likely to heal you spiritually if not physically. Even the miracles of healing at Lourdes are not to be denied.

But wait! Suppose that in your heart of hearts you really don't believe you're going to make it. You'd love to be one of Bernie Siegel's exceptionals, who follow his blueprint for living with illness, and maybe even prolong your life. But you need a talent for it, and you could no more be optimistic than you could sing opera or fix the transmission on your car. "If only I could feel that way," you say.

Amazingly, you can! When you *behave* in a certain way, you begin to *feel* that way. It's a psychological axiom. You can do everything Dr. Siegel's exceptional patients do, even if you don't believe it's going to work. At some point it will—partly because such steps as meditation and exercise actually bestow beneficial physical effects, such as raising the level of endorphins in your blood.

By the way, it's not enough just to use affirmations or say to your friends, "I'm optimistic." You have to take the actual steps *until you are*. Indefinite lying doesn't cut it. And if it doesn't work? Chances are you'll feel a lot better anyway.

So, one advantage of perceiving yourself as living with your disease rather than dying of it is that you may actually live a longer life of higher quality. It is also likely to be a different sort of life from the one you're accustomed to because it includes so many new activities and people.

Other advantages? You become more cheerful and hopeful, whether or not you started out that way. This is reflected in the attitudes and treatment of those around you. They cannot help but act more optimistic, even if they're not, and this makes you feel better—a benign circle rather than a vicious one. Not only is hope a more pleasurable state than anger, fear, or depression, but also you make life easier on your family, friends, and medical personnel. Optimism is part of our country's "right" way to die, and you benefit from cultural approval.

So how can there be a downside? First, as we have seen, optimism doesn't necessarily result in life extension.

Second, you may not like all of the steps I've suggested. Meditation may bore you. If you're pretending to an optimism you don't feel (without *acting* on it), presenting a false front to the world, this is a tough way to end your life. It may be against your values—you may feel it's cowardice. It interferes with confiding your real emotions and with the freedom to deal with them. The pretense may block imtimacy between you and those you love. Many couples end their marriages this way, lying to each other for each other's sake, a kind of emotional gift of the magi.

Then, too, you miss out on the great advantages of *living* your dying.

THINK OF YOURSELF AS DYING

If you choose to think of yourself as dying, of course, you miss out on the advantages of perceiving yourself as living.

Unless you look forward to death (some do) or are, for some reason, reconciled to the prospect, you may become depressed. As mentioned above, *emotional* depression may adversely affect the immune and other bodily systems, possibly translating into a shorter life span.

Additionally, because you are depressed, you may experience more isolation than those who are more hopeful. Nor are you meticulous in following your treatment regimen—"What's the use?" You throw up your hands and gorge on runny cheeses and chocolate (raising your spirits as well as your blood sugar and cholesterol).

There are also major *advantages* to thinking of yourself as dying; most obvious is that you are—if not now, later. You face death with unflinching honesty, truer to your personality style. You take many of the positive steps I mentioned in Chapter 1, do more of what you love, pet the dog instead of meditating if that's a chore, complete practical tasks, plan your funeral, transcend and transform various losses, and create life meaning.

You're less inclined to put off forgiveness and more likely to become closer to family and friends. More honest with yourself, you become so with them (but not cruelly so). You help them rehearse your absence. You relieve the strain of pretense both with them and with the medical staff. You may even have some fun.

And, if it turns out that you're going to live longer anyway, all this is "in the bank." You'll get it done *now*.

LIVING OR DYING? YOUR DECISION

Your choice of how you see yourself may also depend on what your doctor has told you, your personality style, how you have handled previous life losses, the advice of significant others, your ethical and religious beliefs, and the meaning your illness has for you.

Could you tolerate the ambivalence of perceiving yourself as both living *and* dying? After all, we've been doing both all our lives. Sometimes we die a little more, after a great loss, for example. Sometimes we are more alive—when we are in love. All that's changed is our focus on living/dying today, more so than yesterday, and the likelihood that we'll die of one disease rather than another. Even that expectation isn't foolproof. As we've seen, doctors don't claim 100 percent reliability.

We think death is a bullet with our name on it, and it is true that some of us die in crazy, unpredictable circumstances. But many others postpone death until an important anniversary or a child's graduation has passed.[25] Yogis reveal to their devotees that they will die on a specific day at a specific hour, even when they show no signs of illness. Some Native Americans expect to die when they *decide* to. Many are the stories of loved ones releasing the dying from any further obligation to live—and they die.

This modicum of control over when and how we live or die has always been with us. We just understand better that it really exists, and a little bit about how it works.

Of course, if you perceive yourself as both living *and* dying, you'll experience all of the advantages and none of the disadvantages. You'll meditate and make out your will, laugh at old *Cheers* programs, and cry with your children. You may take all the steps toward dying, but be less depressed about it.

4
FOUR

WHAT DOES
YOUR ILLNESS
MEAN TO YOU?

BILL planned to tell his family after Christmas. He didn't want to spoil the holidays for them, so, with heroic restraint, he'd kept the news to himself for a month. When his wife, Peg, commented on his absentmindedness, he blamed pressures at work.

Now, at the Christmas feast, he sat at the head of the table, surveying his family with mingled love and grief. Beside him, Peg served a candied yam to their five-year-old grandson, Zach, then wiped up the few drops of milk he'd spilled on the lace tablecloth. How she doted on that child! Bill worried that Peg was too fragile to bear the news, let alone care for him during his declining two years. She'd been subject to nervousness and depression all her life. Would she give up her position as executive director of the symphony orchestra? Bill didn't want her to, and yet he wanted her with him.

Innocent of his thoughts, Peg passed the casserole to their daughter-in-law, Heather, Zach's mother and Bill Jr.'s wife. They'd help all they could, but they lived three hours away; neither could leave their jobs for long, let alone the three children.

Uneasily, Bill watched Bill Jr. joke with Mark's artsy girlfriend. Bill was quite sure his son had fooled around during Heather's recent pregnancy—he must talk to him about this. Heather was a good wife, and sexual variety, though exciting, was never worth the potential loss of your family. Bill knew from experience. Mark himself, Peg's frayed-at-the-cuffs brother, tried to hide his jealousy. At forty-eight, he'd given up a successful antiques business to throw himself into painting landscapes. The financial roller-coaster ride was worth it, he claimed. Bill must recheck his will. Maybe he should arrange a trust for Mark, whose own children lived with his ex-wife.

"Gravy, Willy? Willy?" His mother nudged him on his right. "You're not eating."

As he took the gravy boat from her hands, she frowned at him, her sight recently sharpened by laser surgery. "Are those tears?" She'd asked in a normal tone of voice, but somehow everyone heard. One by one, conversations around the table broke off, the message of something wrong spreading like electrical impulses through a single system, and they turned to examine him, concern in their eyes.

"I was thinking how great it is to have all of you here. Wish Maddie could have made it."

And they were off on Peg's mother's latest diabetes setback, relieving Bill of the attention he felt he could not handle. Of all those here, he most dreaded his mother's reaction to the news. "No greater sorrow than the loss of a child"—especially an adult child— he'd heard it often enough. Perhaps they could conspire to keep it from her, but for how long? He could almost wish her own death to spare her this.

So the Christmas dinner progressed, revealing to Bill the multiple meanings of his illness and impending death and giving them depth and breadth. When he received the diagnosis, his overriding thought had been that he, the strong one, would die of weakness ("Be strong, little Willy," his own father had urged throughout his childhood). Now he was discovering what his death might mean to the others; to their daughter Tori, for example, single mother of little Angela, Zach's age and today in a red velveteen dress and cascading curls. At twenty-five, Tori was back in college and on track again after a disastrous love affair.

All those present would change during the next year, and the meaning of his death would ripple out to nieces, nephews, uncles, and others far away. And Bill himself would be the unwilling center as they gradually grew stronger, feeding on his weakness, just as his father had warned. "Be strong, little Willy." They would derive their own strength from his decline.

He would still be here next Christmas, although God alone knew in what shape—drooling in a wheelchair, perhaps? That might be how Zach, Angela, Darren, baby Hugh, and Mark's children would remember him, if they remembered him at all.

There was another option. Siren thoughts of suicide lured him. The trick was to squeeze every ounce of living left to him and then kill himself at the last possible moment, while he still had the strength. He'd have to do it cleverly. No car running in the locked garage or Peg wouldn't get his life insurance.

Then Bill Jr.'s laughter, so like his own, boomed toward him across the Christmas table, across the candles, crystal, silver, holly berries, and turkey. Still strong and vibrant, Bill thought the doctor's diagnosis of ALS must be a mistake. Suddenly he was filled with joy.

Thus the meanings of Bill's illness multiplied. What does your illness mean to you? How can awareness ease your suffering?

We have always ascribed various psychological meanings to different diseases. For Freudians, asthma signified "smother love." Back trouble, a universal malady, meant you carried too heavy a psychic burden. Similarly, gastrointestinal disease symbolized a situation in your life you could not "stomach." The cardiac patient has "lost heart" for some enterprise, or a loved one has "broken" it. Tuberculosis once had a romantic aura, indelibly portrayed in Thomas Mann's *The Magic Mountain;* the consumptive, as he or she was called in the nineteenth century, was a melancholy, delicate, thin, feverish, artistic, sensitive, spiritual creature, eyes fixed on redemption. Cancer, on the other hand, as Susan Sontag observes, stigmatized the sufferer. It was an evil, repugnant obscenity, something to hide.[1] AIDS has been called "God's punishment" for a way of loving. Currently, many diseases are viewed as mechanical breakdowns, increasingly intermingled with computer terminology. We may speak of "rebooting" the system, glitches, crashes, "reprogramming" with biofeedback and imagery. Indeed, "viruses" infect our software.

These cultural meanings are difficult to escape, but there are personal meanings as well. We are prisoners of the cultural if we don't identify the personal.

Several exercises can help you get in touch with what your disease means to you. These meanings may be illogical and emotional; don't worry about it. As with the other exercises in this book, there's no right answer.

MEANING-OF-DISEASE EXERCISE

On a sheet of paper, write the name of your illness at the top. As quickly as you can, jot down the first words that come to mind, good or bad. Some will make more sense than others, for example, medical terms like "lab," "shot," or "doctor." Other words may seem crazy. Write them down anyway.

Now for the second part of the exercise. On another sheet of paper, print one of the words on your list. Then dash off all your associations with that word. "Shot" might mean poke, hurt, drug, thigh, gun, punishment, anger, and so on. When the words stop popping, move to the next word on the original list. . . .

Finished? Look everything over. Can you spot a pattern in your answers? The more unusual associations are clues to the deeper meanings of your illness.

PAST-REWARDS EXERCISE

List illnesses you've experienced in the past. Be sure to include minor ones as well as major—colds, flu, and the like. Were there any *positive* experiences associated with them, such as escape from something disagreeable like a nasty work situation or an unpleasant obligation? Is there a similar reward for your present illness?

You might also include the diseases of others close to you. Perhaps you cared for a relative during her dying. Did anything good come of it, more closeness or love, perhaps? Something she taught you about how to live your life?

Whenever I was ill as a child, my mother cut the crusts off my bread. In fact, that was how I could tell my sickness was serious. Crusts off the bread meant she was worried (good!). Thus, chicken pox and pneumonia were oddly transmuted into love, which probably delayed my recovery, but the love I received was worth it.

What rewards are you receiving for your disease?

GESTALT EXERCISE

Ruby was thirty-eight and married with three children. Recently diagnosed with breast cancer, she had been scheduled for a lumpectomy.

This morning she was packing her suitcase and tote for the hospital. The kids were in school and her husband was at work. I'd made a weird suggestion to her. "Sit down and talk to your breasts," I'd said. "Ask them what they want to say to you. Then listen!"

Ruby wasn't about to do this in a roomful of people, even if they were family. But now she was alone. Where was the harm?

Feeling ridiculous, she perched on her bed and sank into a meditative state, as I'd instructed. Then, her attention focused on her breasts, she asked, "Is there something you want to tell me?" In her mind the reply zinged back to her: "We, the nurturing part of you, will kill you."

Ruby gasped and sprang to her feet. She understood immediately. For fifteen years she'd yearned to return to college and study all kinds of things—African history, anthropology, the flute, Buddhism, car maintenance, woodworking. Her enthusiasms were boundless but unfocused, and definitely not career-oriented—a sin in our modern culture, as her parents and husband lost no opportunity to remind her. Why waste her time? So she worked as an airline reservations clerk and put her earnings aside for their children's education instead. Day by week by month by year, she could feel herself shrinking, bits of who she could be dying off like twigs, deadwood, dropping to earth.

Had her psychological dying caused her physical deterioration? Was there a connection? No one could prove it, but Ruby *felt* it.

She would use her remaining time well. Amid protests from her family, Ruby returned to college. She reduced her job to half-time, and everyone at home had to pitch in with the chores. You may imagine how they grumbled about that!

Seven years have passed. Ruby earned her B.A. and is now in graduate school. If you ask, returning to herself did not save her life. Surgery, radiation, and chemotherapy did that. And yet, in another way, her life is saved even if she finds a lump tomorrow.

You, too, can consult with aspects of yourself about your illness (a gestalt therapy technique). Like Ruby, you might save the quality of your life, if not the quantity.

HOW RECOGNIZING MEANINGS MAY EASE YOUR SUFFERING

From the preceding consciousness-raising exercises, and the case examples, you have found that

1. Your illness has conventional cultural meanings for you, as well as connotations unique to yourself, as Ruby's were.
2. Your own experiences with past illnesses not only help you interpret the meanings of your current one, but also alert you to possible benefits of, or rewards for, remaining ill.
3. Meanings are not singular but rather multiple, complex, and many-layered. As Bill continued to discover, the meanings of his disease included the value of strength inculcated in him at an early age by his father, and all the ways his illness would affect his family, friends, work colleagues, and community.

Meanings grow in number and significance, often becoming revelations. How can they help you?

Let me give an example. To some of us, illness means punishment for something we did and for which we have never atoned. If this applies to you, ask yourself, "Do I really deserve this punishment?" You may have taken candy from your parents' room and blamed your brother. You may have lashed out at a vulnerable colleague. One woman discovered she was eternally guilty because, on demand, she'd told the father who molested her that she loved him when she really hated him. (He'd have beaten her otherwise. Besides, she must have loved him to do what she did—right? Then he died when she was twelve—her fault.) The emotions are not logical. Sometimes remembered guilt remains in the body. Does any of your misdeeds merit what is happening to you? Perhaps more serious sins do. Indeed, you may richly deserve your current "punishment." If so, do you regret your action? The hurt it caused? Is there a way to atone? Can you phone the victim? Send her a note? Or suppose it's too late for a practical action; say she's moved or died. Can you write that note and send it to the universe? Burn it, perhaps, while consigning it with a silent prayer to smoke? Can you confess it to your priest, minister, or rabbi? Give to a relevant charity? Meditate on what you did, with true regret? Sometimes the injured person's voice will respond in your mind.

Oddly, as we deal with the meaning of our illness, we may be able to lift some of the negativity from it—and it becomes less weighty. I am not suggesting a physical cure. I am suggesting an emotional or spiritual one.

Gilda Radner searched for causes of her cancer in the things she'd done.[2] Was her illness her fault? Was it due to saccharin? Cyclamates? Smoking? Red dye number 2? Candy, apples, tuna, city living, stress-induced eating disorders, junk food?

For some, a specific disease may signify a form of sacrifice. The person has lived a self-sacrificial life. Frequently, these are daughters of alcoholics. If you discover this meaning, ask yourself, "Will my sacrifice do any good? What is it that will live because I die?" Now that you are aware of the sacrifice, are you consciously willing to make it?

Or does your impending death feel like release? What is the prison you find yourself in? A life disappointment, perhaps? A relationship? Is there a way of knocking down the walls, rather than escaping altogether? Perhaps it would help to discuss this exercise with a friend or a therapist.

Or is your death a great adventure, of which there are not enough in your life? A final sleep? In your time remaining, you might include more adventure (or sleep, relaxation, enjoyment, hedonism, even). Then you will not need death to excite you, relax you, save you.

Or again, if you can benefit from your illness, is there another way of creating these rewards for yourself?

Or perhaps your illness has no other meaning. Perhaps it just *is* what it is, and you accept this.

Most important of all, by understanding the meaning of your illness to you, by gaining full awareness of it, it becomes less impersonal and not quite so unfair. And whatever is negative in that meaning you may be able to change, giving you more control. Any sense of meaninglessness begins to dissolve.

The meaning of your illness extends to life meaning and death meaning, as we shall see.

FIVE

SHOULD YOU

TELL OTHERS?

HOW CAN YOU TELL

YOUNGER CHILDREN?

ONE of the most difficult deaths I've ever encountered was that of Mark, a counseling student of mine in my graduate courses ("Death and Dying" among them). A thirty-year-old mild-mannered journalist, Mark had learned to hide his brilliance until he could be sure he didn't threaten the professor.

One day, Mark noticed a sore on the soft palate inside his mouth. He consulted a physician, and then another. Biopsies and X rays followed. The cancer had metastasized to the brain. Radiation and drugs couldn't halt the inexorable progress of his disease over the year.

Our close-knit graduate group was devastated. Students visited, ran errands, and supported him in every way they could. Our classes often began with news of Mark. It was uppermost in our minds and we had to deal with it before moving on. His attendance faltered, but on the occasions he did make it to school, even if he was too weak to have done the work or, in the latter months, his eyesight was too blurred, he always knew the material in more depth than the rest of us. Experimental treatments were tried, including radioactive "bullets" implanted in his brain. We held our breath, expecting, I think, some kind of fairy-tale ending. This newest treatment would finally work, and together we would celebrate Mark's return. He would be restored, resurrected even, walking among us strong, whole, sighted, and brilliant as ever.

It didn't happen.

We asked one another, "Why Mark? Why someone so good, kind, and gifted, with so much to contribute?" It wasn't a question Mark asked. As usual, he already knew the answer, which was "Why *not* Mark?"

So we talked, grieved, did what we could for him, and supported one another. In return, he shared his dying with us. He told us what was happening with him, matter-of-factly, not too much but enough. He wrote us little notes of thanks in his increasingly shaky scrawl.

When the time came, Mark decided to go home to Virginia to die among his family. We gave him a farewell party with his favorite gourmet lemon meringue pie—he insisted on bringing it. To ease the separation for us, he bestowed little gifts, a book for me with a beautiful inscription inside, thanking me for teaching him about his death. (It wasn't true. He taught me.)

Mark chose not only to tell us about his illness but also to share his passing with us. There were a number of reasons. First, his disease was life threatening and his time relatively short. Second, we'd have noticed his increasing absences and physical infirmity, so we would have guessed at one possibility or another. Perhaps our anxiety would have been worse if we hadn't known the details. Third, his personality made him comfortable with sharing; he was an open rather than a private person. Fourth, even in his extreme humility, I think he recognized his opportunity to teach us. Fifth, he didn't have as much to lose as some do—not his job, not the isolation or embarrassment of a stigmatizing disease. Sixth, I like to think he gained some strength and support from the love we gave him.

Some choose not to tell, often because their circumstances are very different from Mark's. Ellie was also thirty, an administrative assistant on the fast track at a New York Fortune 500 company with nowhere to go but up. She began having difficulties with walking and blurred vision. The diagnosis was multiple sclerosis. Ellie chose not to tell.

It wouldn't do her career any good if word got out. Instead, she became expert at concealing her physical symptoms. Her "leg" problem was due to an old automobile accident.

There were other reasons for her decision. Unlike Mark's, her illness was chronic and long-term, the pace of it far slower, her disability far less obvious. She'd live for years. She'd always been a private person. Her health was no one else's business. If they didn't know, they wouldn't treat her as an "MS." They'd treat her as Ellie. This meant she could often distract herself from her predicament. She didn't want to dwell on it; rather, she wanted to live as normal a life as possible for however long she could. Who knew what medical breakthroughs might occur? Finally, unacknowledged even to herself, I think, there was her pride. She could do as much as anyone else, she didn't need them, she was completely able-bodied. In particular, she didn't need their pity. Her mother had been a woman with unlimited capacity for self-pity over the relatively inconsequential, and Ellie was determinedly her opposite.

Years passed. Ellie's colleagues noticed more frequent stumbles. Sometimes she needed a cane. She persisted in her explanations, but they began to suspect. They asked questions. She put them off. She'd do it *her* way. Some wanted to help and felt rebuffed. When they offered rides, they learned to make excuses: "I have to go by there anyway," "I like company," "I need your advice." At restaurants they forged ahead, apparently without thinking, so they could open doors. They learned to conspire with her and she with them. But, perhaps because of the strain, she fought with a lot of people.

In such circumstances as Mark's and Ellie's, we tend to draw either closer to each other or farther apart, perhaps even severing our relationship. Relationships are *never* static for any length of time. They are always dynamic, even if we are not aware of this. When they *appear* static, they are decaying.

Telling those around you draws some to you and drives others away. But not telling does the same.

The decision is tougher when society places a moral judgment on the disease, as it does with AIDS or liver cirrhosis. If a man with

AIDS tells his co-workers, he may lose his job—and his health insurance. He'll very likely feel he must keep the secret at all costs. Jared, a real-estate broker, at first told no one except his partner and their close circle. But as his disease progressed he told others, and the circle of caring people widened. He never felt alone.

Another reason not to tell is that it might discourage romance. A prospective lover might simply withdraw from you, not wanting the responsibility. You might not want to chance it.

Disclosure confirms your illness to yourself, making it a more important part of your identity, because others see you as ill and treat you that way. You might not be ready for that.

Isolation and feelings of loneliness are strongly implicated in the onset and/or worsening of disease. Gaining a supportive environment is a good reason to tell. Some people, however, fear being shunned or rebuffed, and consequently keep their disease to themselves.

But what about the pryers, the nosies, the busybodies? Ellie felt their curiosity and resented it—a major reason she didn't tell.

Why do people want all the gory details? For the same reason they slow down and rubberneck at the six-car accident on the freeway (for which they're unendingly castigated). It's a form of rehearsal for them. They're seeking reassurance that if the same thing happens to them it won't be as awful as they imagine. They want to know what you're experiencing, and then how you feel about it. They want you to say, "It's not as bad as I thought it would be," or "It's not as bad as it looks," so it won't be as bad for them. The physical details of disease, injury, and death are a mystery. Sherwin Nuland's book *How We Die* gives them to us and is popular for precisely that reason.[1] He reveals what has been hidden.

Once you recognize that people's curiosity about your illness is a form of defensive rehearsal for their own death, you may not resent it as much.

In sum, your decision about whether or not to tell will depend on all of the following factors:

1. How immediately life threatening is your disease? People live for many years with MS, cancer, heart ailments, and diabetes. There are more treatments for these than for the ALS with which Bill is afflicted.

2. How obvious are your symptoms? How soon are they likely to be more so? Will you need more time off work?
3. How communicable is your illness?
4. Is there a stigma associated with your disease, with possible negative consequences, for example, losing your job or health insurance?
5. Whom might you tell—spouse or partner, children, parents, friends, colleagues? How will they receive the news? Will it have a devastating effect on an ill parent?
6. If, like Bill, you told no one for a while, could you unburden yourself to a therapist or a spiritual counselor?
7. How do you *feel* about revealing such personal details? Are you normally a private person, gathering your life to yourself with intense focus? Or are you more open?
8. Do you *feel* you have the opportunity and strength to teach others about your dying? (You're not obligated!)

One caveat: If you begin to tell others that something's wrong, you can't usually leave it at that. You have to finish. People want to name the disease.

As Bill's disabilities became more obvious, he admitted at work to a "little problem," claiming that his doctor was optimistic. When he took time off, it was because a family member was ill. He made an excuse to drop off the company softball team "temporarily." He felt that "discretion" was expected. "Never whine," his father had told him. "Other people have their own problems."

HOW CAN YOU TELL YOUNGER CHILDREN?

If you are a parent, perhaps the most wrenching aspect of your dying is leaving behind your younger child or children—your toddler, elementary-schooler, or teen. Someone else will rear them to adulthood, not you. How can you explain that to them? Since their birth, you have protected them from all harm. How can you protect them from your absence?

It depends partly on their age. Children develop increasingly mature notions about death as they grow older. The very young child, aged roughly two to seven, can't conceive of death as permanent. He assumes that death is like being asleep. If you tell him his dead kitty that you've buried in the backyard will never come back, he may nod as if he accepts it, then later put a dish of fresh milk out on the porch. Somewhere between the ages of seven and twelve (there are wide variations), he begins to grasp the notions that everyone dies, that a dead person can no longer move or breathe, and that she can't be cured by either medicine or magic. The teenager's greater capacity for abstract reasoning helps him develop philosophical and religious beliefs; also, he has a concept of a future time that extends into years, and he figures he has a long time before his own death.[2]

One of the first things you may want to do after you learn of the seriousness of your illness is to expose your younger child to the notion of death as natural and normal (contrary to what he sees on TV). A number of books can help you do this (see the Notes and Resources section for this chapter). I suggest you read these books first yourself, to be sure the philosophy agrees with your own. Then read them *with* your child; make the occasion one of affectionate togetherness, just as you would reading any book with him.

Next, one expert believes you should tell your children three things: that you are seriously ill, the name of your disease, and what you think may happen.[3] Children know something is wrong, and it is reassuring to give a name to it.

Telling children about death is a lot like telling them about sex. Let *them* raise the various issues. Often their questions are immediate and practical: "Why are you in bed?" or "What does the medicine do?" Answer their questions matter-of-factly and truthfully, but don't give them more information than they ask for. If they're frowning after your explanation, encourage them to ask more. If they just say "Oh" and skip off to play, don't call them back for an oration.

When your child knows you're seriously ill, and your illness begins to affect your daily life, reassure him that it's not his fault. Sometimes a child believes a parent got sick because he got mad at her and even wished she'd die. He needs to understand that his thoughts can't cause things to happen.

Also, if you have been fighting with your spouse, or are separated or divorced, let your child know the estranged spouse is not to blame. He'll be needing that parent even more in the future.

He may be terrified that he, too, will become sick and die. Let him know that this doesn't usually happen to most people until they're very old, and that (in most cases) he cannot "catch" your illness from you.

Understand if your younger child is suddenly afraid of the dark; give him a night-light, another cuddly toy, plenty of hugs and kisses. Be patient with other lapses—sleep or eating disturbances, fears, in fact, any very *temporary* changes in his pattern of behavior. One expert believes, however, that failure or trouble at school should never be tolerated but, rather, addressed as soon as it occurs.[4] Often, just talking with the child may be the solution (don't ignore the problem). Changes that persist beyond a few days or weeks may signal that your child is having difficulty handling the stress. A visit with a professional counselor may be in order.

There are some things you will not want to tell younger children.

Don't tell them that you're going on a long trip. Children think you're abandoning them, that you have a choice. Young children can be very literal. At some point, you'll want to tell them you'd stay with them if you could.

Nor do you want to tell them that God or Jesus is calling you. Many children hearing this will then hate God.

Don't tell them that dead pets have gone to sleep, or that you will. They'll fear closing their eyes, that they won't wake up.

Be careful about saying you'll visit them in spirit or watch over them. Some children can develop a terror of ghosts. But if they ask you to watch over them, you might tell them you'll try.

If you believe you'll continue in another life, at some point nearing the end you might tell them that someday, far in the future, you'll all be together again. If you're an atheist or an agnostic, do stay away from moldering in the earth with worms. Saying you "don't know" is honest, and if you feel unafraid or curious, tell them that, too—anything positive.

The thing to emphasize in these last months is love—of each other, pets, nature, play, and friends. These continue after you're gone. It's also important to let them help with your care and to listen to them. These are wonderful gifts.

Hospitals and hospices often facilitate support groups for grieving children and families. You might consider one. They help children know that there are others like them, and that grieving is okay. Ask your hospice, bereavement group, or physician to recommend a counselor who specializes in death and dying.

Most important, you want to ensure that your child will have a stable environment, that someone will be caring for him when you're gone. Assure him of this, and see that he spends plenty of time with that person and in the *place* where he'll be (for example, an ex-spouse's home). In this way, you help smooth the transition.

It's a lot to ask, I know. You're going through your own personal agonies—physical, mental, emotional, perhaps spiritual. But it's an act of love, and love is a marvelous painkiller.

A word or two on how to comfort yourself during this wrenching period:

First of all, take comfort in the most recent research showing that children do not suffer permanent damage from the early loss of a parent, that, on the contrary, they survive intact and flourish just as well as the nonbereaved.[5]

Remember that your children will probably feel your presence, when they are asleep or awake, especially during crises, whether or not you are actually there. In this sense, you will continue to comfort them. And there is always the possibility that you can continue in reality as well.

If you grieve not being there to help with all the problems they'll encounter in the future, you can write a letter to them, to be opened during their teen years perhaps. I did this when I was faced with the possibility; I poured out all the advice I thought they would need about love, school, career, values, everything I could think of, and I sealed it tight. I survived, and when they reached their teens they, of course, listened to their friends and not me. In fact, a letter from a *dead* mother might have had more influence!

This is probably good to remember: We tend to idealize our future, just as we may our past. Our children will be reared mainly by their peers, whether or not we are here, especially in their teens.

In addition to letters, you can update the photo albums so your children can trace their development and yours. You can tape little stories of how they grew, and make videotapes of family gatherings and vacations.

Perhaps you cannot conceive of your spouse remarrying and a fos- ter parent raising your children in your place. But it may happen, and if he chose you, he'll probably choose well again. You'll always be the "genuine original" mother or father, one with whom your children heavily identify and to whom they trace personality traits, values, and physical characteristics (the good and the bad). Since you're not around to discipline, control, and fight with, your chil- dren may idealize you far more than if you were alive. Thus, death may make you a better parent!

LEGAL, MEDICAL, AND

FINANCIAL PREPARATIONS:

PSYCHOSPIRITUAL

GUIDANCE

THE following practical preparations have psychological and spiritual aspects that you will want to consider:

1. Making a will
2. Signing a physician's advance health directive and living will
3. Delegating power of attorney
4. Delegating durable power of attorney (health proxy)
5. Bequeathing your organs for transplant or your body to a medical school
6. Deciding about final disposal of your body
7. Financial planning

To carry out these preparations, you need information and/or professional help from experts in the legal, medical, and financial-planning fields.[1] There are entire books and computer resources devoted to each of these topics; I list some I've found most helpful in the Notes and Resources section.

It's possible, however, for you to complete all these tasks and still not address the emotional and spiritual aspects of your major decisions.

They are yours alone, of course. My purpose is to highlight some major considerations for you in order to shorten and ease the process.

YOUR WILL

In her award-winning novel A *Thousand Acres*, author Jane Smiley tells the story of a father who cuts one of his three daughters from a farm inheritance. This action tears the family apart, sets sister against sister, husband against wife, and exposes secrets whose bleached bones might better have been left in the earth. As a result, the entire family's past, present, and future unravels.[2]

If you are tempted to disinherit someone, you probably have good reason. Perhaps your relative or friend or organization has betrayed you in some way. Or your child would spend the money on drugs. Or your brother is a fiscally irresponsible no-account who has stolen from you.

You have a right to be angry, just as you have a right to any of your emotions. I hope you can express your anger and hurt to those closest to you. The question is whether or not you wish to act on those emotions.

Disowning someone is a way of "getting back"; your final vengeance, your "last word." Too often, though, in whatever way you may rationalize it, it becomes an act of malice that can corrode your soul.

In most cases, your disownment is not limited to the one person who harmed you. It ripples out to those nearest and dearest to him. More important, you are also disinheriting the others in your will to the extent that they identify with him. You show that your love for them is not unconditional—it depends on what they do, not who they are. And no matter how justified they believe you are, they may feel guilty over taking what's his. They may therefore blame him, enlarging his transgressions.

Being disowned, especially by parents, feels like the "killing" thing it is. Symbolically (perhaps actually), it deprives the child of the wherewithal to continue life. Her parent sends a message of regret that she was born. Who of us, even parents of brutal murderers, would kill our child either literally or symbolically? The weeping mother in the courtroom, protesting her child's sweetness, is a commonplace. And who of us would deliberately rip the fabric, however flimsy, of our family relationships? Our relatives need one another, especially when we're gone. But if, in spite of everything, you feel you must disinherit someone, I suggest that you discuss it in family council.

In sum, disinheriting often sets in motion deep family rifts, pitting relative against relative. In vengeance against his three brothers who had always belittled him before their father, one disowned son persuaded a lawyer to take the case on contingency. The case dragged on for years, and even though he lost, his brothers had to declare bankruptcy. The lawyers got the inheritance, and the angry brother was satisfied.

Disownment perpetuates itself. Your children, too, may be tempted to disinherit. This is how you've taught them to deal with those who displease them. The family history becomes twisted, the episode memorialized in succeeding generations through myths, at family gatherings, in photo albums.

Remember that your heirs will be learning of your bequests while they are grief-stricken—yes, even those you don't get along with. Their guilt over their poor relationship with you will make their loss of you especially difficult to bear, as will their shock when your death suddenly ends any possibility of reconciliation. It is common for the bereaved to want to idealize those who have just passed, to spread the winding sheet of love over flaws in the relationship. You are likely to want this too. After all, the love among you, even if it was mottled, scratched, and dented, was important to each of you. Your will might interfere with this final blessing.

Your will includes a separate "letter of instruction," bequeathing your most cherished jewelry, furniture, and mementos. You may want to ask each heir about his or her choice. If they respond with something like "Oh, Dad, I can't bear to think about it," be matter-of-fact, even say it would ease your mind. Give a loving and personal reason for each bequest in your letter: "My bone china goes to Rachel, because she loves antiques."

You may also want to consider bequests to political causes or organizations that you love. This continues work that you value.

One child may deserve more for her care of you. Aside from generous expense reimbursement, I'd be careful. Give her first choice of possessions. Her siblings will probably understand and not resent this. But leave each child the same amount, perhaps setting up a trust for anyone mentally ill or incompetent, with food or rent to be paid by the executor. If you've given more to one child for her education or a home, this is your opportunity to even things out. And don't give more to the unsuccessful child than the successful one.[3]

When you choose a relative as the will executor, explain to the others why you chose him. Even if it's because you have more confidence in his judgment, or you get along with him best of all, try to find a more objective reason: "He lives closer," or "You were your dad's executor, and I'm trying to spread the load."

If you have questions or doubts, discuss them openly rather than harboring them, and invite your loved ones to do the same. Finally, there have been wills bequeathing not material assets but beautiful and favorite things like sunsets. Tell those who remain that they can find you there.

In sum, let your will express loving care for those you leave behind, to be for them a means of transcendence over their loss of you. I don't think most people realize how powerful their last will and testament can be—for good or ill.

Finally, I suggest that you don't wait until the last minute to arrange your will. If you do, you risk seeing this task as a loss of hope. Update periodically.

PHYSICIAN'S ADVANCE HEALTH DIRECTIVE AND LIVING WILL

The physician's advance health directive and living will (usually combined) sets forth your desires regarding end-of-life treatment. It varies from state to state, so be sure to acquaint yourself with the laws in your own. Through this document, if you are adjudged terminal, you can refuse CPR, defibrillation, intubation, hydration, and intravenous nutrition, among other treatments. You can also request "active euthanasia, if it becomes legal." The living will may include a personal statement of how and where you wish to die—at home, for example, or in a hospice. The idea is that you do not want to prolong dying; it is not that you reject living.

Through a different document, the Christian Affirmation of Life, which was approved by the Catholic Hospital Association in June 1994, you can express your religious faith in living for as long as possible.[4] You accept treatments rather than refuse some.

These directives relieve your loved ones of the agony of making such decisions if you become mentally incompetent or comatose. Be sure to discuss yours with the person you designate to see that these instructions are carried out. Explain what choices you've made and *why*. When she knows the why, she'll be better able to make responsible decisions at crucial moments.

Finally, if you do decide on a Christian Affirmation or the physician's advance directive and living will, inform your physician and give her a copy. Ask if she has any religious, medical, or other reservations about carrying out your wishes. If so, you may need to make the hard decision to find another doctor.

POWER OF ATTORNEY

There are two kinds of power of attorney: business and health. A simple power of attorney is a legal document authorizing someone, whom you choose, to make decisions regarding your *finances*, should you become incapacitated either physically or mentally. It allows her to manage property or business, pay your bills from your accounts, enter your safe-deposit box, participate in legal action, and sign documents for you. You may choose a relative or an attorney to do this.

A durable power of attorney, also known as a "health-care power of attorney" or "health proxy," authorizes your representative to make *medical* decisions regarding your treatment, hospitals, physicians, and the like, in case of your disability. She may not be the same person as the one who acts for you financially.

Select someone whose values are congruent with your own, and in whom you have *emotional* confidence. You are putting the end of your life in their hands. I selected one of my daughters. When I phoned to ask her, I had no idea how she'd respond. I'd broached the subject in the past, but she'd gotten all choked up, and we'd dropped it. Finally I told her I had to ease my mind by making these decisions well in advance. (I'm in the field, after all!) Her response was "Mom, it would be an honor." So, my preparation for death was another occasion of love!

BEQUEATHING YOUR BODY

You can make a gift of your body in two ways:

1. By donating organs such as kidneys and eye corneas for transplant to other individuals. You carry a donor card with you. On some state drivers' licenses you sign a form on the back because, in case of an accident, your organs should be harvested as soon as possible. Organs are removed from brain-dead, but artifically "beating-heart cadavers." The United Network for Organ Sharing (UNOS) coordinates organ distribution.[5]
2. By donating your entire body to a medical school for the students to practice on. Make arrangements with the university, which will supply you with proper forms.

Most of us can donate corneas and tissues, no matter what our physical condition (there are exceptions, such as badly burned bodies). On the other hand, relatively few of us die young enough and healthy enough to make such organ donations as lungs, heart, or kidneys. If we do, it's an incredible gift—breath, heartiness, or independence from the dialysis machine.

Thoughts of donating body parts evoke squeamishness. It's hard to imagine we won't feel the snip across the eye or the scalpel down our midriff. Then, too, we've heard stories of medical students trading insults across cadavers—us! If we have any body shame, knowing we will be unable to snap back some withering rejoinder may dismay us. One doctor insists on his students treating bodies with dignity and respect during dissection—the fact is, he's got to insist! Does he keep the guffaws down to snickers?

This is probably the place to mention a little-known teaching method which may be practiced on your body immediately after you have died. Apparently, in some hospitals, physicians use newly deceased bodies to teach medical students such techniques as endotracheal intubation, and other resuscitation procedures.[6] This is done without the patient's consent. As written up in the medical journals, there is conflict over whether or not it is ethical. I suggest you discuss your wishes with your relatives and add them to your advance directives; your relatives may never know whether or not resuscitation techniques were practiced on your body, but they can be alert to the possibility. Also, there must be some effort on the part of laymen to define the ethicality, as well as individual rights in this regard, just as there is in the case of organ donorship.

Donating our organs and bodies is a matter of values. "Doing good" is fashionable, but anger at our human predicament often influences our choices. You may want to consider the feelings of the bereaving. And it's easier simply to do nothing—donation usually requires an action of some kind (not always). On the other hand, you may view your body as an old but still useful overcoat that you're willing to donate, just as you'd give your real one to the Salvation Army.

Wouldn't it be nice if medical students offered up prayerful thanks over our bodies as some Native Americans have done before shooting a deer or plucking a root? Don't we deserve it?

FINAL DISPOSITION OF YOUR BODY

You'll be helping your relatives immensely if you let them know your wishes regarding final disposition of your body.[7] Inform yourself of your state's laws. Embalming is not necessarily a legal requirement, for example. Do you want to be buried or cremated? Should your ashes be scattered or sealed in an urn and stored in a columbarium?

Visit a funeral parlor or two, look at caskets, and acquaint yourself with costs. Consider the possibility of purchasing a cemetery plot. Resist on-the-spot decisions, however, until you've done enough research to make an informed decision. The American Association of Retired People (AARP) has excellent materials you can send for.[8]

What kind of service would you like? Traditional? Religious? Where would you like it held? A church or funeral parlor chapel? Outdoors? Be sure to communicate these decisions, preferences, and advance plans to your loved ones. You will be relieving them of these burdensome duties in the midst of their grief.

FINANCIAL PLANNING

"I am dying as I've lived: beyond my means," Oscar Wilde is reported to have said.[9] Many of us would sympathize.

You may have done long-term financial planning throughout your life, although much may have gone wrong—for example, the extended illness of a spouse or losses on the stock market. You've reached this point in life with whatever financial resources are left, and these are what you have to work with.

As you can see, all of the above practical end-of-life matters involve financial arrangements. For example, if there isn't much left, you may want to choose cremation over burial (cremation's cheaper). You could even join the Neptune Society, or another "direct-disposition" organization.[10] Without a funeral, your body would be cremated in a very inexpensive casket, and the ashes inurned or scattered.

If your estate is substantial, consider setting up a living trust so that the executive trustee can manage finances and avoid probate. Also consider making gifts to your heirs of up to $10,000 per year tax free.[11]

Depending on your health and disability insurance, and the nature of your final illness, your last days or months may eat up much of what you own. You may feel this is worthwhile, even that this is what you saved for, or you may not. You may value a grandchild's college education or a grown child's home ownership over extended treatment for yourself. Therefore, you need to protect yourself and your loved ones by informing yourself, making your decisions, and documenting them.

A FINAL WORD

Most people carry out their practical tasks in a logical and rational manner. It doesn't occur to them that these are opportunities to express love and to improve the lives of others. The *meanings* of organ donations, monetary bequests, and rituals escape them. But as family members help tie up the loose ends of your life, you all remind one another that you will not be together forever, and you draw closer.

Meditate prayerfully on your gifts. Think of them as ways of loving. Then they will be received as such.

The fact is, supposedly practical, concrete, tangible things are never *only* what they are.

7

SEVEN

COPING

POSITIVELY

WITH

DAILY LIFE

FOR the great American novelist Reynolds Price, coping daily with an elongated spinal tumor he called "the eel" became the book *A Whole New Life*.[1]

The personal narratives of those facing life-threatening illness give us insight into meeting the challenges of daily living. How we meet those challenges has an impact on our self-concept and life meaning. Among the narratives I recommend are those of Arnold Beisser, Norman Cousins, Kat Duff, Alice Hopper Epstein, Arthur Frank, Joseph Heller, Jody Heymann, Hirshel Jaffe, Leonard Kriegel, Andre Lord, Paul Monette, Lon Nungesser, Robert O'Boyle, and Gilda Radner.[2] A caution: They *do* stress the ordeals of disease, which may be too depressing or scary for you at this time. Be wise!

Below are lessons we glean from those who have gone before.

POSITIVE REFRAMING

Often the new diet, exercise, medications, treatments, and activity bans can make you feel deprived. Life has become dangerous. The zest is gone. You bemoan the fact that "living takes too much time." Self-maintenance used to be a sideline. Now it's the main event, the center ring of what is becoming a one-ring circus.

One of the most liberating things you can do for yourself is to reframe these daily living changes in a positive light.

For example, Marian learned to envision her dialysis as a cleansing and purifying ritual.

To his new, more time-consuming diet, rest periods, meditation, medical checkups, group therapy, and family time, Wayne adds daily two-hour walks. These strengthen his heart for the things and people he loves. He discovers delight that he had previously missed in the faces of others. When he nods and smiles, so do they. A whole new life!

Charlie's increasing Parkinsonian tremor frustrates him because it takes so much longer to do everything. But he recognizes that he now has more time to think.

Jeff would have turned up his nose at a diet of fruits, vegetables, and grains in the old, pre-AIDS days of fast food. He is fortunate that his partner, Doug, has a gourmet flare with spices. They feast together by candlelight, discovering unsuspected sensual pleasure. A whole new life!

Careful adherence to his diabetic regimen is a form of bargaining for Rudy. If he counts spaghetti strands, he'll survive.

Ellie's medication smashed the staphyloccus in her lungs with the vengeance she felt toward God, fate, and other people for afflicting her with MS; now lobar pneumonia hasn't a chance.

Thus, love, anger, caution, pleasure, frustration, and even cleansing transmute new demands into new rituals.[3]

ASK FOR HELP

Gerontologist Kenneth Doka cites a patient who refused relatives' offers of help. Assuming he was trying to maintain his independence, they didn't press, which angered him. He thought they should. The lesson is, be honest and clear about your needs.[4]

Proud as he is, Bill has learned to do precisely that. A lifelong insomniac, he now sleeps even less than he did and needs more daytime rest. When someone offers to help, he accepts. If it's not what he needs, he asks for something else. Accustomed to taking charge, he is the perfect supervisor for Peg, the children, work colleagues, friends, and volunteers. His family, on the other hand, is careful not to overprotect him or cultivate his dependency on them.

Ellie does it a bit differently. She's far too proud to ask; in fact, she and her family conspire to maintain the fiction that she still does everything she used to. She'll suggest dinner to a visitor, for example. They'll walk into the kitchen, and perhaps she'll get down the package of spaghetti noodles. Then, while she and the guest are talking (thus distracting him from what's really going on), teenaged daughters appear as if by magic and do the actual cooking. If she tells a daughter to hand her a can of tomato sauce, the daughter opens it first, placing it on the counter, where it sits until the onions, green pepper, and ground turkey are browned. Then the daughter pours it into the skillet, and Ellie picks up the oregano. All this may sound a bit pathological to you, but the fact is that most families have similar systems to protect members' self-esteem, just not quite so obvious. Life-threatening illness exposes such systems. We're all entitled.

Ellie's daily coping methods illustrate that we die as we have lived. Our personalities do not change. Some fight illness, some ignore it, others accept it or even welcome it, right to the end.

It's true that most people are too busy to add one iota of extra work to their stuffed lives. In the new lean and mean economy, they're doing half another person's work as well as their own, and raising families besides. But you need and deserve their help, and it will do them good to give it. Then when their turn comes they won't be too shy to ask. Think of all the assistance you've volunteered in the past. Time to call in your markers (although not necessarily from the same individuals).

We're an extended human family. If each of us spends a day on your chores, takes you shopping or to the doctor, together we'll cover your care without too much personal sacrifice. We owe this to one another, and we reap the rewards of your teaching.

As for you, you must maintain that delicate balance between doing all you can, retaining your autonomy, and leaning on others when you're weak, exhausted, or hurting. If you do less, you risk dying before you're dead. If you overdo, you risk medical setback. Most of us are strangers to our bodies. We hear gross needs for food, sex, and sleep, for bladder, bowel, and pain relief, but are oblivious to subtler cues. Now, if we don't listen, our body punishes us like a loudly insistent child diving into the swimming pool and screaming, "Look at me!" We must learn to play our bodies like instruments, attuned to every nuance.

SHOULD YOU EXPECT THE WORST SO YOU WON'T BE DISAPPOINTED?

Expecting the worst is called "cognitive defensiveness." You rehearse the most horrible outcomes of every facet of your disease so you'll be accustomed to them and develop tactics to fight them.

Ellie currently walks with a limp and occasionally uses a cane. She imagines herself slipping from her wheelchair to the floor, alone, unable to reach the phone, eventually puddling as evening fades to night. (At this point, a director yells, "CUT!")

Research does *not* show that such dreary imaginings either protect or prepare. You might gain some desensitization to the awful, but you pay dearly for it in pessimism, which can lead to depression and even the ordeal for which you prepare yourself.

HOW TO COPE AS ENERGY FLAGS

You've always prepared meals, cleaned house (more or less), done laundry. Now substitute quick and easy for gourmet, frozen dinners for homemade (if they don't violate your diet too much), raw for cooked when you can tolerate it. Welcome the neighbors' casseroles, and yes, tell them the minute they offer that you don't eat salt or sugar. They'd rather substitute than do all that work for nothing. Let the rain wash the car and water the yard. If it gives you pleasure, putter around the flower beds, nothing heavy. As for your home, when it gets too dirty, you could be like a guest at Alice's mad tea party and move to another chair—or room, or house, even. If you're not dust-sensitive, think of the layers as mounting thick enough to hatch something—and then keep them around as pets. As for dust bunnies, kick them out the back door and watch them roll down the walk like tumbleweed.

Cleanliness is a frame of mind. It takes on whatever value you assign to it. Remember that weeklong camping trip with the kids? Grit and grime? You and your "home" were much dirtier than now.

Maintain personal cleanliness, however, so you don't drive others away, particularly if you have special problems such as an ostomy or incontinence. By the way, we were taught at our mother's knee that these things are nasty; they aren't, in and of themselves—witness the sexual practices of some people! Think of a once-worn shirt as pretty clean, or a thrice-worn as merely gamey, to be put in the laundry hamper before the guests arrive.

Extensive research with seriously ill patients shows that you are likely to adapt to your illness by simplifying your life, doing less, staying home, juggling chores, perhaps moving to a place more compact and easier to care for, adding a ramp to stairs, seeing fewer people, pacing yourself, timing problematic body functions when you do plan to go out, and the like. What you used to take for granted—a few hours without having to go to the bathroom, for example—you no longer do.[5]

Some people plan one additional chore a day—for example, treatment on Monday, recuperation on Tuesday, soup preparation on Wednesday, phone calls, bills, and letters on Thursday, marketing on Friday. Make good use of chore services, relatives, volunteers, neighbors, and friends. Have a list so you can organize your helpers. Call and ask; offer a choice of services and days so they can work you into their tight schedules. Be grateful, even if you're feeling envious and resentful. They have their burdens, too.

REMEMBER—IT'S NOT NECESSARILY PERMANENT!

Every time Ellie gets a new MS symptom, she thinks she'll always have it. Maybe, maybe not. You're more likely to have your good days and your bad days, and you need to organize and plan for the good and allow yourself to "veg out" on the bad.

You may follow one of five different illness trajectories: gradual decline, speedier decline, remission and relapse, decline and stabilization, or recovery with the realization that the heart attack or cancer may recur.[6] You don't know yet which of these paths is yours or if you'll switch from one to the other. No matter which, your comfort level is likely to fluctuate.

With each serious episode, you may wonder, "Is this it?" Probably not. You'll know when "it" is.

YOU'LL NEVER HAVE SEX IN THIS TOWN AGAIN!

In our culture, sexual activity is an occasion for bragging and self-esteem; inactivity is a source of secret shame. If we have a good sex life, it rarely occurs to us that this may change. But sooner or later it changes for everyone.

Surgery, treatment, or medication may lower your libido or potency; sex may be painful. Don't hesitate to confide in your doctor. Ask her what you should expect. Perhaps she can change your medication. Do read the excellent American Cancer Society booklets (rose-pink for women, aqua-blue for men).[7]

The nature of your sexual activity may change, at least temporarily, with more emphasis on the wonderful pleasure of simple touch, or even new sex aids or fantasy. Did you know that, in some paraplegics, orgasms may happen anywhere in the body, even in a shoulder? Orgasms for both partners each and every time are not necessarily the most important end result. The mind is the major sex organ, and your mind may be giving you more trouble than your body is. Talk openly with your partner, and get counseling if that doesn't work.

AIR OUT YOUR MIND!

One of your greatest risks during this period is that you'll allow your great life adventure to shrink to the dimensions of your disease and its treatment. Your thoughts can fill up with nothing but a constant monitoring of your condition and what you can do to ameliorate it. A new pain you'd have paid no attention to before takes on ominous meanings, and your imagination fills in the blanks. Family and medical staff ask about your illness, which you report in grim detail. Suddenly you're a depressing bore to everyone, especially to yourself.

Save the story of your illness, its mileposts, highs, and lows, for your doctor and your journal, where you write your "illness chronology." Some friends ask about your progress politely, or as a kindness, to allow you to ventilate. Others crave gory details to reassure themselves that they're different and will not die. Still others use your experience to prepare. Limit your ventilation, paying attention to their reactions. Ask them to talk about themselves, politics, whatever has always interested you, even if (temporarily) it doesn't. They'll revitalize your interests. Go to live in their experiences for a time (and, by the way, they'll be more likely to visit yours). Their lives are your windows on the world. Keeping interested may help you live longer, and will certainly lend a better quality to your remaining time.

Don't, however, waste energy on negative people or others you don't want to see. *Screen your calls!*[8] Don't be afraid to tell someone you're not up to a visit. Let family and friends rebuff the persistent curiosity-seeker or the lonely illness-ghoul. At this stage in your "whole new life," don't waste precious moments being polite.

One reason you're tempted to stay at home, besides the good ones of conserving time and energy, is that your illness is becoming more obvious. I'd like to suggest that you brave the public, however. If more people stopped hiding out and exposed their esophageal speech, their shakiness and ostomies, their canes and wheelchairs, they would become more usual, even normal.

Finally, take your mind for an airing to your local library. Not just for information on your illness, but also for access to the Internet, travel videos, CDs to lull you into altered states, concerts, talks, films, and mysteries to escape into on rough days.

IF THEY SAY YOU MUST MOVE

The day may come when your children tell you that you must move to some form of assisted living. You may feel devastated. Many patients say they want to remain in their homes to the end of their lives. "I don't care if it's a closet—it's my own," one told me. The great majority feel this way, but 80 percent do die in hospitals and nursing homes. Somehow you never thought this would apply to you. You feel hurt, resentful, and betrayed, no matter how gently or reasonably they explain it.

In all probability, your children are acting in what they sincerely believe are your best interests. They're afraid you'll burn the house down while heating water for tea; or that you'll be the victim of the next con man with a roofing scam; or that you'll fall and be unable to call for help. They are entirely focused on preserving your life and welfare.

There's a big problem here that you can't communicate to them: Your independence and quality of life may be more important to you than a few more years of life. You might honestly prefer to take your chances rather than give up your home, with all its ghosts, presences, textures, mementos, light, and dark—all that's precious to you. This is where the fights erupt.

From your children's point of view, you're being unreasonable. From yours, you're opting for higher quality over longer life. And you're not supposed to. The fact that you do argues for your frailer mental abilities (they think). Meanwhile, you have this awful vision of yourself stuck in a chair, with a bunch of quavery voices singing "Happy Days Are Here Again" at you, or enduring watery mashed potatoes beside someone for whom incessant talk is a religion, or compelled by some overenthusiastic nurse to join in whatever passes for "exercise" or "activities." "Fate worse than death" is the phrase that comes to mind.

I have several suggestions that may ease your decision:

- Immediately make a list of priorities, in case you have to go. Privacy may be more important to you than anything else. Or bringing your cat along. Or having a place for art—*real* art, not their pot holders. Different facilities offer different advantages; let your children know loud and clear what's most important.

- Remember that this arrangement may be only temporary. (Then again, you may return home for a few months, only to reenter the hospital, hospice, nursing home, or convalescent center.)
- Try to consider all points of view. You are quite reasonably attached to your own, but your loved ones have other responsibilities and nerves stretched taut as tightwires. Not only that, but also you can almost bet they're feeling guilty, which marvelously empowers you. Solve the problem cooperatively.
- At least consent to a visit. In all probability, you'll meet people you like, with similar or interestingly diverse backgrounds, talents, personality quirks. You may even make friends—real ones.
- Finally, remember that you will never be compelled to stay where you don't want to be. Even prison convicts "fly" outside prison walls, and as your journey, your dreams, your spirit, and your inner life take over, so will you.

EIGHT

BETRAYED BY THE BODY:

DISABILITY,

DISFIGUREMENT,

AND STIGMA

MARIA'S father measured her growth against the kitchen doorjamb. Every birthday, the pencil mark was higher than the one before. It never occurred to her that this year's mark might be lower. You only grew, you never shrank.

At puberty, Maria's nipples rubbed sore against her sweaters, her breasts pushed out, and she faced the dismaying prospect of an ample bosom like her mother's. She had no control over these bodily changes, not even on the morning she awoke to bed sheets saturated with blood. "Now you can have babies," they consoled her. She was becoming someone else.

She did not regain her girlish figure after her third child. In her forties, she complained that she was suddenly invisible to men. Back pain became chronic, bifocals were a necessity, and she no longer received quarters under her pillow for each lost tooth.

These earlier physical changes are rehearsals for the later ones, although we don't know it at the time. As we pass a mirror, we're caught off-guard. Our mental image of a younger, more vibrant person is contradicted by our sagging reflection. The process of bodily change moves inexorably on, and though we can fool others and even ourselves for a while, the body isn't fooled. We become split between our appearance and our identity.

Maria was one of the lucky ones. By the time she was fifty, a friend had had a mastectomy, another had died of a heart attack, and her son's best friend, only seventeen, had contracted AIDS.

Maria's adaptive solutions to the gradual changes in her body were the ones most of us opt for—diet, exercise, hair dyes, makeup, concealing clothes, plastic surgery perhaps, and younger ways of behaving—all to make us appear more youthful, sexually desirable, jobworthy, respected, admired . . . and more distant from death. Friends promise us we haven't changed, even that we've reversed sags and wrinkles. That's what friends are for!

But as we age, and particularly when debilitating illness takes over, these old solutions become less and less effective. We must develop others. Furthermore, illness and disability breed more of the same. For example, Danny's hip surgery for arthritis laid him up, dramatically increasing the heartbeat irregularities that aerobic exercise had always prevented ("sedentary heart," his doctor termed it).

WHAT BODY CHANGE DO YOU DREAD THE MOST?

The possibility of being confined to a wheelchair terrifies one of my athletic daughters. I, on the other hand, feel I could tolerate restricted mobility as long as I could read and write. Raising such differences to consciousness clarifies our values and assists us in rehearsal and planning.

Below is a list of our most common fears concerning bodily change and loss. Which ones apply to you?

1. *Mutilation:* Loss of a breast, limb, or jaw exposes us to critical eyes. We may fear less the loss of a hidden organ, such as a kidney. Fear of exposure puts us on notice that we are mortally dependent on the approval of others.

2. *Dysfunction:* A colostomy or urostomy might gurgle or leak, drawing attention to our excretory processes, of which we have been conditioned to feel ashamed. Smells, often imaginary, repel others.

3. *Loss of independence:* We may develop the inability to care for ourselves, to perform the simple tasks of bathing, toileting, preparing food and eating it, combing our hair, and covering our nakedness with clean clothing. Our culture values cleanliness (supposedly next to godliness) as well as independence.

4. *Being sexually unattractive or repulsive:* Sexual attractiveness draws others to us, unites us with them, gives pleasure, and, in this culture, is a major measure of our worth.

5. *Loss of the senses that inform us of the world around us:* Eyesight to read, hearing to listen to other people's thoughts and responses to us.

6. *Loss of viability in the workplace:* If we are unattractive or disfigured, we are less likely to be hired; if we are too disabled, we cannot perform the work.

7. *Inability to pursue other activities that give life meaning:* We may no longer be able to play sports, travel, cook for the family, paint, listen to music, grow flowers, keep up with the world.

You must find ways to control whichever of these losses is especially important to you.

WHY AGING AND DISEASE FEEL LIKE BETRAYAL

All my life I've been myself, bones and muscles to move me from one place to another, mouth and stomach to take in sustenance, lungs to breathe, head to think, skin to feel, hands to caress and work, and genitalia to pleasure, connect, and reproduce. All my life my body has felt like who I am, a body-mind unity, a complex tool or set of them, to perpetuate my precious existence.

Now, suddenly (it feels sudden, but often it isn't), parts of my body that I've never even laid eyes on are rising up in open rebellion—

weakening, thickening, breaking, growing out of control, blackening, twisting, bleeding, bruising, demyelinating, lesioning, swelling, shutting down. They refuse to recognize that they are me and I am them, and also that I'm the boss and know best. They've launched a war of independence, even if it means their (and my) destruction. They're no longer me but themselves, with their own agendas and trajectories. I didn't plan this, I can't control it. Like the Addams Family's crawling hand, my body parts break away and are on their own.

But a natural defense comes to my rescue. I stop thinking of my body as myself. I begin to experience a mind-body split (if I haven't before). I'm me, but I acknowledge (with great regret) that my body is expendable. This leaves me outside my body, surviving it. Serves it right! My body is now the rebellious child, the weak link, the black sheep of the self, the remittance man sent to a foreign shore, even the enemy. I'm engaged in a civil war!

This split is a potent defense. While the body betrays, sinking lower and lower to the earth, the loves, emotions, thoughts, and spiritual beliefs continue, even soar. They may be based in the brain or (as most recently discovered) in the entire central nervous system, but they *feel* independent of our bodies. The "I" can mourn the body, then give it up.

COPING WITH MUTILATION AND DYSFUNCTION

1. Confide your feelings to those closest to you. Don't hide them. Let your husband know about your fear of being no longer attractive to him. If your young children seem repelled by your appearance, smile and acknowledge this: "I know I look different, scary even, but I'm still the same mother who loves you very much." Your own words are best.

   If you allow fears of rejection to fester out of sight, they won't be of any use to those around you. Use? Of course! Your fears give them the opportunity to discover that the person they love is much more than appearance and physical ability.

Therefore, so are they! You invite them to express and renew their love for you. This is a gift for you both. It will serve them infinitely well when their own time comes. Remember that this is a period when you either draw closer to each other or split farther apart. Intimacy benefits those you love as well as yourself. And it heals.

2. Whatever your disease(s), there are specific coping methods, many based on the experiences of others. You'll be enrolling in a "course" you hadn't planned to take. As Bernie Siegel says, "Death is not an elective."[1] The catalog title is *Coping with Cancer* (or congestive heart disease, hepatitis, stroke, injury). Like all courses, it requires attendance (at information meetings and doctors' appointments), homework (including reading and keeping a journal), computer time, and the laboratory of trial and error. You discover what works for maximum function and comfort. There are tricks of the trade. You need to learn them.

3. Recall other illnesses you've had, perhaps a chronic one such as a back problem. At first, the thought of living with it for the rest of your life was insupportable. But you learned to bend at the knees, carry lighter loads, wear flats, and do your special exercises religiously. Bit by bit, the significance of your condition waned, with occasional flare-ups (unless you needed surgery). Your coping became automatic.

   Now your illness is more serious, with myriad symptoms—different kinds of pain, nausea, difficulty breathing, and the like. Each symptom has its own range of helpful solutions.

   It's natural to resent having to "take time out of living" for these new tasks. But this *is* living!

4. Keep a health-management chart. Note your symptoms, treatment—whether it works or doesn't—and any side effects.[2] Ask your nurse for help.

5. Most important, as the body deteriorates we fall back on *inner* resources—thoughts, emotions, and spiritual feelings. Often, inexplicably, these rise to meet the challenge of physical disintegration, giving us more control. In later chapters, we will learn how to access these resources and strengthen them.

STIGMA

Larissa couldn't bear to leave her San Francisco apartment in the light of day. Her reddish-purple Kaposi's sarcoma lesions were hideous to her and advertised her condition. At night she bundled a scarf around her head and throat, wore dark glasses, and ducked down to the all-night deli for food.

Charles learned to unobtrusively support one shaking hand with the other, holding his sandwich between the thumbs and fingers of both hands rather than just one. Unfortunately, his shakiness increased under stress, especially when he had to fight the school board on a policy issue. The board would think he was afraid of them, or that his position was as shaky as his hands. The secret, shameful truth was that he'd always been terrified of a fight, the legacy of a strict childhood during which his parents beat any opposition out of him. He'd triumphed over this terror countless times. Now his shakiness, which had always been due to fear, was the symptom of Parkinson's disease, but it felt like fear. One night, during a particularly nasty meeting, he walked out. Board members, not knowing the circumstances, never forgave him.

Agnes tried not to wheeze as she mounted the stairs with her neighbor. She exclaimed over the view of Lake Michigan as her excuse for frequent pauses.

Loss of her hair bothered Gilda Radner more than any other side effect from her fight with cancer.[3] It's the part of our body that identifies us and seems most visible that we stroke the most.

Emma covered the melanoma on her forehead with makeup in the morning, against her doctor's stern instructions. Oddly enough, it had been a beauty spot before it was diagnosed.

As Bill's voice weakened from ALS, he tried to boom out his opinions heartily, so he would not seem so changed.

Beauty and strength, two of our cultural ideals, were new failings and challenges for Larissa, Charles, Agnes, Emma, Bill, and Gilda Radner.

Thus, the body not only betrays who we thought we were but also stigmatizes us in the eyes of those we care for.

* * *

As our dysfunction and mutilation become more obvious, we feel marked as different, in ways distasteful to others. We forget that we are stigmatized from birth: fat, bony, scarred, from the "wrong" country of origin or a different race, disabled, too bright, retarded—with signs of Down's or fetal alcohol syndromes— blind, deaf, epileptic, or ugly. As we grow older, our stigmas increase. We stammer, develop acne, or make the repetitive motions of tardive dyskinesia that mark our treatment for schizophrenia. We are ex-convicts or the "wrong" religion, we have alcoholic parents, we smoke, age, lose our hair, love the "wrong" sex, work as garbage collectors, and make horrible mistakes.

Then there are all the differences others can't see that affect our behavior. We feel stigmatized by them, although we aren't.

Currently, AIDS is our most stigmatizing disease, because some attribute it to what they consider immoral behavior. But the world has a long history of such diseases.[4] Jews were accused of spreading bubonic plague in Rome in 1656. Africans were blamed for syphilis in the 1930s, and polio was blamed on the poor in 1916. Blame can repress certain groups of people.

Six dimensions define how people become more or less stigmatized. We can apply these to the terminally ill.[5]

First there is the dimension of *concealability*: to what extent can you hide your condition? Probably, as it progresses, it becomes more visible. If you can conceal it, you cannot be marked.

Second, what is the probable *course* of your disease? If a person improves—a stutterer obtains speech therapy, for example—he experiences less stigma (unless he's among children). Others calculate the probabilities of your surviving your illness.

Third, to what extent does the illness *disrupt* the normal course of your relationships? For example, must you take frequent breaks at work, or impose on friends to assist you? The emphasis here is on "normal" functioning.

Fourth, how has your condition made you *aesthetically* less pleasing? Are you marked by disfigurement, mutilation, or other forms of "ugliness," according to societal norms?

On November 11, 1960, Rod Serling aired a marvelous science fiction story on his TV show, *The Twilight Zone*. A woman undergoes surgery to correct her hideous abnormal face (which we do not see) to make her look like other people. At last the bandages come off and we hear the gasps of the medical personnel. The surgery has failed. The camera pans to her very beautiful face, then to the "normals" with their pig faces, snout noses, and hideously misshapen mouths. They offer her consolation and compassion. The story is entitled "The Eye of the Beholder."[6]

Fifth, what is the *origin* of your illness, and to what extent are you held responsible for it? If someone gets AIDS from a blood transfusion, *that's* considered a tragedy. The person, suffering from hemophilia or involved in a bad car accident, is not to blame for her condition. However, she may have to prove her "innocence." For this reason, newspaper accounts document the hospital, date, and circumstances to "unmark" her. Infants born to HIV-infected mothers are not responsible, but they have the aura of being marked about them. This is stigmatization by association. Some attribute certain personality traits to cancer as a form of blame.[7] The person rebelling against such stereotyping says, in effect, "They think they know my character just by knowing my disease."

The sixth and final dimension is *peril.* What danger do you pose to others? Can anyone be contaminated by you because your disease is plague or tuberculosis? Is your emphysema contagious? At one time it was thought that cancer was a virus you could catch. Now that we know some ulcers are bacterial in origin, will ulcer victims suffer ostracism? If the mode of contagion is uncertain (airborne versus secretory, for example), people stay away. People with a specific disease may be labeled as more similar to one another than they actually are. This protects the stereotyper; if he doesn't smoke or eat fat or have unprotected sex like the diseased, he won't get it. So stigmatizing is an excuse for distancing the "healthy" from disease and death; it is a form of defense.

Stigma can work in reverse. It can be claimed that an illness is catching, even if it isn't. Such behavior may be punitive and malicious. Thus stigmatizing becomes a weapon, particularly effective with mental disorders. For example, a woman I know counseled victims of severe sexual harassment in her workplace; she was labeled paranoid by her guilty colleagues, a common accusation in those situations. It got around that she was "mentally ill," even though she wasn't. She was "marked" and fired.

Is there a stigmatizing aspect of your illness? Do you feel it as defense or as attack?

SHAME

The effect on the stigmatized is shame—shame over nakedness, exposure of hidden weaknesses, loss of control over bodily functions both sexual and excretory. We feel stigmatized by our new uselessness, undesirability, dependence, and incapacity. What else about our lives, about our most private moments and innermost thoughts, will be exposed? Even in the doctor's office we feel ashamed. We must stand or lie naked before him so that the faults and imperfections wrought by our disease may be examined. Indeed, our illness provides us with a never-ending succession of occasions on which to feel debased. The things in which we took pride we can no longer do—or be.

We feel demeaned, lower than we have ever been, because of our lost capacities. Having so little value now, it is almost as if we never had any. If feels like a cancellation. It may feel like a visitation by God for secret, entirely unrelated sins!

The cruelty is that stigma spreads like chicken pox, from one area of our lives to another. Because we cannot lift a plate with our left hand, it is thought we cannot paint with our right. Because we can no longer run the Boston Marathon, we can no longer walk to work. Because one set of actions or abilities is discredited, all of them are.

True story: A young woman named Ellen Stohl was in a terrible car crash some years ago. Her neck broken in five places, she became paraplegic, confined to a wheelchair. Increasingly, she raged at people's assumptions about her limitations. In rebellion, she agreed to be the *Playboy* centerfold for July 1987. Then, because people assumed she was unable to have sex, she made a *Playboy* video that showed her doing exactly that.[8]

COPING WITH STIGMA AND SHAME

When stigmatization increases because of our illness, we find our-selves in conflict between two broad coping methods:

1. We can *hide* our physical changes, wear wigs and prostheses, dress in big clothes to conceal weight loss, and take refuge in our homes. We do this not only to deflect disapproval, but also out of concern for others, so as not to horrify them with the truth. Why should they know any sooner than necessary? But be aware that when they eventually find out, they can feel hurt or angry that you didn't level with them sooner, particu-larly if they fear some form of contagion.

2. We can remain *public*, even confrontational, refusing to con-ceal our condition. We can say to the world, "Hey, look at me! I'm human, too, just a different stage, another form of life. This is what illness does to us all, eventually. You, too." In fact, if everyone were more open and accepting, then, when our own time came, we'd be much less shocked and afraid of disap-proval.

Additional solutions:

- Join socially with "like" others, forming a "tribe" or community or "leper colony." For the terminally ill, this can be a support group of people with the same affliction. We can get together at Thanksgiving, or in one another's homes on Friday nights, or chat on the phone or via computer. We will also be with family, friends, counselors, and medical and religious staff who grow ac-customed to us.

- If our appearance has become ugly, we can surround ourselves with what is beautiful to us and concentrate on that. We can meditate on what is beautiful inside ourselves, and on the tempo-rariness of this outward condition.

- Recognize that other people have looked worse—probably! If you doubt this, read Lucy Grealy's account of her extraordinary triumph over childhood cancer and disfigurement.[9]

- Stay strong enough so that you don't begin to believe the stigma yourself. It's hard to resist seeing ourselves as others see us, but it is important not to stigmatize ourselves. We are more than our temporary appearance.

Lon Nungesser wrote wonderfully about coping with his own experience of stigma.[10] Diagnosed with Kaposi's sarcoma, he was given a few months to live and survived many years. He suggested that you:

- Act in such a way as to contradict the stereotyped expectations people have of you. Be helpful rather than appearing to need help.
- Don't share any more information than you feel comfortable in sharing, especially if others can use it to blame you for your illness. Mutually disclose.
- Allow people the opportunity to assess you covertly and adapt to the difference you represent. When Nungesser focused his attention elsewhere for a minute, people had the chance to observe his wheelchair and were more comfortable with him.

The above solutions either conceal or boldly reveal our defects on the outside while we come to terms with them on the inside.

When we must be out in the world, exposing our disfigurement to the eyes of strangers, perhaps it is best to think of ourselves as teachers. Veterans often sport their scars proudly. Surely, we also are veterans of wars. Surely, we too deserve honor, if only for what we've survived.

ISOLATION VERSUS CONNECTION

A major consequence of being stigmatized because of physical losses—of beauty, function, privacy, sexual attractiveness, senses, work viability, and beloved activities—is isolation, both real and imagined. Our bodies are our means of connecting, but, one by one, people distance themselves. Perhaps unfairly, it becomes our responsibility to take the initiative in assisting them to remain in our world. The following are reasons for isolation, and some possible solutions:

1. Our progressive disability may prevent us from frequenting accustomed places, for example, our church, the bowling alley, or a bridge tournament. We can correct this by adapting to the activities. We can invite the bridge game over to our house!
2. Others may treat us as a child or a pariah. We can calmly assert ourselves, realizing that others are probably acting out of ignorance rather than malice.[11]
3. Often, people don't know what to say. Bodily losses and death are embarrassments. We can show that we are open to whatever they *do* say. We can encourage them, even when then say "the wrong thing." At least they're trying. We've stumbled, too.
4. They don't want to face their own mortality. If they're having trouble with this, we can talk about the good stuff, the reordered priorities. Others will probably invalidate anything positive, however.[12] They'll say we're "courageous" (implying that we're not truthful). They don't believe there's ever anything remotely positive about death, and they assume we're glossing over our real experiences just as they claim they were laid off rather than fired, or that they're innocent of all charges. We must remember that, in revealing our positive discoveries, we're doing them a favor, although we shouldn't act superior about it.
5. Don't assume people don't want you around anymore. Even if they don't, you can change their minds. Annamarie is confined to a wheelchair following a stroke. She speaks haltingly out of one side of her mouth, and she certainly isn't the beauty she used to be. But she rolls out into the street every day to chat and joke with people. Some respond kindly at first, because they feel sorry for her. But her humor is infectious, and pretty soon they're enjoying themselves. The street is Annamarie's water cooler.

6. People think they might catch your dying from you. Your disease need not be contagious for them to feel that way. Where death is concerned, sometimes we are thrown back to a superstitious way of thinking, by which mere exposure, mere thought, is dangerous. Of course, you combat this by laying out the parameters immediately, explaining either that liver cirrhosis isn't contagious or that specific precautions must be taken. You want them to feel safe around you, so at least they don't have *that* excuse.

7. Employers with ill employees fear a rise in insurance rates, so you keep quiet about your illness and stay in a job you hate. If you have cancer and the boss finds out, you might quote the National Coalition for Cancer Survivorship, which claims that six million cancer survivors are alive today. AIDS survivorship, deemed impossible a few years ago, is also a growing phenomenon.

8. You're afraid to initiate a new intimate relationship because the opportunities and grounds for rejection are too numerous. Then deepen the old and creep up on the new so as not to scare it away.

9. To doctors, the dying patient represents failure. One patient I knew told his doctor, "Dr. Mason, I know you're doing the very best you can, and I just want to tell you how much I appreciate it." The shock on the doctor's face was replaced with a determination to continue to do her best. She can't save everyone from death. In fact, she can't *save* anyone—she can only postpone.

Dying can be a transformation from the physical to the spiritual. And yet its signs are stigmas, filling us with shame and resulting in our isolation as if we were engaged in nefarious activities.

We would do well to think of signs that stigmatize us as stigmata, the grace of prophecy—our sacrifice for others in order that they may see their own future.

NINE

TWENTY-SEVEN RULES FOR DYING THE "RIGHT WAY": ONE RULE FOR DYING YOUR WAY!

CARRIE'S mother, Marian, was dying of kidney disease. Because Carrie was the only child who lived close by, and even though she had a job and three teenage children to raise, the burden of her mother's illness fell to her. She had known it would but hadn't planned on it happening quite so soon. Her brother promised to come "when it gets more serious." "It *is* serious." "Yes, but it could be months, Carrie. We can't hang around all that time. We have jobs and a family to raise." "So do I," Carrie said. "You're closer." He cut her off.

Carrie was determined to do it right. She visited her mother at home or in the hospital every day, took her for dialysis, consulted with the physicians and nurses, talked cheerily about how well the children and grandchildren were doing, and read up on the disease.

A friend handed Carrie the book *On Death and Dying* by Elisabeth Kübler-Ross, widely respected for bringing the subject of death out of the closet.[1] Carrie learned that people go through five stages: denial (that they are dying); anger (that other people are alive and well, including crooks); bargaining (with God or their physician to let them live until the next important life event—a child's graduation or a holiday—or until a cure is found); depression (they're in mourning for all they leave behind); and acceptance (a period of peace signaling final transition).

Carrie tried to figure out what stage her mother was in. Not denial. She'd had kidney disease for a long time now. It had worsened only recently and she seemed aware of this. Not depression. And it was too soon for acceptance. As for anger, Marian had always been angry, finding just cause for resenting everyone else's good fortune, victimized by her ex-husband, neglected by her children, and ignored by salesladies. So her occasional outbursts over her predicament were nothing new.

If Carrie could identify the stage, she would know what to expect next. She could explain it to her mother and help her through it. "I think Marian's been depressed for a long time," the doctor said in response to Carrie's question about what stage Marian might be in. "Anger is often a defense against depression."

There has been a lot of research into these five stages of dying. And it's been found that they just don't hold up. The problem is that the research is published in professional journals no one sees except physicians, nurses, psychiatrists, psychologists, and social workers, whereas On Death and Dying has been in the book stores for twenty-five years (and is still of great value).

Denial, anger, bargaining, depression, and acceptance are common mental *states* during the dying process, along with fear, hope, guilt, envy, regret, humiliation, and even joy. But they don't happen in an irreversible sequence, so they are not "stages." One can be depressed at one point, then become angry, and many dying people go in and out of acceptance.

Many medical personnel no longer believe in these stages, but family members, struggling valiantly to understand what their beloved dying relative is going through, still stumble across this theory of dying and accept it as fact. It sounds logical. It is comforting to think that something as messy as dying can have some predictability about it, that there can be order in the ultimate chaos.

The danger in such belief is that it can actually be *imposed* on the dying person. It can, and has, become prescriptive: "You've been in the bargaining stage long enough. Aren't you feeling at all depressed?" Just as we push our year-old baby to take her first step, we may push our dear, dying father to stop denying and get angry. As a culture, we have an obsession with advancement. It's superior to be advanced—although I've yet to run into two relatives bragging in the hospital corridor, "My aunt's in the bargaining stage." "Well, my great-grandfather's depressed already, and he's only been dying for three weeks!"

If you find yourself in a situation where your dying is being "staged," or you're being told you should behave or feel in a different way, know that this may be the source. If you are the one reading about such stages, know that they are not required of you. Read for permission to be angry or depressed, or even for permission to deny, bargain, or accept. But you do not have to feel that, since you are only just getting over the kind of stunned shock, numbness, and even denial that Bill initially went through when diagnosed with ALS, you're going to get angry. It may *help* you to get angry. We are more powerful and in control when we are angry. Anger feels good when we've just learned that we're going to be helpless. But it isn't a requirement. You may pass anger and go directly to bargaining if you choose (you may even collect $200 if you can find it!). You can do anger later if you like, or never. It's your choice, not your physician's, not your loving child's or friend's or partner's.

Dying in a sequence of stages isn't the only prescription you need not follow. When you think of it, there are a lot of other rules. You learn them in the doctor's office, the X-ray lab, even at home when friends and relatives come to call. In other words, we are socialized into dying well, just as we are socialized into sharing toys in nursery school, polite table manners, appropriate dating behavior, child-rearing practices, the work ethos of our particular company, and participation in our community. We choose either to follow these rules or to take the consequences, and we may be willing to do the latter. So, we have plenty of experience in socialization and behavior choice. The rules for dying simply make up another behavior code.

These rules aren't written anywhere. They are part of the fabric of our society. For example and in no particular order:

1. *Don't make waves.* Don't argue with the medical staff. It wastes time they could be using to save your life. There's a system; don't try to change it. There are specific days and hours when things get done for you (or to you), and there's a reason for this. You're not the only dying person, you know.

There are a number of ambiguous rules, such as:

2. *Ask questions, but only the appropriate kind.* Basically, you may ask questions about your treatment, but only proper ones. If the response is, "That's a good question," it means the doctor or nurse knows the answer. If your question, about sex say, is met with hesitation, a sigh, another question, or referral to your husband, it's not proper. (You're on the verge of dying and you're thinking about sex?)

3. *Don't throw food trays.* You're just projecting your anger at death onto the unfortunate besmeared and drenched, and you should be more mature. (Proper ways of dying are often char- acterized as "mature." Did you know that you can be a hun- dred years old and die immaturely?)

4. *Complain.* How else are your doctors going to know if you're in pain or if that new medication makes you see stars?

5. *Don't complain unless it's important.* You're supposed to know what's important and what isn't. (Don't ask me how.)

6. *Follow all orders to the letter.* Take all medication at specified times, exercise where and how and for however long you're supposed to, and keep all your appointments.

7. *Take responsibility for your own health, but leave the treatment to your doctor.* For example, it may be okay to read up on alterna- tive health treatments, but not to act on them; since you al- ready are, be sure to tell her; since you've decided not to, reconsider. She might be more open to alternatives than you imagine; or, she might have a hissy-fit.

8. *Don't worry.* Let your doctor do that for you. After all, it's her life, isn't it?

9. *Talk about the near future only.* If you have a month to live, talk about that but not about next year (although you may very well be around for another year or five—physicians are justifi-

ably modest about the accuracy of their estimates). If you have only a week, talk about that. It's in bad taste to mention a future you don't have, because it makes those around you feel guilty that they have one. Besides, then they're plunged into this horrible conflict about whether to collude with you on a future you don't have or be silent. Admit it: Collusion was what you were angling for.

10. *When people knock on your hospital door, graciously say, "Please come in."* If by some chance they enter without knocking, say just as graciously, "Please come in."

11. *If you're sick and tired of all your visitors, be dreary, and talk unendingly about your symptoms, treatments, test results, surgery (step by step), what the doctors say . . . (are you bored yet?).* It's only natural to be enthusiastic about your new learning experiences, and people are usually interested in hearing about them—unless it's the progress of your disease. In short, discussing your illness at length is in as bad taste as showing home movies of your vacation.

12. *If you want to keep your visitors coming around, when they ask how you're doing, be short and vague.* I knew one patient who could describe her treatments in such vivid detail—it was a talent she had—that everyone exited her room nauseated.

13. *Act interested.* Your visitors have been socialized into what they're supposed to talk about—the outside world, politics (but not enough to upset you), the most recent pointless mass shooting or child molestation case, the latest episode of your favorite television show. This may not be your idea of appropriate conversation but you're expected to play along. (Don't blame me. I don't make these rules.)

14. *Don't smoke, don't drink anything except water, and don't do recreational drugs.* If it tastes good, don't eat it (this goes double for chocolate and butter). If you smoke pot to relieve nausea, don't share. Face it, your destiny is that quivery strawberry stuff.

15. *Follow the rules for the management of your own specific disease— or mess of them.*

16. *"Save your life" with such self-healing methods as visualization, prayer, and meditation.* If you die anyway, people will be able to praise your "courage."

17. *When you first find out about your illness, act the hero.* Say, "We're going to beat this thing," and "If the treatments don't work, the doctors are bringing in the big guns." Use plenty of war terminology. It's acceptable to be "feisty" as long as you're entertaining and don't break dishes.

18. *Don't cry where someone is likely to barge in on you.*

19. *Stay off the phone to your place of business just as soon as your opinions no longer count.* You can tell when this is so by being alert to the questions they ask you. They begin with panic, such as "Where's the Morrison file?" or "Did you get that shipment out to Guiana Holding?" Sooner or later, these questions taper off into "What did you do with the paper clips?" They're trying to make you feel useful.

    You've moved to another country, at least for a time. Don't try to pretend you haven't. It's bad form. And face it, they don't want to be in the same country with you.

20. *Know the meaning of "Relax," "Take it easy," and "I'll do it."* They all mean the same thing: "Don't waste my time doing what I'll have to do anyway, but faster."

21. *Smile at everyone so they'll be willing to stay around you and do what you need them to do.* Sometimes you'll feel manipulated, but 'fess up, you're doing some manipulation, too.

22. *Crack a joke.* If you're famous and sick enough, it'll be on TV.

23. *Conspire with everyone to be cheerful.* The weather may be miserable, but it'll clear—within a few months, anyway.

24. *Act as if you actually believe your doctor's optimism, or your son's.* After all, they're making all that effort to act optimistic, so the least you can do is behave as if they're succeeding. It makes them feel better.

25. For some reason, we have the word "bereaved" for those who have lost a loved one, but we don't seem to have a word for those who are still going through the *process* of losing someone. So I am coining the word "bereaving." The bereaving are those who are losing to death someone they love. So *help the bereaving go through the process.* You do this by relieving their guilt about all the dirty rotten things they've done to you. You say you don't remember, or it was a long time ago, or you forgive them (even if you don't). You tell them what a wonderful

friend or person they are. You thank them. You talk to them even if you don't feel like it because, likely as not, they're following the bereaving's first rule, which is to listen.

26. If you are into Eastern thought, you *"open to the pain" (whatever that means), let go of control, and meditate.*[2]

In other words, adding up all of the above, when you are dying you behave in a more saintly manner than you ever have in life. You bestow last words that will be taken for wisdom (and perhaps they are). In any event, you will be assured that they are received as such, if your bereaving is doing his job.

As you can see, dying can be a very busy period of your life. After all this, if there is time . . .

27. *Get some sleep.*

These are just a few of the hidden rules for serious illness and dying. We learn them as we go through the process. Have I left any out? Let me know what they are. Perhaps I can get them into future editions.

Now, of course, there are good reasons to follow these rules. First, some of them may save your life or ease your passage. Second, you don't want your caregivers angry at you when you're helpless; they're only human, and you may fear they'll delay your pain medication or ignore you altogether.[3] You're in their power (not that they ever think in those terms, even subconsciously). The great majority of caregivers have large doses of kindness and compassion in their makeup, and you'd like to think yours are in that majority. But are you absolutely sure?

DYING YOUR WAY—ONE RULE

What about your own rules for dying? How can you create them? How can you die your way, instead of someone else's?

You might begin with who you are as a person, not as a condition.

This may be a mystery to you, however. You may not have given it much thought until now. We tend to think of ourselves as a collection of roles—daughter, mother, computer analyst, part-time actor, soup kitchen volunteer. But our deepest selves are not about these roles. They are about what we love.

Here is a simple exercise to help you determine who you are at your deepest level. On each of a batch of three-by-five-inch index cards, write a sentence that starts with "I love." Let's say you use seven cards, although you might use five or fifty-three. You might begin with the people you love (you might not—it's *your* list). Then move on to other things. When I do it, I write on one card "I love my family," and I list them. On another card I write "I love my friends" (another list). Then, "I love to hike in the mountains, along the shore, in national parks, and at historical monuments," "I love to write stories," "I love to read," "I love to teach," "I love to love," "I love to listen to music—soft rock, classical, and New Age," "I love surrealist and nineteenth-century American landscape art," "I love foreign films," "I love rich chocolate, pizza, smoked salmon, burritos, turkey, brie cheese, mangos, champagne, Thai curry, gourmet coffee. . . ." I have trouble limiting this one.

Mainly I note activities, people, or things that arouse the emotion of *love* in me. I may be other things, but I am, at my deepest level, what I love.

It is this love I want to die with. And it is this love that is the immortal part of me, the part that will not die. There will always be dancing and daughters, mine or someone else's.

Now that you know a bit of who you are at your deepest core level, now that you can name it, it is time to arrange to die *your* way. There will be many rules for dying your way that you create, as we shall see throughout this book. But the first and most important rule is this one: **Create in your life as much as you can of what you love.** If you love surfing but can no longer do it, ask a friend (whom you love) to take you out on a boat or to the seashore where the surfers are, watch tapes, exchange surfing stories with other surfers, read books, look at pictures.

In the same way, incorporate into your daily living whatever other people and activities you love in whatever way you can. Hang the pictures on your walls, put the music on your tape deck, read the books (have someone read to you if you no longer can).

A word of caution: Typically, when we are critically ill, we have good days and bad days. On the bad days, we may want only to watch TV, whatever is on. TV is a great anesthetic. But whatever you are doing in these last days goes into your mind and becomes who you are. On your good days, limit the TV and become more of what you love.

Actually, I hope you have been including in your life plenty of what you love for many years, but perhaps you haven't had the time. Now, suddenly, you perceive how important are the activities and people you love; now, suddenly, you have the time.

10
TEN

POWER

OVER

PAIN

IN my hospital bed, I relived for hours the unimaginable pain of giving birth to my daughter. A shortage of nursing personnel and a sudden influx of mothers-about-to-be had left me in the labor room far too long without drugs or anesthesia of any kind, not even natural childbirth training. It's a torture chamber, I realized, panicking amid the screams, some of them my own. I'd wanted to die. Now I wanted to hold my baby, but in these wee hours of the morning I must comply with hospital regulations and wait until ten o'clock.

In the darkness relieved only by dim light from the hall, I discerned a placard on my night table. Reaching over, I picked it up and barely made out these words: "Pain is God's way of bringing us closer to Him."

In that precise instant, I lost my faith.

The rest of the night I raged at the God I now denied. This was the God who allowed so much pain, which I multiplied by six million Jews, the Inquisition, the rack, wars, plagues, witch burnings, impalements, iron maidens, lynchings, cattle prods, floggings, electric instruments such as the "telephone," and other barbaric tortures down the ages.

That was decades ago. "Labor relations" are better now, I'm told.

Pain is a four-letter word. One of our great fears as seriously ill and dying people is that pain uncontrolled may escalate beyond our wildest imaginings, that we may cry out, and that our children may not recognize us in our agony. In her seminal book on torture, Elaine Scarry tells us that the etymology of pain is *poena* or punishment, and for some of us, pain is precisely that.[1] Extreme pain so fills up the mind that the world is "unmade," ceasing to exist as it was. When we are ill, we may grow to associate commonplace objects or places such as a bed or bathroom with nausea or dread, and no longer with refuge or comfort. Their meanings are changed, and so are we. Thus our pain can overwhelm the mind and "shrink the consciousness."[2]

Pain is no stranger to us, and we have relieved it in a number of ways in the past. But in our last weeks, we become dependent on someone else who doesn't feel our pain as we do, on medical staff who use the word "discomfort" to describe *agony*. "People tell you to 'work with the pain,'" grumbles Maggie, who suffers from arthritis and cancer. "They never had anything worse than a broken fingernail!"

Nor does it help that, over the past few years, the "undertreatment of pain" has been bruited about by the medical community.[3] Pain afflicts ninety-seven million people per year. In a 1994 survey, the Agency for Health Care Policy and Research (AHCPR), a branch of the U.S. Department of Health and Human Services, found that 42 percent of 1,308 cancer patients received inadequate pain medication.[4] A flurry of articles in medical and nursing journals proposed specific aggressive treatment solutions. They hadn't known before?

In other words, the bellyachers, the whiners, and the cowards were right all along!

In this chapter, a questionnaire helps you identify your beliefs about pain and its relief, the major myths and realities. I conclude with the emerging revolution in analgesia, and how you can cope successfully.

QUESTIONNAIRE: YOUR BELIEFS ABOUT PAIN AND PAIN RELIEF

Mark the following statements T (true) or F (false).

1. People who complain about pain are just a bunch of whiners.
2. A man (or woman) should be able to bear most discomfort until the next shot.
3. The doctors are aware of my pain and have decided my condition necessitates it.
4. God never gives us more than we can bear.
5. I'm afraid of getting addicted.
6. If I take too much medication, it will stop working. I'd better save it for when I need it more.
7. Pain is God's way of drawing us close to Him.
8. Here's my arm—give me your best shot.
9. I deserve to suffer for my sins and all the nasty things I've done.
10. If I shut up about it, the doctors and nurses will tell me I'm a good girl (or boy) like they did when I was little.
11. The side effects of analgesia are worse than the disease!
12. Pain in this life is unavoidable.
13. To bear excruciating pain without complaint is saintly.
14. I don't want to upset my family, so I'll keep quiet.
15. I don't want to bother my doctor, or he won't have time to cure me.
16. Actually, I look forward to pain because it gives me something to complain about.
17. Increasing pain shows that my disease is progressing, so I'd rather think it's just my imagination.
18. "I would hate that death bandaged my eyes and forebore, and bade me creep past" (Robert Browning).[5]
19. Wake me when it's over.
20. I don't want pain relief, because I hate shots.
21. I'm a coward. I've always been a coward, I always will be a coward. So do as my dentist does, either give me laughing gas or knock me out.

22. I want enough medication to dull the pain without making me dopey, so I can finish this project.
23. I want to control my own medication as much as I can.
24. If a specific treatment—say, ten weeks of chemotherapy or six weeks of radiation—that's very painful and sickening will give me a *reasonable* chance of resuming my life, it's worth it.
25. If such a treatment give me a *slim* chance of resuming my life, it's worth it.
26. If such a treatment gives me a *slim* chance of resuming my life, it *isn't* worth it.
27. If you use opioids (narcotics), you can die.
28. I take my pain medication only when I really need it.

In reviewing the answers you checked, you may find that you fit one of three pain profiles emerging from this questionnaire:

No-Pain-Tolerance Profile. You really do not want to endure any pain whatsoever. Nothing is worth pain, including life, loved ones, and activities. Perhaps you believe in life after death, perhaps you have a low pain threshold, or your life isn't that wonderful anyway, or you've already had enough pain to last a lifetime.

Life-at-Any-Cost Profile. You'll do anything to stay alive. You want every treatment. Perhaps you're far more afraid of death than anything they can do to you in this life. Or life is too rich for you to leave.

Midrange Profile. You're willing to endure a certain amount but not a whole lot, or maybe a whole lot but not everything they throw at you. Your life, afterlife beliefs, pain experience, and tolerance might be midrange.

THE MYTHS AND REALITIES OF PAIN AND ITS RELIEF[6]

A number of the above questions reflect myths or misconceptions about pain—all shared by patients, families, and professionals. You need to recognize those myths so you can (1) educate your caregivers and (2) suffer less.

1. We tend to think pain is *inevitable* and unavoidable, so we may endure it as long as possible before seeking relief. Not true! Interestingly, if our loved one is in pain, we're more insistent on treatment for it.[7]

2. With the current emphasis on drug *addiction*, we're afraid of becoming addicted ourselves, even during the last weeks of life. But addiction is a craving for *psychological* effects, and the craving most terminally ill patients have is for *physical* relief.[8] Addiction occurs in less than 1 percent of patients.[9] Is addiction in even these few people during their last weeks worse than intractable pain? This is a value judgment many of us would not wish to make. You may become *physically* dependent on your medication (not psychologically), but this is overcome by *slow* rather than abrupt withdrawal.

3. We fear increasing *tolerance* to narcotic pain medication, that we'll need higher and higher doses. Actually, studies show that, if the disease is stable, the amount of narcotic medication needed often levels off, or even decreases, as anxiety over pain proves unnecessary. If you *do* need increasing doses, "effectiveness . . . is not limited by a ceiling."[10] The dose can be increased for more relief.

4. Most *side effects* of both treatment and medication—drowsiness, mild nausea, moderate diarrhea, uncomfortable mouth sores, itching hands, and a host of other symptoms, all forming a constellation of misery—are either temporary or *can be relieved* by changing medications or with adjuvant medication. A ninety-year-old man I know suffers from bone cancer of two years' duration, for which he undergoes monthly chemotherapy; he still works and doesn't want morphine because he's heard it would make him sleepy. Actually, with continued medication, this drowsiness usually lasts only a few days.[11]

5. An increase in pain may or *may not* show that the disease is *progressing*; either way, you owe yourself pain relief.

6. No, relieving your pain won't *distract* your doctor from curing you; pain relief is part of her job.

7. If you *fear shots*, know that most pain relief is administered orally, because this is more effective.[12] Other routes include

intravenous, suppositories, sublingual (under your tongue), transdermal—a fentanyl skin patch—and epidural, used in childbirth and even radiation and surgery. PCAs (patient-controlled analgesia pumps), possibly implanted, allow the patient to self-administer medication.

Combining opioids like morphine with other medications such as NSAIDs is an increasingly effective art in pain relief.

8. Plan to be a good boy or girl *after* your pain is relieved!
9. Only rarely does a patient *die* of opioid administration.
10. Analgesics (pain relievers) do *not* cause a decline in mental functioning—*but pain may!*[13]
11. Don't postpone pain medication until your pain is severe. It's "easier to control when it is mild."[14] (I know, I know, you'd like to see if you can do without; or you fantasize painlessness, the way it used to be. On the other hand, if the pain is getting worse, it will let you know.)

PSYCHOLOGICAL FACTORS THAT INFLUENCE DEGREE OF PAIN

Psychological factors can actually raise or lower your *experience* of pain.[15] The two major factors that *intensify* the experience of pain are fear and depression.

Fear: Some researchers believe that anxiety and depression can "make pain seem worse," while not actually causing it.[16] Others show that negative emotions don't necessarily make you feel more pain, or have less success at pain relief, but do make you believe the pain has a greater impact on your daily living.[17] Why is it important to understand this distinction? In the past, some doctors have discounted patients' reports of pain, saying, "You're just depressed." This led to less prescribed pain relief! Now, if anyone blames your pain on your anxiety or depression, you can tell him it isn't so.

Your fear, however, can *focus your attention* on your pain. As you weigh its implications, you tighten muscles you didn't know you had. The resulting intensification is not your imagination, making you fear a still greater increase—a vicious circle. New pain signals new physical invasion and destruction, new metastases, for example, *which may or may not be true in fact.* The pain could be harmless, but your imagination is working overtime. An ache you wouldn't otherwise notice becomes a menace.

Finally, fear *breeds* other fears and can lead to depression.

Depression: Depression makes you give up. You believe there's nothing you can do, and you do not work to lower your pain and improve your lifestyle. Research shows that pain itself is depressing. You may contemplate suicide.

Endorphins are major factors in *lessening* pain. As you may know, these are the brain's natural opiates. Their release is stimulated in several ways. One is pain itself. Another is called the *placebo effect.* Simply swallowing a pill or getting a shot may relieve your pain, even if the pill is sugar or the shot is water. The *belief* that your pain is being relieved elicits the endorphins. Acupuncture may do the same.[18] Other endorphin-inducing or -enhancing activities apparently include laughter, kisses and other expressions of affection like hugs, relaxation exercises, prescribed stretching exercises or yoga, touch, meditation, guided imagery, and massage—whereby your body is positively acknowledged and pleasured rather than condemned as diseased.[19] Select your own humor. Norman Cousins chose Marx brothers comedies.[20] I'd choose infinite reruns of *Cheers* and *Night Court.* What makes *you* laugh?

The above activities *distract* you from your pain as well. Your dentist's procedures are the same whether or not he pipes in music, but we know it makes a difference.

Laughter, massage, meditation, music, and the like all induce *relaxation;* you do not fight the pain or tense yourself against it, which can increase it; you relax with it, and relaxation *eases* it.

While fear and depression serve to *intensify* pain, and endorphins, distraction, the placebo effect, and relaxation lessen it, there are four additional psychological factors that may either lessen *or* intensify your experience of pain.

One factor is the *meaning* your pain has for you. As we have seen, if your pain increases or spreads to other sites, you may interpret this as a worsening of the disease itself. Or pain may mean punishment, or it may remind you of a painful relationship or make you relive previously painful situations you have not worked through—war experiences, for example. On the other hand, your suffering may mean an opportunity to atone, or to share in Jesus' agony, or it may mean payback time for a good life. The laboring mother interprets her pain as imminent birth of new love. Perhaps for you, a new love in another dimension is also imminent.

Expectations also influence your perception of pain. If you expect a downhill course, with pain culminating in an agonizing death, you set yourself up. If you expect to control it, however, you take steps to do just that. *Control*, if you exercise it, results in your communication of your pain to your caregivers; your adherence to prescribed medication; your faithful participation in additional modes of pain relief, such as meditation and group activities; or perhaps a TENS unit (Transcutaneous Electrical Nerve Stimulator) or a pain-relieving intravenous drip set to run faster or slower into your system according to your own judgment of need.

Finally, *anger* is a two-edged sword. Like anxiety, it can rouse you to demand the pain relief you believe is not forthcoming. Studies show that angry patients in institutions live longer. Anger is the flip side of depression, and it feels better. On the other hand, anger can alienate your caregivers, making you feel guilty and even depressed. In heart, stroke, and hypertension patients, anger may precipitate a physical crisis. Use it *wisely*.

We deal with these emotions at greater length in Chapter 12.

WHY IS PAIN UNDERTREATED?

There are numerous reasons for the undertreatment of pain, including communication problems, ethical and legal issues, and "the system."

COMMUNICATION

Some patients suffer in silence, determined to be staunch and brave; they may even try to conceal their pain.[21] This attitude is a relic of earlier centuries when there wasn't much for pain relief beyond whiskey and laudanum. Patients weren't kept alive (and in pain) by extraordinary medical technology. The first life-threatening illness killed them off at age forty, and they didn't have to endure today's serial multiplicity of illnesses and treatments.

Some patients are too embarrassed to complain. What's hurting you is in a place that's either intimate or "dirty." You were scolded for having problems in those places as a child. Besides, you may feel that if you're labeled a complainer, the medical staff will get angry and withhold painkillers. Then, too, you fear you're not using the "right" vocabulary, that there are buzz words you don't know.

Many patients believe in the myths I've outlined above. They say they're satisfied with pain relief even when it's inadequate, often not realizing that more relief is possible.[22] They need to educate themselves and become aware of treatment options and of potential side effects. They must learn to (1) *listen* to their bodies, and (2) *take action* by communicating to family and medical professionals.

But communication is a two-way responsibility. Some patients are not heard. Medical schools do not adequately train physicians in pain assessment and management. And many medical personnel also believe these very same myths concerning addiction, tolerance, side effects, and the rest—as do family members and caregivers! They may also believe they can't relieve the pain unless they know the cause. Not true!

In a series of courageous articles, Margo McCaffery, R.N., and her colleagues have alerted nurses to the many factors affecting their pain-control decisions, including gender, lifestyle, age (women, adolescents, and elderly undertreated), and whether the patient may be exaggerating.[23]

ETHICAL AND LEGAL ISSUES

Physicians suffer "opioidphobia"; they fear disciplinary action for overprescribing narcotics; they fear being blamed for a patient's death. To be on the safe side, they *under*prescribe.[24]

Some states severely restrict the use of narcotics, even for pain relief. What are the regulations in your state?

The System

One in seven people in this country suffers from "chronic debilitating pain."[25] But in these days of cost-cutting, insurance companies and Medicare are increasingly reluctant to finance additional pain relief, especially newer, nontraditional forms. So, some patients cannot afford them. The federal government is denying and capping patients' pain medications at the same time another federal agency, AHCPR, is pushing for more aggressive pain treatment.[26] Patients and caregivers need to fight for the financing of adequate pain relief.

While the AHCPR survey (see page 94) concluded that pain could be controlled in 90 percent of patients, there seems to be an underlying expectation, especially by some euthanasia opponents, that all pain can be eliminated or at least satisfactorily minimized. There is no proof that this is so. One recent study investigated a group of over four thousand patients "in advanced stages of one or more of nine illnesses," and who were estimated to be six months from death. In spite of supportive interventions, family members reported "moderate to severe pain at least half the time" in 50 percent of conscious patients who died in the hospital.[27] Some pain, such as that of thoracic outlet syndrome, causalgia, trigeminal neuralgia, reflex sympathetic dystrophy, and other conditions, is more difficult to manage, although not impossibly so.[28]

Much suffering can be relieved, but not all.[29]

THE EMERGING REVOLUTION IN PAIN RELIEF

Thanks in large part to hospice, founded by Dr. Cecily Saunders in Great Britain in 1969, the emphasis on pain control has grown in recent years.

Now pain relief is moving in a newer direction still, from a humane concern for the suffering of the dying to a recognition that pain is actually unhealthy. Pain is stressful; it can inhibit improvement or recovery, limit physical activity, decrease appetite, interrupt sleep needed to fight the disease, raise blood pressure (implicated in strokes and heart attacks), increase anxiety over future pain, thereby increasing pain, and cause depression that alters the immune system; it may result in suicide, and may even promote tumor growth. Pain can damage the nerve cells—permanently, if it is chronic—resulting in increased pain from future injuries. Pain used to be thought secondary to disease: heal the disease and the pain will go away. Now pain is recognized as an ailment in itself with negative consequences. According to Ada Jacox, R.N., Ph.D., and her co-authors, "Patients in pain are reluctant to cough, to breathe deeply, or to move, for fear of exacerbating the pain. And immobility contributes to complications, such as pneumonia, thrombosis, and ileus."[30] Pain can interfere with normal functioning, relationships, thinking, and work.

The medical community used to believe that pain relief could be harmful. The current thinking is that pain itself is harmful. As Jane Cowles points out, if your pain is treated you "heal faster, have fewer medical complications, spend less time in the hospital, . . . enjoy a better quality of . . . life."[31] Proper treatment of pain also can lower medical costs.

Typically, pain medication has been scheduled every four to six hours, or ordered PRN (as needed); this meant the patient had to feel pain first, suffer for perhaps an hour or two until the busy nurse could get to him, and then wait for the medicine to take effect. The current goal is to *preempt* pain, either by giving relief earlier than needed or by using a continuous method of delivery. Anesthesiologists may even inject a local anesthetic into the surgical wound site or epidurally before the patients leaves the OR.

Your timing may be more clever than you realize. Alarmed by increasing demands for "death with dignity," including both passive and active euthanasia (by, for example, the Hemlock Society, and physicians Jack Kevorkian and Timothy Quill), many anti-euthanasists are now calling for better treatment of pain. They reason that fewer patients will want to end their lives if their pain is relieved. In my view, they often dismiss or forget the psychological suffering. What all of this means to you is that you are dying at a time in history that promises better pain relief than ever.

THE BASIC PAIN-RELIEF INFORMATION YOU NEED

As you know, different kinds of pain and suffering have their own modes of relief. Some modes can interact, or neutralize or weaken each other. Many physical ailments listed below are the result of *treatment* rather than disease; the solutions depend on the cause. Your physician, nurse, anesthetist, and pharmacist can give you the information you need to help you make choices.

You need to be able to talk with them intelligently, to ask the right questions, and to understand the answers. That's a tall order. Obtaining the right information is, unfortunately, your responsibility—not fair, in that you may feel too ill to do so, but all is not lost. To the extent that your pain is and has been *chronic* over a period of time, you're already familiar with some analgesics. Further, you may also have experienced *acute* pain such as that of childbirth, surgery, or the physical trauma of an accident—all of which are distinguished from the pain of life-threatening illness, in that acute pain is usually temporary. Should your pain become *extreme* and/or *intractable*, you may need methods you haven't used before.

The following is a broad outline of available pain relief. It differs from other outlines you may have seen in that it includes not only traditional, allopathic medications, but also so-called alternative treatments, those for which I feel there is enough scientific evidence about their effectiveness to try them (some disagree). Margo McCaffery, however, advises you to relieve pain with medication first, and then add alternative methods.

This is by no means a comprehensive list. I offer it as a basic survey chart to demonstrate the wide variety of frequently used methods available to you, depending on your medical condition, your preferences, and your doctor's advice. This should both comfort you and increase your knowledge. I have not included naturopathic or herbal remedies, which may relieve some symptoms. Always consult your physician, and remember that there is often controversy.[32]

SYMPTOM-TREATMENT CHART

Mild Pain: Aspirin, acetaminophen (Tylenol), nonsteroidal anti-inflammatory drugs (NSAIDs such as Ibuprofen), topical applications (capsaicin—from chile peppers!), salicylate menthol (Ben-Gay), biofeedback, appropriate stretching and physical reconditioning, relaxation exercises, music, imagery

Moderate Pain: See above. Codeine and other opioid analgesics, some combined with NSAIDs (Percodan, Darvon), appropriate adjuvants—such as antidepressants, anxiolytics, anticonvulsants, and corticosteroids—TENS units, physical therapy, meditation, support groups, biofeedback acupuncture, hypnosis, massage

Severe/Intractable Pain: See above. Opioids (narcotics including morphine, methadone, oxymorphone, levorphanol, fentanyl, Demerol, Dilaudid), PCA (patient-controlled analgesia), implanted pumps, nerve blocks, trigger-point injections, radiation, surgery. Amphetamines may reduce sedation from the above.

For years, novelist Reynolds Price suffered intractable pain from a spinal tumor that had been partially resected and treated with radiation. He rated the pain an 11 or 12 on a scale of 10. Then, through biofeedback, he found freedom—not from the pain itself, which still "roars" continually, but from awareness of it. In an average sixteen-hour day, he's aware of it for perhaps a total of fifteen minutes. Hypnosis and self-hypnosis also helped.[33]

Constipation: Laxatives, stool softeners, enemas, suppositories, fiber, psyllium (Metamucil)

Nausea/Vomiting: Antiemetics (Dramamine), THC from marijuana (cannabis), Marinol, Compazine, Phenergan, and others

Cannabis relieves the severe nausea of patients treated with chemotheraphy in AIDS and cancer. (It also relieves eye pressure in glaucoma patients as well as muscular sclerosis spasms.) Even though cannabis is illegal (without a doctor's prescription), underground sources exist for those with evidence of medical conditions. For example, the San Francisco Cannabis Buyer's Club has 3,200 members; laws against them are "low priority" for enforcement, by resolution of the city's board of supervisors.[34]

Anorexia (poor appetite): Corticosteroids, *moderate* alcohol intake before meals, favorite foods, allowing patient to eat when hungry rather than on schedule, cannabis

Diarrhea: Antidiarrheal medications (Pepto-Bismol, Lomotil, Immodium), fiber, surgery if necessary

Inflammation: NSAIDs, steroids

Cough: Expectorants and suppressants (Robitussin), codeine, hydrocordone
Hiccups: Haldol, Thorazine, surgery
Dry Mouth: Artificial saliva, ice chips, lemon drops
Mouth Pain: Prescribed medicated lozenges, mouthwash, and topical agents
Itching: Antihistamines, cortisone creams, and others
Depression: Close supportive relations with family, friends, and groups; psychological and/or pastoral counseling; cognitive behavioral therapy; acupuncture; antidepressants such as tricyclics (Elavil, Tofranil), MAO inhibitors (Nardil), Prozac
Anxiety: Anti-anxiety agents such as Librium, Valium, Equanil, and Xanax, counseling
Insomnia: Antihistamines, Dalmane, Nembutal, Seconal
Dyspnea (breathing difficulties): bronchodilators, morphine

The goal of pain relief during the final months is to relieve your pain without making you too sleepy, so you can "live" your dying, interact with family and friends, make decisions, engage in limited activities, and gradually close your circle.[35]

COPING WITH PAIN

Pain is a subjective experience, not an objective one. Just as there are easily observable differences among people's physiques, so it is logical to presume *physiological* differences among pain thresholds. Your pain is your own, no one else's. Recognize this and ask for relief when you need it, not when someone else says you do.

A doctor I adored told me a week after my surgery, "You shouldn't be feeling so much pain." He was wrong; he subsequently discovered an unsuspected complication.

The following methods will help you cope with and control your pain:

1. Pain and suffering take different forms. Raise your awareness of the various areas of your body. *Where and how does it hurt?* Is

it a stabbing, burning, aching, gnawing, shooting, crushing, tingling, throbbing, sharp, steady, tender, pricking, pulling, tight, hot, or grinding sensation?

2. *Communicate* with your nurse, physician, or other caregiver. Tell them *what* hurts, how badly, and what the pain is like. How else are they to know?

3. Be prepared to *describe* it on a scale of 0 to 5 or 0 to 10. People tend to pick a lower number, just as they undermedicate themselves. The advice I am about to give you is philosophical, not medical. Pick a higher number, particularly if you feel you are undertreated. If you're feeling pain at 6, choose 7. But don't choose 8, because you really don't want overmedication's possible side effects.

4. Ask to see the AHCPR policy guidelines for aggressive pain management (see the Notes and Resources for this). They call for (1) a collaborative interdisciplinary approach to the care of patients with cancer pain (apply to your own)—this team may include the *patient* (my emphasis), family, surgeon, nurse, psychologist, anesthesiologist, general practitioner, and pharmacist; (2) an individual plan of management; (3) continued assessment of pain; (4) use of both drug and nondrug therapies; and (5) institutional support for these policies. "A patient's report of pain should determine pain control," says Jacox.[36]

5. Demand your *Patient's Bill of Rights*—to a pain history, assessment, measurement, plan adequate timing, and control—and to explanations of how much pain to expect from all treatments, as well as side effects and alternatives. You have a right to answers, to be believed, to secure a second opinion, to refuse treatment, to view records, and to receive "compassionate and sympathetic care."[37]

6. Set specific pain relief goals with your doctor and nurses—for example, your goal may be to be able to walk, and you figure lowering your pain to 2 (on a scale of 1 to 10) will help.

7. Consider the pain clinics and therapy groups discussed in Chapter 11. They often use alternative approaches such as behavior modification, support, meditation, and visualization.

These work for some who never thought they would, but not for others. "They'll just tell me to love my pain," said Maddie, but to her surprise the clinic proved effective. Many of us know from experience that some pains we get rid of; others we work with.

Bill Moyers was talking with psychologist Jon Kabat-Zinn, who leads one of the most lauded stress-reduction-through-meditation groups. Moyers quoted a friend as not wanting to relax into his pain: "I don't want *any* [pain]. . . ."

"Lots of luck," responded Kabat-Zinn.[38]

8. Keep a *comfort-assessment journal* with the date and time of entry, how you're feeling, and the medication or exercise and results. Your nurse may be able to help you set this up.

9. Reject myths and remember realities. Don't worry about addiction or tolerance. Most pain relief is by mouth, but for severe pain, if your doctor agrees, a slow, continuous method of pain relief may be best, via a patch, implanted pump, or the like. Patients who control their own pain relief often under-medicate themselves, waiting too long to take those pills or press that button. But don't worry, you can't overdose on the pump; built-in regulators and adjustment mechanisms increase or decrease the amount. You'll actually need less, because the greater frequency of delivery lowers both pain and anxiety over pain.

10. "The squeaky wheel gets the grease." Unless you've decided to suffer bravely, *complain,* and have all your relatives do the same. If that doesn't work, change hospitals and physicians. (Many years ago I worked in a hospital where a woman screamed down the halls for weeks, while my friend, the nursing supervisor, assured me, "She doesn't feel a thing." She really believed that.)

11. Depending on where you are on your life-threatening illness trajectory, consider hospice. (See Chapter 14.)

12. In many ways the psychological pain and suffering during the dying process is far worse than the physical, but you must relieve the physical first. Unresolved relationships and conflicts greatly magnify suffering. Much of the rest of this book is aimed at relieving psychological pain.

THE SPIRITUAL USES OF PAIN

Not all suffering can be relieved. So a review of the possible spiritual uses of pain may be helpful to some of you, although, to be honest, I'd rather not have to go through this spiritual lesson.

Pain arouses compassion in others, which, if they act upon it, may be the salvation of their souls.

Pain, if it doesn't shrink our minds, makes us pause and evaluate our lives, selves, and relationships. It gives us the time and justification to do so.

Pain may open us to others, and them to us, bringing us closer to one another.

Finally, pain snips at the threads that bind us to this life—snip, snip, and we are less and less attached, bits of us floating skyward like a bouquet of balloons, released one at a time, until they are too far away for us to see them pop in the increasingly rarefied atmosphere.

ELEVEN 11

HOW TO BE

IN A SUPPORT GROUP:

THE "NOT-EXPECTED-

TO-LIVE CLUB"

AT fifty my friend Vicki, a brilliant novelist, had just begun receiving the recognition long due her. When I phoned her about a volunteer project we were both working on, she confided her alarm at pain down her left arm. She thought it might be her heart.

The verdict numerous tests later: a virulent liver cancer. Struggling to live, she sought help from the foremost specialists around the country. At the same time, she prepared to die.

Vicki joined with two friends to form the Not-Expected-to-Live Club. Several times a week they met in the warmth of each other's homes and shared the latest news of their tests and treatments, how their spouses coped, problems with how and what to tell their children, their funeral plans, and speculation on a life beyond. Weaving in and out of disbelief (after all, they had always been saved before), they shared fear, faith, and grief over all they must lose, mingled with flashes of hope. Often, incredibly, there was laughter. Meanwhile, their families, interacting casually at first, gradually drew closer, forming a community.

At the end of each meeting, the three women held hands in a circle of love, offering silent prayers for each other. One day a husband joined them, and another day a child, and so the circle widened. One by one the women passed, but the family circle continued.

For the great majority of people, support from others makes their illness more endurable. Feelings of isolation (whether or not based on fact) increase pain. People with support from families, friends, and special groups actually live longer than people without such resources. Bernie Siegel's "exceptional patients" demonstrate this, as do psychiatrist David Spiegel's groups, detailed below. It may be because people gain more crucial information, or because they can express their feelings rather than keep them bottled up, or because positive emotions such as love, faith, and determination alleviate depression and even strengthen the immune system.

Oddly enough, the dying often find themselves surrounded by more love than they had when they were healthy. Those who care about them now let them know, as they didn't before. While many people withdraw from the dying, those who stick with them draw closer. The growth of caring community around those stricken with AIDS is a shining example.

WHAT CAN YOU GAIN FROM A SUPPORT GROUP?

First, support groups keep you up to date on *information* about your illness. In fact, some, like the group I Can Cope sponsored by the American Cancer Society, have as their primary mission the dispensing of information about the disease, its diagnosis, treatment, choices and possible side effects, and other resources.

One new source of information is the computer. You can tap into medical libraries all over the country. Also, you can connect with others who have your disease. One woman on chemotherapy requested suggestions for explaining to her children why her hair was falling out. She received a response from another woman whose daughter had found a use for the fallen hair; she'd made a birds' nest of it!

Even in information groups, your increased knowledge helps you emotionally; you feel more in control.

Second, many groups focus on *emotional* support and the sharing of experiences. You have the opportunity to ventilate your anger, grief, and feelings of loss, which you may be concealing from your family. You overcome a sense of isolation. Most important, you have the chance to help others, even to teach. But you gain helpful information that you wouldn't find in libraries from these groups as well, particularly on handling the "micro-aspects" of your illness, based on the experiences of fellow patients and often unknown to the medical community.

Third, participation in groups focused on *pain relief* may indeed accomplish that end, as we have discussed.

Fourth, an unexpected effect of support groups may be *extended life*. Dr. David Spiegel led a group of women with metastatic breast cancer at Stanford University.[1] He taught them pain control with self-hypnosis, imagery, and relaxation. In comparison with a control group of patients (who had the same treatments except for his group interventions), Spiegel's group experienced less pain intensity and a rise in mood. But in addition, to his utter amazement, members of his group lived twice as long as members of the control, treatment-only, group. I suspect, however, that if you focus on achievement of benefits rather than the actual group experience, you might negate those benefits. Therefore, I strongly suggest that you attend support groups for the *experience*, not to extend your life.

If you've never participated in a group before and wonder what it might be like, one way to preview the experience is to rent a tape.[2]

IF YOU DON'T WANT TO JOIN

Some people don't want to join a group. They say they're not joiners, not organization types. They're private about their lives. For them, letting it all hang out is tantamount to washing dirty linen. They don't want to relate to people on the basis of disease. They don't feel close to strangers, resent possible intrusions, are ashamed of their emotions, and fear "standing naked" in public. For some, their independence is a matter of pride. Nor do they want to deal with other people's devastation; they have plenty of their own, thank you!

Others don't want to concentrate that much on their illness. If they do, they feel that the symptoms will intensify, and this may be true. Distraction eases fear and discomfort. A good solution for these people might be to attend a group only as often as necessary to get vital information and reap the benefits of emotional support.

You should never join any group as a result of pressure, and you should never feel pressured to "share," to some people a nice word for "spilling your guts to a bunch of voyeurs."

HOW DO YOU CHOOSE A GROUP?

You can find an appropriate group through your hospital's resource center, your physician, the national society for your disease, recommendations of private therapists, or from friends. You may want a group of people who are in your stage of the disease—early, middle, or late.

Studies that evaluate the efficacy of groups show that the personal qualities of the facilitator are better predictors of member satisfaction than anything else, including school of psychology, methods employed, training, and location.

What are the qualities of a good support group facilitator?

1. He doesn't come across as the only one in the room who isn't dying!
2. He is warm, welcoming, and nonjudgmental.
3. He interacts easily and effectively with the other members.
4. He doesn't blame anyone for their disease.
5. He doesn't pressure members into his own philosophical, religious, or other beliefs.
6. He *LISTENS!*
7. He honors the contributions of the various members.

8. He doesn't promise cures.
9. He doesn't force anyone to speak—although he does offer. For example, he may say, "Larry, Rose's experience seems to have brought up strong feelings in you. Would you like to comment?" If Larry says, "No" the facilitator moves on to something else.
10. Usually (not always), he allows each person to be where she is. If she's talking of getting healthy, he'll go with that. If she's talking of dying, he'll go with that as well.
11. He is realistic, but focuses on the positive.
12. His fees aren't astronomical.
13. He's willing to be *taught*, even if it's something he already knows.

This last point is very important. The seriously ill and dying are going through this experience for the first time. Often, they want to share, inform, and *teach*, transforming their loss and grief into transcendence for themselves and others.

HOW TO BE AN EFFECTIVE MEMBER OF A SUPPORT GROUP

If the facilitator agrees, attend a few meetings to see if you will fit in. She will know if the group would welcome or resent your provisional participation. It will be somewhat artificial; probably you will not take part as much as if you were one of them. Once you do decide to join, the following guidelines may help you to contribute and to benefit:

1. Monitor your comfort level. If you are uncomfortable because you are facing your illness, grieving over losses, or venting your anger, that's probably helpful. If, on the other hand, you feel manipulated, blamed, or compelled to thoughts or actions you disagree with, take a break. How do you feel on leaving the group at the end of the session? At the prospect of the next one? Are you looking forward to it or dreading it?

Charles, newly diagnosed with Parkinson's disease, joined the local group, but found himself very depressed at meeting people who were in a far more advanced stage of the illness. This is why stage of illness may be a criterion for your selection. Charles switched to a group dealing with chronic illness.

2. Exposing your feelings to a bunch of strangers can be scary at first. Go at your own pace.

3. Really listen to what others have to say, and respond to that. If you're preparing for your next point, you won't hear the others and you won't get as much out of the session.

4. Those in the group are going through trauma and ordeal, just as you are. Soften toward them and make allowances.

5. Offer your suggestions, but don't inflict them.

6. Honor each person, and extend to each your care and support. You'll find yourself filled with your own love as well as theirs. This is one way groups heal.

7. Recognize that your time together is limited and that you are in the process of losing each other. You will value each other more.

8. Allow others to teach you what you already know. I've done this many times. You give them the gift of giving. If this seems insincere, remember that the experience of dying is different for everyone. The cancer patient may want to talk about learning the value of each day—which, of course, you already knew. But it's different for her, and what she brings to it—her entire, unique self and life—will enrich your own experience.

9. Finally, remember that being part of a group is merely a formality. All of us already are.

THE BLESSING OF GROUPS— CONNECTION AND CONTINUITY

Ultimately, groups connect us to larger and larger circles of living, and connection works. It shows us we do not die alone, that we do indeed have companions for most of the hard journey, and that our

responses are normal. Connection reminds us that we are individually part of something much bigger than ourselves—our community,
our causes, and all the other things we love—and that these survive
us. They continue.

The daughter of the man in the seat beside you will survive, and
to the extent that what you say becomes part of him and he is part of
his daughter, you survive also. You continue.

Connection brings out the best in us. It offers warmth, hope, and
faith.

The day after Charles left his group because it depressed him, he
sat in his living room watching the Clarence Thomas hearings. Senator Robert Byrd rose to speak, hand and voice shaking. "He has benign essential tremor, you know," someone said. The Senator, that
great, grand orator, nearly eighty years old, kept both Charles and
the Senate spellbound with his passion and eloquence. He showed
Charles that he could continue to be the best he was. A couple of
years later, Billy Graham, afflicted with Parkinson's, inspired Charles
with the possibilities for courage, dignity, and a continuing sense of
mission.

OUR HEROES LEAD THE WAY

A hero is someone who descends into the valley of death and returns, often with a gift for his people.[3]

Whatever your disease, connect with the hero who *continues* in
spite of it rather than stops (until he or she must)—Mary Tyler
Moore with diabetes, Magic Johnson with HIV, Mother Teresa with
heart disease, Annette Funicello with multiple sclerosis, Katharine
Hepburn with benign essential tremor, Ronald Reagan with Alzheimer's, Christopher Reeve and James Brady (of the Brady bill)
with paralysis, Steve Fox of *Good Morning America* with arthritis,
actress Patricia Neal with stroke, novelist Joseph Heller with
Guillain-Barré syndrome, Ann Jillian with breast cancer—it's a roll
call of people we'd like to know. Read their books and articles,
watch their public appearances, gain sustenance from them, emulate

them. These are all members of your greater support group. With them, you are not alone.

You, too, can be a hero such as these to those around you.

But if time is short, perhaps you, like Vicki, will want to form your own "Not-Expected-to-Live Club."

12

TWELVE

RIDING THE

EMOTIONAL ROLLER

COASTER

I could handle it if I weren't so depressed," Bill confided. Normally bluff and optimistic, accustomed to inspiring confidence in the "troops" during the leanest times, he was laid low by his ALS. After all, the mortality rate was 100 percent, and even now, progressive weakness slurred and softened his speech. Nor did it help that he awoke at two or three every morning to peer out the window, hopeless under the night sky, the stars colder and more distant than ever. Chronically weary, he took no pleasure in anything anymore. A drag on Peg, Bill Jr., Mom, Tori, and the rest, an unfair burden, why should he continue?

Suicide seemed increasingly logical. In secret he reviewed his life insurance policy. If he killed himself, they wouldn't get the money. So he had to make it look like an accident. Moreover, he must do it before he got too weak. This was his greatest worry, that he wouldn't have the strength to precipitate whatever mishap he thought up. Dr. Kerr promised he'd do all in his power to see that Bill didn't suffer, but what did that mean exactly? Bill knew Kerr was limited by law.

Besides, the good doctor defined pain as physical; he was oblivious to Bill's *mental* suffering.

At night in front of the TV, he stared at his wife until she asked, "What is it, Bill?"

"It's been a good run, hasn't it, Peg?"

"And not over yet." She got up, came around to the back of his chair, and put her arms around his neck.

"But, the best is *not* to come," he warned.

"Our marriage has been my best. I wouldn't have had it any other way."

She'd proved amazingly strong throughout the ordeal. He hadn't given her enough credit. Now he wondered if she could do it, whatever "it" might be. Administer the injection when his throat was too weak to swallow? Point the gun and fire? No, no, he shook his head. Peg would sooner put a bullet through her own heart. Nor could he ask her to break the law and possibly endure a trial, publicity, and prison, with the kids losing their mom as well as their dad.

In New York's Lenox Hill Hospital, Marian, dying of renal failure, was in a different mood. She raged at her devoted daughter Carrie for flipping her into one stage of dying or another, and for flirting with the doctors instead of seeing to it that her mother had the simple comforts, like a bottle of Johnnie Walker Red. She was furious at the doctor for not doing more, just because she wasn't a pretty young thing of thirty, like Carrie, to whom the hospital staff paid more attention. Marian fumed at the nurses, who took their sweet time answering her buzzer and expected her to eat slop she wouldn't feed to a dog, if she had one, but they were too damned much trouble, and how in hell was she supposed to care for a dog, sick as she was?

At this rate, she was getting worse, not better!

Ellie continued pretending she didn't have MS, even when forced to use a cane, which her spasticity made increasingly problematic. Her husband, Art, feared she'd fall and break something.

"Why don't we *rent* a wheelchair so you can try it out?" he pleaded. "You might even like being pushed. You've never objected to me doing all the work before," he joked.

"I don't need it!" she blazed. "So shut up about it, okay?"

Thus she kept her demons at bay. If no one mentioned MS, life could go on as usual. She might even return to work, from which she'd taken a "leave." But at night the demons stuffed in her closet came out to play, like Maurice Sendak's wild things, only more vicious. Ellie lay there in bed, shrieking inside against the death of her acting dream, which she blamed on MS (but had actually forsaken years before because she couldn't stand the insecurity). One night she gave herself over to terror, waking Art.

"What is it? What's wrong? You're shaking the whole bed."

He'd leave her. It was only a matter of time. Already he was involved with someone else—from the office, she thought.

Depression, grief, rage, denial, and terror—each is a common response to the face of death. Methods of coping include cultivation of such positive emotions as hope, love, and joy.

DEATH ISN'T FAIR—BUT NEITHER IS LIFE

Jeff's resentment wasn't directed at people so much as at the outrageous unfairness of the universe. At thirty-two, a successful computer programmer climbing the corporate ranks and a would-be photographer, he'd been stricken with AIDS. Not given to promiscuity, he and his partner, Doug, had been together for seven years, did no drugs, and rarely touched anything stronger than exotic liqueurs. When they donned their nuns' habits for Mardi Gras and waltzed down Bourbon Street, their huge ornate crosses swinging and swaying, people applauded, but otherwise Jeff and Doug remained observers.

No, it wasn't fair that Jeff must die on account of love, but is any death fair? Is it fair that a young nurse gets blown to bits in a war on foreign soil? That the baby next door is born without a brain? That the ten-year-old is stricken with leukemia or the high-schooler is hit by a car in the crosswalk while joking around with her friends? Is it fair that comedian Gilda Radner, in her prime, should have died of ovarian cancer? Or that Charles's wife should have been in the last stages of Alzheimer's just as he was struggling with Parkinson's? But, for that matter, is it fair that the boss's son gets your job? The carjacker picks your Honda? Your enemy wins big in Las Vegas? Junk crowds art galleries while your paintings can't find a home? Is it fair that you get audited and real crooks don't? The waiter serves the later-arriving party first? It rains on your vacation?

For that matter, is it fair that the average human being grows in skill, experience, and understanding, then gradually loses these to old age and death?

No, death isn't fair, but then neither is life!

Yet we're raised to think it is. When we were toddlers, our parents taught us to share and to play fair—in order to avoid the chaos of a lot of flailing little bodies and to keep the noise below deafening. Painstakingly, they explained the equality of their gifts to rivalrous brothers and sisters. Perhaps they should have trained us in how to manage injustice.

We'd like to think the universe is fair, because fairness is "good" (not a cultural universal, by the way; in some cultures clever manipulation is superior to foolish fairness). And we want to think the universe is good. We may even develop an afterlife complete with Judgment Day, on which the rotten winners in this world get "theirs" while we glory in our just reward, especially if we've been meek, poor, and charitable. But there's so much injustice and cruelty that we're left with another possibility, and that is that the universe itself isn't fair or even good. It just *is*, and so are life and death. This way of thinking leaves room for individual accountability, for choices between good and evil.

It also leaves room for religious doubts, which may be more painful than the assaults on our bodies. How can an all-powerful, all-knowing, all-compassionate God allow so much human suffering? Rabbi Harold Kushner, who lost his fourteen-year-old son to progeria, has one answer. He rejects the arguments that "bad things happen to good people" as part of God's (good) design, or because God is testing us, or as an instrument of (brutal) teaching, or to get rid of some bad fault we have (blaming the victim), or even to elicit our compassion.[1]

Instead, Kushner gives a reasoned argument that God cannot be both all-powerful and fair. Perhaps He is still in the process of creating order out of chaos, but He hasn't completed it and random evil still exists. God doesn't cause our trials, but He can help us through them.

In all probability, the illness that afflicts you now is unfair. At first you respond to this unfairness with depression and anger, which are flip sides of each other.

ANGER, THE CHAMELEON EMOTION

Anger is socially unacceptable, so we fold, spindle, and mutilate it. Its manifestations include:

> Subtle torture and blame of caregivers.
> Arousing caregivers' guilt, sometimes very sweetly.
> Depression, which may be anger focused inward—Bill might do violence to the body that betrays him.
> "Displaced" anger—at the government, for example, or on apparently unrelated issues, such as the plight of others.
> Loss of faith—we want to punish God with the same nonbeing!
> Projection—the anger we see in others may actually be a manifestation of our own frustration and depression.
> Resistance—you don't take your medicine; you miss treatment appointments.

A word about resistance: It often disguises itself as anger toward caregivers and the medical staff. If you resist treatment, explain that you are doing so and why. But be sure this is a choice you want to make. Resistance seduces, in that it is a way of seizing control—ultimately even power over death, possibly your real aim. Can you accomplish this in another way?

IS DEPRESSION A NORMAL RESPONSE TO LIFE-THREATENING ILLNESS, OR IS IT ANOTHER ILLNESS?

In the current controversy raging over euthanasia, the point is frequently made that depression in the seriously or terminally ill is a *mental illness*. If treated as such, with antidepressants and therapy, patients won't want to die, and they'll stop demanding "death with dignity" or physician-assisted suicide.

Often cited is the *DSM-IV* (the *Diagnostic and Statistical Manual*, with which mental health professionals diagnose mental illness).[2] Sections quoted include those on the symptoms of Major Depressive Episode, which typically "follows a psychosocial stressor, particularly death of a loved one, marital separation, or divorce." One section of the *DSM-IV* that I've never seen cited as diagnostic of the terminally ill is V62.82, Bereavement, defined as "a reaction to the death of a loved one." The bereaved person may suffer depressed mood, insomnia, poor appetite, weight loss, and diminished capacity for pleasure. In fact, such bereavement reactions are considered "normal." A diagnosis of Major Depression is not made unless the symptoms last longer than two months (after death) and are accompanied by survivor guilt, feelings of worthlessness, thoughts of suicide, psychomotor retardation, severe functional impairment and/or hallucinations other than transient experiences of the deceased.

My question is this: Isn't the dying person undergoing bereavement? Isn't he facing the loss, through death, not just of himself, his physical functions, and his abilities, but also his spouse or partner, children, grandchildren, siblings, and friends? Add to this the loss of well-loved work and places, dreams, and a future. And further add that the common symptoms of Major Depression—insomnia, anorexia, significant weight loss or gain, fatigue, and the like—are frequently symptoms of the physical disease and/or its treatment.

Then the question becomes: Is depression in the face of life-threatening illness really "abnormal"? Isn't it, rather, the most normal reaction in the world, a "normal reaction to the death of a loved one"—*yourself*? Kübler-Ross considers it a stage of dying. Is it really necessary to add "mental illness" to the diagnosis of the terminally ill patient?

The distinction is important, first, because almost half of the dying are diagnosed as suffering from "mental illness." The fact that *depression* is the most frequent diagnosis is not mentioned. Because of this diagnosis, many patients are judged *not competent* to make decisions regarding their treatment, including the decision of "rational suicide."

Second, the treatment of Major Depression is often an antidepressant medication. For me, there are serious ethical issues around administration of antidepressants to the dying. They can interfere with the patient's processing of what is happening to him, his closing his circle. Psychotherapy, on the other hand, compels the patient to deal with and solve his problems rather than draw a curtain across them.

Antidepressants may artificially lift the mood or numb the feelings, and cause side effects. Psychiatrist Peter Kramer claims that the antidepressant Prozac not only relieves symptoms but also changes personality.[3] Your personality characteristics are partly inborn, partly the result of experiences, for example, childhood loss and trauma. Kramer's patients on Prozac became more confident, assertive, cheerful, aggressive, outgoing, flexible, sexually attractive, energetic, sociable, rejection-tolerant, less inhibited, and better able to cope with problems.

Psychiatrist Peter Breggin is highly critical of Prozac. He sees it as acting as a stimulant similar to cocaine and amphetamines; he points to side effects in some people such as nausea, insomnia, agitation, diarrhea, and lowered libido, as well as disturbing evidence that there may be a higher risk of suicide in Prozac patients. Breggin writes: "Prozac disrupts two of the neurotransmitters most involved in frontal-lobe function—serotonin and dopamine—and in that process can rob us of our sensitivity, self-awareness, and capacity to care or love." This is the opposite of what the dying person needs in her end-time.[4] He also advocates psychotherapy over antidepressants: "Drugs are a euthanasia of the soul."[5]

To a lesser extent, other medications change personality as well. The self becomes less of a stable constellation and more malleable. Even the patient's history can change: if self-esteem is higher, so is his reevaluation of his past, and perhaps consequently his values and memories. This throws us into questions on the nature of truth and reality.

The result can be that the dying person, rather than struggling through the psychological and spiritual conflicts I discuss in this book, dies as "not himself." He misses the opportunities for true self-examination and revelation, all crucial to end-of-life development. "One cannot heal the soul with medication."[6]

On the other hand, we relieve physical suffering chemically, so why not mental suffering? Psychologist M. Brewster Smith cites his own experience of a relative who seemed depressed due to the medications administered to her. At a stage of dying when she was far too close to death for further self-reflection and processing of her life, the antidepressant helped.[7]

You may find that there is a rush to solutions by many people around you, a rush to operate, radiate, chemicalize, and antidepress. These solutions may respond more to other people's needs than your own. They wouldn't be able to face what you're going through. They want to deny it by fixing it—so death doesn't exist anymore.

Having said all this, however, we need caveats. First, even "normal" depression or bereavement merits counseling. By all means, seek out friends and family, a therapist or minister, to help you cope with the terrific constellation of major losses that you're enduring. Second, some experts believe that if a depression lasts, it actually results in biochemical changes that *intensify* the depression, converting it from a normal emotional reaction to a more biologically-based one for which treatment is mandatory. If you are receiving counseling for normal depression, your therapist will be alert to the length of your depression, any deepening of it, and, particularly, "stuckness" with no movement (even anger is movement).

Unfortunately, you may feel too depressed to seek help—a sure indication that you should. If loved ones, physicians, and nurses are urging you to, they're seeing something you don't see in yourself. Getting help is an act of faith in their judgment.

If your depression lasts with no ups, or you sink deeper and deeper, or if in the past you've been diagnosed with depression, bipolar disorder, or another serious mental illness (mentally ill people die, too), or if you're contemplating suicide (and I don't mean just the passing thought most of us have), or if you just can't seem to get going in the morning—each is a sure sign that you need immediate therapeutic help, possibly including medication.

I'M UP ONE MINUTE, DOWN THE NEXT: WHY IS THAT?

The most obvious reason is that you're experiencing a lot of different stresses whose meaning you don't even know. You await the latest biopsy results, but you're having a good day. Chemo's over, replaced by a troubling new symptom. Anxiety between you and your lover eases—last night was the best—but your disapproving dad hasn't called. Pain wanes, then returns with a vengeance; some days you need all your energy to deal with it. And through good and bad, hope flits in and out, light and shadow, playing hide and seek among the ruins of your life.

Your *whole existence* is up and down, so why wouldn't your emotions be?

Actually, our basic negative emotions are *adaptive defenses,* that is, their purpose is to keep us alive. Any threat to our survival arouses them. When parts of us start breaking down, we feel *fear,* which prods us to action—see a doctor, gain information, swallow medicine, undergo treatment. We're created with fight or flight mechanisms; if something of dinosaur proportions lumbers toward us, we flee, but if *we're* the dinosaur, we stand and fight. *Anger* has the same adaptive value; attack arouses it. Since we're human, attack need not be physical. A rival at the office takes our job, our livelihood; our response looks like *jealousy* or *envy,* but it is really defense of our physical or psychological survival. Disrespect threatens our identity as strong or good or capable of life skills; we respond in kind.

In other words, *any* prospect of loss—physical, psychological, social, or even metaphorical—arouses a variety of emotions.

Some emotions actually *defend* us against others. Freud believed that depression was anger turned inward. When we turn our anger outward, we feel energized and more in control. People who express their anger may in fact live longer.[8] Using one emotion to defend against another is something we do without realizing it, contributing to the roller coaster effect.

Additionally, some medications, opioids, for example, are notorious precipitants of mood swings. Others cause anxiety, jumpiness, euphoria, spaciness, depression, even hallucinations. If you're on medications for emotional disorders, these affect you as well.

Another reason for the roller coaster effect is that, through trial and error, we discover that certain emotions attract other people; we need others so we hone our gallows humor. When they laugh, so do we. We keep our conversation positive to make them feel better. We express our love, they reward us with affection, and so we love them more.

Serious illness intensifies the emotions we normally have. If we are loving, our *love* deepens. We feel even greater *humiliation* over things done to our bodies by strangers—worse than our stinging exposure when the boss reamed us out in front of the entire department. Our *envy* of others' health—the bloom in their cheeks, their ability to stride into our room without a wheelchair, to eat as they please—intensifies and corrodes our souls. We feel *scared* of the next unpredictable symptom, *overwhelmed* by the plethora of treatments, *hurt* that a special friend hasn't called, *frustrated* by slow lab results, *triumphant* in remission, *proud* of surviving with identity intact, *abandoned* by an adult child, *bitter* that all our kindness should be rewarded with pain, *guilty* over the financial drain, *confused* about contradictions in advice and treatment, *euphoric* over rising dreams, fantasies, and visions that signify impending transition.

Meanwhile, caregivers are responding emotionally as well. They're getting annoyed, angry, and even using your upsets as an excuse to abandon you. Sometimes, they imagine your pain is worse than it is—it certainly *looks* worse to them. Magnanimously, they make excuses for your moodiness. Or else they take it as a sign of weakness. They demand your equanimity in the face of odds that would throw anyone, themselves included. Forever guilty, they fight among themselves, ostensibly over your welfare but actually over old issues never resolved (how you favored one brother over the others), making you take sides. They're working out their own issues through your dying process. This in turn makes you feel guilty over all the trouble you're causing. What a stew!

HOW CAN I COPE WITH MY EMOTIONS?

Some people like roller coasters. Others get sick on them. Which type are you? Do you prefer an even-keel life, or plenty of excitement?

You're entitled to feel sad, glad, mad, or rad. They're *your* feelings, no one else's. No emotion, in and of itself, is good or bad. So don't let anyone tell you to stop crying, be brave, grow up, or the like. How they handle your emotions is *their* problem. What counts is what you do with yours. Act on them, verbalize them, or keep them to yourself. What matters is how you make others feel and whether that's what you intend. Finally, do you want to change your emotions, and, if so, in what direction?

Exercise: Define for yourself why you feel as you do. On a sheet of paper write down how you feel, and the reason. "I feel depressed because . . ." Spell out those reasons. Then ask yourself if they're *true*. Are you really angry at your treatment—or your disease? Are you really depressed over life ending—or a failure of some kind? Are you really afraid of death—or have you been afraid of life all along? When you write it out, or verbalize it to a friend, you externalize it, and put it out there where you can deal with it.

In the course of performing this exercise (which you may do over a number of days or weeks), you are likely to discover unresolved emotional issues. Past losses, if we haven't worked them through, reactivate past emotions and intensify present ones.

We need to deal with the past as well as the present. You can do this in the following ways:

1. Acknowledge your emotion. Admit to yourself that you are feeling it.
2. Express it aloud to yourself and to those with whom you feel comfortable. Use your instinct to select these people. Remem-

ber that this is good training for them!

3. Express your feelings in other ways. Paint them, act them out, write a poem, make a collage; or you can beat a pillow and scream, but do these in the presence of caregivers who can handle it.

4. Crying releases endorphins, opioid substances from the brain, and can comfort you.

5. Dream expert Jeremy Taylor believes we can experience our emotions in the dream world, and deal with them there.[9]

6. Different emotions call for different methods of handling. With fear, for example, I find it useful to describe the symptoms to myself: "Oh, I'm afraid. Look, my hands are shaking, my heart's fluttering, it feels like there's a stone in the pit of my stomach, I can't think." In this way, for me, fear passes magically.

   Consult books on handling specific emotions.[10]

7. Ask yourself if you are really angry or frustrated or upset about what you think you are, or about something else. If it's something else, deal with that.

8. Ask yourself if you are being rewarded in any way for your emotions. If your tears bring floods of help, perhaps you need to rethink them. Yes, I said "rethink."

ACTIVE HOPE

Another major thing you can do for yourself is to engage in *active hope*.

But hope isn't something you can turn on and off like the TV set, is it? Yes, as a matter of fact, it is.

In the past, you either lay around and hoped for money to pay the bills or you went out and got another job or asked for a raise. That's the difference between plain old *passive* hope and *active* hope. Passive hope is wishing, active hope is taking steps to get what you want. What I'm recommending to you is active hope, *doing* something. It doesn't have to be physically demanding.

Of necessity, your hopes are different now. Many of the old ones are dashed, so you may say you have nothing to hope for. That's be-cause you're defining hopes as they used to be. But many new ones can take their place. Your big surprise may be that because they're within easy reach they're better than the old.

So what *can* you hope for?

- A cure, of course
- That your T cell count is up, or that the mass will shrink, or . . .
- A grandchild's visit
- That the birds gather at the feeder outside your window
- That your Christmas cactus blooms
- That your loved one does
- A good day
- Another meaningful dream like the one you had last week
- A Republican (or Democratic) victory
- That *Cheers* returns with the entire old cast
- That wherever you're going, there's sex—lots of it!
- *Healing* (not cure; rather, a spiritual awakening)
- Increased connection with God or Spirit

Add to or amend this list to suit your own hopes. Make it several pages long. Fill in important names. As you progress through your illness, you will find that the future shrinks for some of these hopes—from next year, to next month, to tomorrow. Others, the most important, are eternal.

Phrase your hopes positively rather than negatively. Don't hope for less pain, hope for more pain relief. This is *active* hope, so badger doctors, nurses, and friends, if necessary.

These hopes don't extend into the far future, as your others did. But they're superior in that they (1) are much easier to actualize, and (2) bring you far greater, deeper, and extended satisfaction. Think about it. How long did the buzz from that raise, promotion, or honor last? There was the celebration—and then what? You went back to living in the future! Now you're blessed with the opportunity to enjoy the present.

Of course, some people tell you hope is futile. That's because they're so tangled up in the practical, material side of life (just as you used to be—don't deny it) that they see hope only as recovery. And that's not practical, at least not permanently (not even for them—but they don't know this and there's no point in telling them). But you're *here*, not *there*, and you're discovering every day how much more hope there is.

The great psychologist William James cautioned against "forced optimism." In fact, you may feel compelled by those around you to exude a phony hope. If you do, be sure *you* know it's phony, otherwise as Marc Ian Barasch says, it can result in emotional anesthesia, the antithesis of healing.[11] On the other hand, physicians and relatives are often afraid to arouse "false hope." Their implied definition is that the only hope is cure. But as you know now, there are many other rich hopes, like healing and spiritual connection, that are far more important.

THIRTEEN

AID-IN-DYING:

DO YOU WANT IT?

AT age forty-three, Canadian Sue Rodriguez was in the last stages of Lou Gehrig's disease (ALS), confined to a wheelchair, her speech barely understandable. Dependent on visiting homemakers for feeding and personal grooming, she was unable even to hold a cup. Her estranged husband, involved with another woman, had moved back into the house to help with their nine-year-old son. Sue petitioned the Canadian Supreme Court to allow a doctor to help her die. They turned her down, five to four. She procured this help anyway several months later, in February 1994.[1]

In 1991 physician Timothy Quill wrote an extraordinary article, which was published in the *New England Journal of Medicine*.[2] He told the story of Diane, a long-term patient with a history of vaginal cancer, family problems, alcoholism, and depression. At age forty-five, Diane developed leukemia. After exploring all options, including treatments and their side effects, she decided she did not want any. Instead, she requested barbiturates for "insomnia." Fully aware of her intentions, Quill prescribed them. Some months later, when she was ready, she took her life.

In 1990 Janet Adkins, age fifty-four and in the early stages of Alzheimer's disease, for which there is currently no cure, mailed her medical records to physician Jack Kevorkian and asked him to help her end her life. She and her husband flew to Michigan to meet with him. The next day, in his specially equipped van, Kevorkian started an intravenous saline solution. Janet pushed a red button, which replaced the saline with sodium pentathol, a painkiller, and one minute later this in turn was replaced with a mixture of potassium chloride and succinylcholine. Just before she died, she thanked Kevorkian.[3] In April 1995, the Supreme Court upheld Michigan's ban on assisted suicide. At this writing, Kevorkian has been present at or has assisted twenty-seven suicides.

In 1983 Nancy Cruzan, age twenty-five, was thrown from a car and went into a coma from which she did not recover. Her parents petitioned the Missouri Supreme Court for removal of her feeding tube, but the request was denied. In 1990 the U.S. Supreme Court finally granted them the right to discontinue her respirator, nutrition, and hydration.[4]

Terminally ill with cancer, eighty-eight-year-old William Meyer, Jr., of Connecticut wanted to die. He followed the Hemlock Society's prescription for barbiturates plus a plastic bag over his head, but a reflex made his hands pull the bag off. In anguish, his son, William F. Meyer III, held the bag over his head. At first the death was ruled a suicide. Then the younger Meyer admitted his part to a magazine reporter.[5] Charged with manslaughter, he pleaded not guilty but was given two years of accelerated rehabilitation, a form of probation. The strong support of his community, including four hundred encouraging letters, has helped him through his ordeal.

These five cases all encompass euthanasia, Greek for "the good death," but there are major issue differences.

Sue Rodriguez was no longer physically capable of killing herself, that is, of pulling the trigger of a gun, swallowing pills, or leaping from a window. Her death may have been hastened by "active" euthanasia; it appears that a physician administered Seconal and a massive dose of morphine.

The ruling in Nancy Cruzan's case followed similar state rulings across the country, including Karen Quinlan's in New Jersey; it was an instance of "passive" euthanasia, the discontinuation of treatment. DNR, or "Do not resuscitate," orders on a patient's chart are another common form.

Quill's method qualifies as "physician-assisted suicide." The physician prescribed the pills, but Diane killed herself while she was physically capable of doing so. Kevorkian's method was technically somewhat similar: he provided the device, but Adkins pushed the button. The two cases are seen as vastly different by many, however. Quill knew his patient well, explored all options with both patient and family, and the patient was terminal. Janet Adkins was still playing tennis and had years to live, although the quality of her life would have become increasingly poor.

The case of William F. Meyer III may be seen as "relative-assisted" suicide.

In the following pages, I outline briefly the legal status of euthanasia, followed by an analysis of the arguments for and against it. The chapter concludes with a discussion of current trends and how these affect your own decisions.

LEGAL STATUS

Active euthanasia, such as that provided to Sue Rodriguez, is currently illegal in all states. It is considered murder. Physician-assisted suicide is specifically banned in more than half of the states.[6]

In November 1994, Oregon passed a physician-assisted suicide law, allowing patients prescriptions of lethal doses of medication under specific guidelines: According to at least two physicians, the patient must be terminally ill, with six months or less to live. Additionally, she must make at least two verbal requests separated by fifteen or more days, sign each request before two witnesses, one not a family or hospital staff member, be advised of options, and be urged (not compelled) to tell family members. The Oregon Department of Health must survey written records of such deaths and publish a statistical report, thus demonstrating the results of law.

An injunction stayed execution of the law, and finally a federal court ruled it unconstitutional. At this writing, proponents of the law are appealing. In March 1996, a federal appeals court struck down as unconstitutional Washington State's ban on assisted suicide. According to Reverend Ralph Mero, Executive Director of Compassion in Dying, Oregon and New York laws are also under appeal for similar reasons. They prohibit physicians from prescribing medication to terminally ill patients for self-administration. Meanwhile, patients who had hoped to benefit continue to suffer. Various other patients' rights laws have been enacted over the last five years. The 1991 Patient Self-Determination Act requires medical institutions receiving Medicare or Medicaid funds to tell patients their rights regarding life-sustaining treatments (and refusals of same). In the 1990 Cruzan case, the Supreme Court affirmed the right of competent patients to refuse life-sustaining treatment, including nutrition and hydration, but this authorization needs "clear and convincing evidence." The major mode of this evidence is a set of advance directives.[7]

As you can see, both the *refusal* and the *discontinuation* of life-sustaining treatments in case of terminal illness are your new, hard-won legal rights. *You must claim them,* however. Furthermore, the waters muddy if these rights contradict the policies and/or values of your physician and/or your hospital, and even, in some cases, your relatives (if you are no longer competent). Dr. George Burnell recounts the horrendous story of his own elderly mother, age eighty-eight and diagnosed with Alzheimer's: the manufacturer of her pacemaker threatened to sue if Burnell did not replace the battery, so she was compelled to live on.[8]

In Holland, euthanasia, while not legal (as commonly believed), proceeds along specific guidelines. If the patient suffers unbearably from terminal illness and repeatedly requests death, the physician himself administers an injection. It is too early to evaluate this system, but both opponents and advocates of euthanasia are weighing in with predictably opposite accounts and judgments. Indeed, the *facts* of euthanasia are vastly different, depending on the values of who's reporting them.

Many physicians claim to have witnessed assisted suicides similar to that provided by Quill. Typically, the doctor administers medication for relief of severe pain, and if, as a by-product, the terminal patient dies, the principle of "double effect" applies. Dr. Judith

Ahronheim and Doron Weber recount the explanation of a Catholic priest.[9] Father John agrees to the administration of morphine to relieve suffering, even if it would result in the patient's death by depressing respiration. The *intent* is humane, not murderous. Ahronheim and Weber believe that many physicians are not aware of this principle, but, as Dr. Burnell points out, even the pope has sanctioned such relief. It is the illness that kills, not the pain-relief medication.

Few such cases are prosecuted. Some believe they should be left under the *threat* of legal action. As for relatives who assist suicide, juries tend to release them on technicalities.

To summarize, when a physician deliberately *prescribes* medication to relieve pain, even if it results in death, the act is considered ethical by many. On the other hand, when a physician prescribes with the *intent* to cause death, the act is termed physician-assisted suicide and is highly controversial. The actual *administration* of the medication for this purpose is considered a crime both legally and, by many, ethically. Others, however, believe that it constitutes humane relief and, as such, is more ethical than withholding that relief or allowing the patient to suffer by withdrawing hydration and nutrition.

The presence of others at the moment a person takes her own life is another growing practice. The organization Compassion in Dying counsels patients and their families about pain management, rational suicide in "desperate cases," and how "a humane death can be accomplished." If the patient requests, members of the organization are present in the final hours, providing spiritual and personal support so the patient need not take her life alone. (They do not provide or administer barbiturates or other means of ending life.)[10] Their advice on suicide is based on Derek Humphrey's explicit instructions in *Final Exit*.[11]

ARGUMENTS IN FAVOR OF AND AGAINST PHYSICIAN-ASSISTED SUICIDE

The arguments for and against physician-assisted suicide cluster around fifteen major issues. Below, I present the major pros and cons around each issue. The next section suggests steps you might take in making your own decision. Last, I discuss whether or not euthanasia will become legal.

1. **Pain:** The major argument *in favor* of physician-assisted suicide is that it is the humane relief of severe and intractable pain in a terminally ill person. It is estimated that between 10 percent and 15 percent of patients endure such pain during their last weeks.

Opponents admit to the undertreatment of pain, but believe that physicians are becoming more informed and aggressive. Dr. Kathleen Foley, a leading expert on pain management, maintains that the new age of pain relief is at hand; pain leads to depression to hopelessness and then to the wish to die; she maintains that patients whose pain is relieved do not request assisted suicide.[12]

Patients *favoring* euthanasia counter that, unfortunately, these arguments do not persuade them; they fear that the new pain management will miss them as it has in the past, and that they'll be in the 10 to 15 percent group with inadequate control. They also reason that, if doctors can't provide enough relief for the pain of childbirth, arthritis, back disorder, lupus, and the like, how successful will they be with my agony?

Pro-euthanasia forces further see the claims of new aggressiveness toward pain as contradicted by the need for pain clinics. They point to the 81 percent of 1,400 doctors and nurses in five hospitals who admitted that patients were undertreated for pain; 70 percent of these confessed to medical treatment beyond patients' best interests or wishes. Anti-euthanasist Foley herself observes that the patient's insurance coverage may control the degree to which his pain is or is not relieved: "By rationing pain management on a financial basis, patients are being forced to consider death."[13] Then there are the books *How We Die*, Dr. Sherwin Nuland's grisly account of how death *really* happens (biologically), and *The Gifts of the Body*, Rebecca Brown's haunting novel of AIDS suffering.[14] Add contemporary personal narratives by such notables as Reynolds Price and physician Jody Heymann.[15] Thus, the proliferation of pain clinics, the admissions to overtreatment of medical conditions or undertreatment of pain by doctors and nurses, the increasing control of pain medication by insurance companies, and the personal accounts of pain, all make claims of adequate pain relief seem unconvincing to those who favor euthanasia.

If and when pro-euthanasists see their own relatives receiving entirely adequate relief, they may be willing to trust that the new pain-management will alleviate the need for euthanasia.

2. Suffering is often mentioned in the same breath with pain by those who favor euthanasia. Suffering includes mental and/or existential anguish, as well as "indignity, confusion, disorientation, sedation, immobility, . . . boredom, loneliness, lying in your own excrement, inability to function on any level that allows enjoyment."[16] Sue Rodriguez suffered not only physical pain but also losses of control and physical abilities, the prospective loss of her son, and the daily reminder that her husband was no longer hers (they separated shortly before she was diagnosed). She could barely communicate, and faced the possibility of gradually smothering to death. She had no realistic hope of remission.

Former Oregon Governor Barbara Roberts watched her husband suffer psychologically and emotionally because his medication relieved his physical pain but deprived him of his abilities to read and communicate.

Those *against* euthanasia argue that relief of pain will relieve suffering and that, besides, suffering is inherent in the human condition. They further believe that, with enough love and caring from relatives and friends, suffering will be lessened.

3. Clinical Depression: It appears from written accounts that Sue Rodriguez was (understandably) clinically depressed.

Many *anti-euthanasists* argue that anyone who wants to die is, by definition, clinically depressed, a *medical* condition. Some quote statistics suggesting that more than 40 percent of terminally ill people are also mentally ill (no mention of the predominant diagnosis, depression!); further, the percentage rises as the dying come closer to death.[17] They argue that there's no such thing as "rational suicide," that depression is a pair of gray glasses darkening all evaluation; that in the terminally ill, it is a *disease* that should be treated with antidepressants. When the patient feels more cheerful, he will not want to die.

Those *favoring* euthanasia agree that, certainly, such a change of mind is true of people who are *not* terminally ill. We've all known the young man whose girlfriend left him, who has "nothing to live for and never will." We've been there ourselves. Then love returns in a new and wondrous guise, along with adventures and blessings he never dreamed of, and he thanks us for saving his life. Curiously, it is with examples like this that anti-euthanasists propose to make their point: attempted suicides who are *not* terminally ill! The terminally ill will not live long enough to be grateful! Sue Rodriguez could not have the young man's hopes or expectations; indeed, if she had, we would have said she was in denial.

The *pro-euthanasist* sees depression over *bereavement* in the face of these losses as utterly normal. Suicide is perfectly rational in a situation such as Sue Rodriguez's, and the patient does not need the added burden of a mental illness diagnosis.

Nor should a history of depression (the "common cold" of mental illness) disqualify a patient from any resources, including prescriptions, to help her end her life.

Finally, some of those *favoring euthanasia* ask, should there be a rush to treat this type of bereavement with antidepressants, artificially lifting mood so that the patient does not want to die? Is the goal of making him agree to live a little longer worth his loss of ability to process what is happening to him?

4. The Slippery Slope: Those *against* euthanasia argue as follows that if it became legal, its use could spread to those with more than six months to live, like Janet Adkins. They ask, What's so sacred about six months? Euthanasia could be *allowed,* and then even *prescribed,* for those deemed by some to be "less alive" or "less human," perhaps the anencephalic, the comatose, and the developmentally disabled. Once we label any human beings as less worthy of life-preservation, where do we stop? If physicians and weary caregivers possess the legal option, they'll exercise it far more frequently than is common now.

Recent concerns around rising Medicare and Medicaid costs may make the slope slipperier still. Since most euthanized would be older patients, Medicare could be cut "in anticipation" of such decisions, thereby sentencing many to poorer health care and earlier death. The elderly could become even more marginalized.

Pro-euthanasists maintain that while the "slippery slope" arguments may be valid, today's dying should not be penalized for future misuse.

5. Abuse: Those *against* euthanasia point to greedy relatives who are after Aunt Nelda's money or are sick of caring for her; institutions that are not paid enough to tend her because of Medicare/Medicaid cuts; insurance companies that seek to end their obligations; physicians pressured or bribed to "do the right thing."

Those *in favor* argue that so-called passive euthanasia, now widely practiced, is susceptible to the same abuses. They ask, What's so passive about pulling the plug? To them, the distinction is a fine one. They venture that guidelines and laws can protect us against abuses of both passive and active euthanasia.

6. Safeguards: As mentioned above, those who *favor* physician-assisted suicide argue that with enough safeguards in place there will be less abuse. Euthanasia will be restricted to the terminally ill who request it. They point to the format of the proposed Oregon physician-assisted suicide law and others.

Opponents ask, Human nature being what it is—political, money-minded, and susceptible to corrupt influences—can *any* laws guarantee safety?

To which the *pros* respond, Maybe not, but must those in the throes of terminal illness suffer with no assistance because of prospective corruption?

7. Economic Considerations: Economic resources are becoming scarcer. They can't keep up with technology. Who gets organ transplants, intensive care, new drugs? A survey of medical directors yielded some suggested criteria: patients of greatest value to society, the young over the old, the more psychologically able, those with a supportive environment (that is, not alone in the world), those who can best benefit from the procedure, those who have the ability to pay, those with special responsibilities such as being a parent, and members of a favored group such as veterans.[18] Perhaps we should add to this list parents capable of mobilizing the media for publicity of their child's plight. Some believe random selection is fairest.

Health care rationing is a fact that few admit. The heaviest expenditures are for life-threatening illnesses, more often in older patients who undergo expensive treatment, organ transplants, and bypass surgery, while young families lack basic preventive care. *Pro-euthanasists* argue: Doesn't it make sense to allow those elderly *willing* to forgo such expensive treatments to die a few months sooner, so that others yet to live their lives can be saved?

To which the *antis* reply: If active euthanasia were the law and the practice, wouldn't those who want everything possible done for them feel unjustly pressured, guilty, and blamed as selfish?

8. Sanctity of Life: Some who are *against* euthanasia argue that human life is bestowed on us by God and therefore is sacred. Through suffering we may attain redemption. We do not have the right to play God ourselves and end life at our own will. This religious precept is supreme over all others for those who believe in it, although the principle of "double effect" (intent to relieve, not kill) brings some relief.

On March 30, 1995, Pope John Paul II issued his encyclical "Evangelium Vitae," or "Gospel of Life," affirming that life is sacred from conception to death and specifically condemning euthanasia. The document supports a "culture of life," over what he sees as a current "culture of death."[19]

Many *pro-euthanasists*, however, do not believe that sanctity includes terminal suffering; is it right to compel them to follow the precepts of a religion to which they do not adhere? Is it right for one group to foist its beliefs on another? Doesn't this threaten separation of church and state?

Further, the *pros* ask, Must sanctity always imply *quantity* over *quality* of life? Might not life be too sacred for extended suffering, even that which includes systematic starvation and dehydration? Is there no sanctity in relieving the suffering of others?

9. Hippocratic Oath: ". . . I will give no poisonous or deadly medicine, even if asked, nor make any such suggestion . . ."[20] *Antis* believe physicians trained in and dedicated to healing should not be compelled to kill. They perceive a contradiction between the mission to heal and the mission to relieve suffering. Indeed, some treatments intended to cure or improve health intensify suffering.

Further, patients might not trust a life-giving physician who they know could be death-dealing. Further still, as Foley points out, Quill's Diane had to assume that his willingness to prescribe death for her meant she had no hope for recovering. Hope may extend lives; hopelessness may kill.

Pros suggest a solution to the dilemma: only physicians who perceive euthanasia as humane and as another aspect of their healing responsibility should euthanize openly and without condemnation.

10. Constitutional Right: It is argued by the group Compassion in Dying that the constitutional right of liberty includes the freedom to die.[21] In Washington State in 1994, a federal district court ruled that a ban *against* physician-assisted suicide violates constitutional rights, although in a catch-22, physicians could still be prosecuted for it. A law banning assisted suicide was upheld in March 1995 and ruled unconstitutional in March 1996.

On the other hand, the *antis* remind us that "the right to die" could become the "duty to die." Nor would a right to die grant to the terminally ill the right to compel someone else to kill.

11. Legalizing Reality: The *pros* assert that passive euthanasia, assisted suicide, and even active euthanasia are already common practice in this country, and we can't be sure that the circumstances are always abuse-free. Legalizing, safeguarding, and exposing to public scrutiny these practices might minimize abuses.

Legal decisions *against* euthanasia, however, often claim that society's concern for preservation of human life outweighs individual autonomy.

To which the *pros* respond: When did the protection afforded by the "social contract" become a mandate to suffer hard or long?

12. Humaneness: Those *favoring* assisted suicide feel that it would be more humane than the current practices of "pulling the plug" and depriving the dying of nutrition and hydration. Thus the dying suffer needlessly, and all to preserve the consciences of those around them.

Opponents maintain a much sharper distinction between *allowing* to die and *compelling*. Not only this, but dying patients occasionally recover.

13. Relative-Assisted Suicide: If euthanasia were legalized (say those who *favor* it), relatives would not bear the horrific burden of either helping or refusing their relatives, both seeding massive guilt. Nor would the dying be compelled by their agony to beg loved ones to risk life, liberty, and conscience to aid their passing.

But those *against* argue that the suicide of a relative, for example a parent, leaves a terrible mark on children that endures for years.

Pros agree that this is so, especially when a parent takes his life after a business failure or for a reason other than terminal illness. The child feels haunted, abandoned, unloved, even compelled to repeat the act. They argue, however, that if well handled, suicide of the terminally ill can be the exception.

14. Whose Life Is It Anyway? Arguments for and against euthanasia often seem to take place across the suffering body of the patient! Then he may weigh in by asking, "Whose life is it, anyway?" as in the play of the same title.[22] The implication is that it is *his* life and *his* decision to end it earlier if he so chooses.

15. What Constitutes Humanity? Opponents of euthanasia argue that, because of our unique abilities to reason and communicate in complex ways, human life is unique and therefore should be preserved at all costs. We do not put humans "out of their misery" as we do pets. Those *favoring* euthanasia rebut: When human faculties are gone, as in coma or severe mental impairment such as Alzheimer's, is the life still human, in need of preservation? They may not think so.

In fairness to both sides of the whole euthanasia issue, not every anti-euthanasist subscribe to *all* the anti-euthanasia arguments; nor do those favoring support *all* the pro arguments.

WHAT IS YOUR DECISION?

For some of you, any form of aid-in-dying would not be an option. Your religion bans it, you're a "fighter," you have much more living to do, your time is precious, you find great value in the process you are undergoing; you hope for resurrection, or reincarnation, for example, or even a cure; your pain and suffering aren't that great, and your living's greater.

Others of you want the security of control over the end stage. If so, take the following steps now:

1. Determine the laws in your state (ask your library).
2. With the help of your attorney, draw up your advance direc-

tives: the physician's directive and living will, a letter of instruction, power of attorney (for business), durable power of attorney (health proxy), standard will, and perhaps an organ donor document and a trust. Update these every few years. Give copies to your physician, executor, and durable power of attorney.

3. Discuss your directives with your spouse, children, or closest relatives, making clear your desires. *Now* is the time for argument, not when you're comatose.

4. Discuss your directives with your physician, making sure that he and whatever hospital he attends have no basic disagreements with you. Burnell recommends ferreting out his attitude toward "pulling the plug." Does he object to plenty of pain medication, or does he fear your addiction? How does he feel about your living will? Is he willing to prescribe enough medication to let you die?[23]

5. Remember your rights to refuse/discontinue treatment.

6. Avail yourself of information regarding suicide methods, so you don't botch it and end up vegetative.

7. Recognize that, when you're actually in the situation, your opinions and priorities may change; that's also your right.

WILL EUTHANASIA BECOME LEGAL?

The rights to refusal and discontinuation of treatment are already legal, with restrictions. I believe physician-assisted suicide will be legalized eventually for the following reasons:

First, it's *humane*. Pain management may improve, but the combination of psychic suffering, physical disability, and terminal diagnosis will most likely always be with us.

After a decades-long career as a physician, Francis D. Moore, eighty-one years old and Mosely Professor of Surgery Emeritus at Harvard University, declares his convictions: "It is my credo that assisting people to leave the dwelling place of their body when it is no longer habitable is becoming an obligation of the medical profession."[24]

Second, it's an *economic* necessity. Now before you blow up at the crassness of this statement, hear out Jenny Parker, a sixty-five-year-old social worker and successful professional artist:

"I'm a grandmother of five. Emphatically, I don't want my family's funds used to prolong my dying, not at the expense of my grandchildren's education or my daughters' welfare. I feel that way about the children of the world, too. The government can't pay my expenses and theirs as well.

"Money isn't just money. It's not just cellular phones and trips to Australia. It's food, clothing, shelter, health care, and education, and it's limited. I've had mine. We're squeezed in a lot of resources— wood, paper, fish. I think they'll get worse unless we return to zero population growth."

Third, legalizing euthanasia will eliminate the secrecy in which it now flourishes, with all the potential for abuse; and it will ease a lot of the guilt of family members in conflict over helping their terminally ill loved one. Safeguards can make the system publicly accountable, minimizing abuse, although they will not eliminate it.

I believe that if the elderly and the so-called less productive (narrowly defined as churning out goods and services) were valued for all their experience, love, and insightful wisdom, there'd be less danger of terminating them prematurely. Guilt over devaluation seeds the struggle.

Fourth, the overwhelming majority of "terminal" patients are going to die in the foreseeable future. We must stop denying that they will. We talk about "saving lives," but that's false talk. It's *denial*. No one has ever "saved" a life! We *extend* life, as well as suffering and dying.

Fifth, if euthanasia is legalized, giving people control over their end-stage, they may be willing to live longer, even in suffering. Now, they panic at the thought of losing control, and some of them foreclose earlier, as Janet Adkins did.

Sixth, we cannot expect physicians to become psychiatrists. They're under enough pressure to cure. Sorting out such emotional decisions takes time, and many physicians aren't that gifted in relating and communicating, nor are they trained to be. Most personal narratives star at least one physician as an "unfeeling clod." The average doctor obtains about three hours of education in the study of thanatology, the psychology of death and dying, in medical school. It's not her field. She's not necessarily a compassionate Bernie Siegel. Few are.

I'm troubled by the notion of one physician making all the decisions for a patient. I believe we'll eventually set up a system of clinics staffed by physicians, nurses, chaplains, and counselors specializing in thanatology; Quill calls them "oversight committees." They would assess the extent to which the patient's appraisal of her situation is realistic, how her psychological and spiritual resources might be improved, and finally come to an *agreement* with her about her final decision. Like Planned Parenthood, there will be many options and services—religious and psychological counseling, information, group support, and the like—but also death planning and assistance, if necessary. More lives may be "saved," if clinics reduce the need for extreme measures. Perhaps in the far future we will perceive the administration of lethal medication as more merciful than removing life support systems and allowing the patient to waste away.

The point is often made that, with enough love from the patient's circle of relatives and friends, he will not want to die, even if he is in extreme pain and suffering. There are problems with this. We are urging the circle to manipulate him with love into their own ethical position. Often, this urging is couched in terms of the circle's needs, rather than the patient's. "We love you, we need you here. Don't leave us." Sometimes, even, "We know how you feel." Not likely! The patient may feel guilty putting his needs above those of his loved ones. His loved ones may feel guilty that they did not "love enough" if the patient rejects their pleas.

Elisabeth Kübler-Ross liberated us from much death denial in the sixties. But not all! I see a lot of it in the passionate and compassionate efforts of those *not yet terminally ill* to keep everyone else alive as long as possible, even in the face of great pain and suffering, as if life could be eternal. They fight for other lives with the same energy they'd fight for their own. They hope they wouldn't want to die under, say, Diane's circumstances. Perhaps they imagine that Diane, who died in 1991, would still be alive today . . . and a hundred years from now.

I have presented many arguments for and against euthanasia in this chapter. But in the last analysis, they are all beside the point. *No one has the right to decree extended pain and suffering for another—not the concentration camp, not the hospital, not the hospice, not the family.* Compelling people to drag out the whole process of dying, to live as long as *we* want to live, is misplaced caring. I believe it is immoral and acts out the needs of the caregiver rather than of the patient. I believe it is a sin to impose our own morality on the dying person, who may be in no position to fight back.

Having said all this, and although suicide is your personal right, I hope that for most of you it will not need to be your decision. If your pain is not so great that it shrinks your consciousness, much can be positive for you in your dying process, as the rest of this book shows. If you feel depressed or suicidal, check in with your crisis clinic, suicide prevention center, or physician. At least talk it over with an intimate.

Even in sharply restricted physical circumstances, the richness of your inner life may amaze you—it may be the beginning of that much-heralded transition.

14

FOURTEEN

WHERE WILL

YOU DIE?

WHO WILL

CARE FOR YOU?

YOU would probably like to die at home, surrounded by all that is familiar and part of you—the photos of those who have gone before, the pets, furniture, dishware, blankets, nightclothes, and souvenirs—all that has made life good.[1] Nine out of ten prefer their own home or a relative's. Hospice and other home health care can help; 340,000, or 14.8 percent, of those who die each year do so in a hospice setting, most of them suffering from cancer or AIDS. The following options are available to you:

1. Home—either your own or a relative's—with or without home hospice care, visiting nurses, home health aides, and the like, to provide respite for your family
2. Hospital or hospital hospice wing for pain management
3. Inpatient facility or residence

4. Nursing home (possibly in a hospice section) or other long-term institution. About 5 percent of people die here, often those afflicted with organic mental disorders such as Alzheimer's who need continuous care.

The National Hospice Organization offers the following definition of a hospice: "Hospice is a holistic, team-oriented program of care which seeks to treat and comfort terminally ill patients and their families at home or in a home-like setting." If you select hospice care, I recommend that you make sure it is licensed by the state (thirty-five states currently have hospice licensure laws), and certified for Medicare reimbursement. Some institutions call themselves "hospice" because the concept is so popular.

Be aware that whereas hospitals may be dedicated to invasive treatment and *cure*, hospices focus on easing your dying with symptomatic relief, *comfort care*, and aiding your spiritual development. You need certification by your physician that you are within approximately six months of death. Medicare and many insurance companies now pay hospice expenses; hospice is cheaper than traditional institutional care (although there's some controversy over this).[2] Mainly, this is because 90 percent of hospice care takes place in patients' homes rather than inpatient facilities; hospices use trained volunteers working under the direction of physicians, nurses, social workers, and religious staff; and they use far fewer technical procedures.

The outlook of hospice personnel is one of spiritual hope, but you will not be subjected to a deathbed conversion; indeed, you define your own spiritual needs. If you are Roman Catholic or Eastern Orthodox and request it, a priest will administer "the anointing of the sick" (formerly "extreme unction"), hear your last confession, and recite the absolution of sins. Members of other religions have access to their own practices, the reading of religious texts, spiritual discussions, praying together, perhaps. Some hospices are sponsored by religious groups, but all are nonsectarian and nondenominational.[3]

Long-term institutional care may be an expense beyond your means without the specific insurance, which most of us don't have. We don't want it. Subconsciously, we may figure that if we're not insured, our relatives can't warehouse us. If it's going to cost them or our estate too much, they'll find some way to keep us out. We may even hope we're lucky enough to die rather than linger on sans wits.

If our spouse is frail, however, if the children are working and their home is cramped, an institution may be our fate. We depend on them to select the best after considerable investigation—a place with no record of abuse, where sheets are changed, bodies are rotated to avoid pressure sores, and patients are fed, hydrated, and medicated. Recently, Consumer Reports published a review of fifty nursing homes, only seven of which they approved. The investigator advises a sniff test. There should be no smells of urine, but also no smells of air freshener, which might be covering up others. Insist on seeing a state inspection report and check out possibilities with the state nursing home ombudsman if there is one.[4] (See Chapter 7, "If They Say You Must Move" section, page 69.)

THE REVIVAL OF PERSON-TO-PERSON CARE: CAVEATS

With the proliferation of hospice programs, AIDS activism, the sheer increase in numbers of dying both now and projected, and the financial crunch in health care, the outlook for more personal care may be improving. I really do think the nineties are a better time to die than the seventies or eighties were. But a few caveats are in order.

Whether or not to tell a patient the truth about his medical condition used to be at the discretion of doctors, who didn't always want to tell, and relatives, who often feared that the truth would so depress their loved one that she'd die. As we have seen, this was not an unrealistic worry, considering the suspected negative influence of depression on the immune system. In the eighties, a more balanced approach revealed the truth to patients *if they asked.* Medical staff followed the patient's lead, rather than inflicting truth on him. Currently, when there is either no treatment left or it would result in severe side effects, physicians may broach the subject of shifting from curative treatment to palliative or comfort care. Oncologists call this "the conversation."[5]

I seem to detect, however, a crusade toward forcing the truth on the patient for his own good: he can exercise more control over his dying if he knows he is. Toward this end, some recommend repeated leading questions, such as "What did your doctor tell you about the outlook for your condition?" and "What do you think this means?" The goal is to push the patient into facing up to his mortality.

While I admire the "truth movement," I worry that in some cases it is becoming too aggressive. Amazingly enough, even patients in a hospice program, well known as an institution for the dying, may deny their condition (and occasionally survive).

My point is that you have a right to deny, if this is what you want to do. "Positive illusions" may even benefit you. Believing you will continue living may be one. I don't think anyone should force the truth on you as they see it. Like beauty, truth is in the eye of the beholder. It's in flux, anyway. Nor is it necessarily an unmitigated virtue. Because your caregiver wants truth at her dying time doesn't mean *you* have to have it. Your own conscious and subconscious are making these decisions for you, and you know best how you'll fare. Unrelenting focus on a painful truth may bore you or seem pointless.

Psychologist Lawrence LeShan, in *Cancer as a Turning Point*, suggests *permission* rather than *imposition* as the helpful style of the caregiver. "How do you feel about what is happening to you?" gives you the option to talk, lets you know that your caregivers are comfortable with anything you have to say. It is not "assaultive or demanding."[6] It is merely an offer. You can talk about the food.

Another worry I have during this wonderful rise in person-to-person care (partly replacing the mechano-technical) is what I perceive as the occasional intrusiveness of the professional caregiver in your final decisions. Some seem to feel that, because they have been at the bedside of a hundred or a thousand dying patients, they know what "the dying" need and want. "Despite good intentions, some hospices end up bullying patients who won't pass away gracefully," writes journalist Vicki Brower, whose mother underwent such an ordeal, partly because of "the Medicare mess."[7]

Another example: Lily was devoutly religious and dying of cancer. She believed she should live her life to the end; death would unfold for her according to God's will, and He knew what was best for her. But her brother encouraged her to make a living will to save herself from pain and allow the plug to be pulled if it came to that, to raise her morphine however high she needed it, even if it meant her death. Lily was firm in her commitment to her own beliefs. She shouldn't have had to fight for them.

"The dying" are not you, and you are not they. No one's expertise, experience, credentials, virtue, or love entitles them to foist their "proper way of dying" on you, especially not in your weakened state. Their taking advantage of their power is hubris of the first magnitude, and I believe it is a sin. You have a right to be aware, resist, blow up, get another caregiver.

My third concern is the way in which some therapists employ the "family systems" approach to dying.[8] The theory is that the problems of one member are the result of the entire family dynamic and can be alleviated by changes in the family interactions. Some therapists, however, now recommend treatment of the dying patient, perhaps heavy sedation, *for the benefit of the family* rather than for the dying person! The reasoning is that the members must live with this last (perhaps traumatic) vision of their loved one, whereas the dying person is considered beyond help. The risk here is that the patient's last stage—growth of being and development of soul, as LeShan phrases it—as well as his continued meaning-creation, are cut short and discounted as not valuable. Ironically, the family members themselves will eventually recall that their loved one's development through the dying stage was not valued . . . and conclude that neither will theirs be. I believe, for the sake of the family as well as the dying patient, that this last stage of development must be facilitated, honored, and held sacred.

Forcing you to admit to a "truth" you do not feel, or to die in accordance with a caregiver's values rather than your own, or to place your family's feelings above one of the most important passages of your life—all these are truly playing God, and (unintentionally) abusive in the extreme.

It is currently fashionable for relatives to say to the dying, "Let go" and "Go to the light," but, if premature, you could take it as rejection or abandonment. Encourage your loved ones to ask the medical staff whether you are truly near the end.

Finally, I worry about Americans' adopting Eastern religions, which tell us that the ego is the source of all death fear. If we weren't so attached to our selves, we would not fear losing them. To my Western ears, the ultimate answer seems to be meditation into blankness. Few people ever define the "ego" they warn against, but I think in this context it means a sense of I-ness, that is, all the hopes, dreams, concerns, worries, resentments, beliefs, and values that make you different from others, that make you an individual person.

For some, the Eastern way of living and dying works wonderfully. Others feel guilty and ashamed when their rotten egos interfere with their "good death." That brilliant author of the Pulitzer Prize–winning *The Denial of Death*, Ernest Becker, understood the problem for Westerners. He wrote: "Religions like Hinduism and Buddhism performed the ingenious trick of pretending not to want to be reborn, which is a sort of negative magic: claiming not to want what you really want most,"[9] but believe you cannot have.

We are whole people—bodies, souls, minds, emotions—but are told to sacrifice one aspect of who we are, the ego in all its manifestations, in order that *something* may survive. Better something than nothing. But this is no better than superstition, or propitiation of the gods; the truth is that we long to survive entirely, not in parts.

I have raised concerns in regard to increasing person-to-person care because I feel most of these concerns relate to our changing ways of dying; the dangers have gone mainly unrecognized. It is probable, however, that most of your caregivers will try their hardest to be generous with their time, their respect for your unique needs and preferences, and their compassion. They hope for the same treatment when their end-time comes.

FIFTEEN

CONTROLLING THE

UNCONTROLLABLE

LOSING control is the most terrifying aspect of dying. We envision uncontrolled pain, uncontrolled body functions with uncontrolled smells, uncontrolled power of others over our food, treatment, medication, information, even nakedness. We see disease rampaging through our bodies with unpredictable results that may take our speech, our sight, our breath, liver, kidneys, heart, breasts, muscles, our very bones, as well as our capacities for thought, memory, action, and pleasure. All this before whatever is left of ourselves spins off out of control into the universe.

Control has been a significant goal for us throughout our lives. When we were toddlers, our parents clapped and gleamed as we spoke, took our first steps, manipulated a crayon, used the potty. What isn't usually recognized is that we also controlled our parents, seducing them into caring for us, reveling in mutual delight. But how do we seduce our caregivers now?

Relinquishing control to others requires trust. Some of us hesitate. If we cried for hours in infancy, went hungry, endured abuse, we learned distrust. The same caregivers continued untrustworthy into our childhood and teen years. If we could not trust them, how can we trust strangers at life's end?

In the past, each developmental achievement extended our control over our environment. By the time we reached school years, the control required of us was more social and emotional. We learned to express jealousy, anger, and frustration (over someone else's control) in acceptable ways. The teen years posed a major conflict over sexual control, followed by control over specific behaviors in order to retain a job.

As we grow older and struggle to gain or maintain control over our lives, we become more aware of the control others exercise over us—parents, teachers, peers, bosses, spouses, physicians, even the pilot of the airplane. The terror of the flyer is that he is helpless and dependent. But at least the flight has a probable secure end-point—dying does not.

Needs for control, dominance, and leadership are personality traits, stronger in some than in others. If our control over our work is limited, if we are subject to the whims and caprices of the boss, the machinery, or the market, we are more susceptible to burnout and stress-related illnesses such as ulcers (possible lowered immunity against a bacterium) and high blood pressure. Perceived control is health-promoting, even at life's end.

The dying process is one of losing the very control we struggled so hard to achieve in those first decades of life. Is our relinquishment recognized as the developmental achievement that it is?

UNPREDICTABILITY

Before ALS, Bill lived by the clock. His appointment calendar regulated his life. So, for their thirty-fifth wedding anniversary two years hence, he and Peg had planned a tour of Australia, New Zealand, Southeast Asia, China, and Japan. Daughter Tori's second marriage was scheduled for next summer. They'd looked forward to buying a motor home one day and becoming snowbirds, Arizona refugees from the harsh winters. Save for the occasional disaster, life had proceeded along an ordered time line, with no reason to start expecting death until their seventies. Now death is at their door, ringing the bell. Bill's disease restricts his family as well as himself.

Their lives have become painfully unpredictable, full of surprises, most of them nasty. Symptoms appear without warning. Planning even the next few weeks is tentative. The sudden paralysis, the just-discovered hemorrhaging, the new pain—all may signal the spread of illness and more losses. One patient was eloquent on the dilemma when he noted the paralysis creeping up his body: "I can move my arms. Will that go, too?"[1] Even if he accepts the loss of his future, it's hard for him to accept the apparent capriciousness of his illness's progression. How long must he drag through the process? How many more losses must he endure before it finally, perhaps blessedly, ends, and how will this ending come about?

In the past Larissa could escape intolerable situations, and she did. She simply left her brain-dead boss short a waitress during the dinner hour one night; she left her dead-end husband a year later, and several lovers after that. She left her pregnancy at the clinic and blew her roach-infested apartment. She left Los Angeles for a new start in San Francisco, elated . . . until her AIDS was diagnosed. She can't leave AIDS.

She says, "God may have a plan, but I don't."

She's compelled to live in the present, a restriction, yes, but a surprisingly delightful one at times. Wise and religious men and women, philosophers, and poets, adjure us to live in the "now," proclaiming it a separate level of being with its own joys and beauties. Most of us never had the time; our days were mortgaged to the future. Now that the future is no longer solid, a mirage, we must "be here now," reaping unexpected rewards.

THE ILLUSION OF CONTROL

So, at the end-time, we lose control but, in reality, it has always been illusory, hasn't it? We think we have a choice, we make it, and then we find out that the job, the house, the neighborhood are different from what we thought. We defend ourselves by forgetting how vulnerable our lives are to unpredictable exigencies—the arsonist, the black ice on the freeway, the false arrest, the doctor's slip, the "other" man or woman, the stock market collapse, the declaration of war.

We live with the illusion of control because we must move in some direction. Action takes planning. We forget how illusory control is until the next crisis.

CONTROL EXERCISE

Remember your recurrent fears, phobias, or obsessions? What threat to your survival did they connote? That the elevator will fall? That the germs will give you a fatal disease? Note that these are disasters over which you had no control. You may try to control them by avoiding them: if you take the stairs, you're safe, you'll live. Ironically, your fear is barely controllable. This out-of-control feeling is the most terrifying aspect of phobias.

A simple exercise can help you deal with control issues. List your fears over loss of control during the terminal phase of your illness. Most of them fall into three categories: physical, social, and psychological. Let's discuss each in turn.

PHYSICAL CONTROL

Pain, technology, bodily processes, and treatment decisions involve special control issues for patients:

1. Pain Control: Some people become upset by their dependence on pain medication. They see themselves as controlled by those who administer the medication, and by the medication as well. This is normal. The new pain revolution puts you in charge of your own pain-relief administration, making you more confident and less needy. Remember that the control by others throughout your life and over every facet of it has simply been a little less visible than it is now. Think about it!

2. Treatment Decisions: You must decide if the discomfort and/or side effects are worth the possible benefit of a particular treatment. Resist pressure by loving relatives and concerned medical staff. They may have different values, and in any case they can't really experience things as you do. If your doctor opposes you, you can get a new one, although I don't advise getting a new family.

3. Technology/Prolonged Dying: Employ advance directives. Be alert, however, to the possibility that physicians and relatives can and do countermand such documents and thus prolong your dying in spite of your wishes. Even if you have an organ donor card, your relatives may refuse the harvesting. Evidence shows that adherence to a DNR (Do Not Resuscitate) request may depend more on your doctor's values than your own.[2] In late 1994 Catholic bishops told Catholic hospitals not to honor advance directives that contradict the church's moral teachings.[3] This is why clarifying your requests very specifically can minimize misadventure.

4. Control Over Bodily Processes includes treatment for diarrhea, constipation, nausea, sleeplessness, and the like. As you move away from curative treatment to palliative or comfort care, you may want the assistance of a hospice affiliated with the National Hospice Organization and approved by Medicare or your insurance company.

Sociologist Anne Munley's book *The Hospice Alternative* gives a Roman Catholic nun's compassionate account of the challenges, tribulations, and triumphs of life and death in a hospice. She is eloquent on patients' longings to be whole again, to walk outside and be free of being "done to." Patients chafe at physical limitations that restrict their freedom; their abilities to perform even simple acts are unlikely to improve.[4] Just a little farther down the road, however, many people in their dying time begin to discover that they are achieving a transformation from a physical existence to a spiritual one. The most frequent manifestations are in dreams and visions.[5] Your disabilities may be a temporary stage of transformation; old growth dies off so new can green.

SOCIAL CONTROL

Control can be another word for power. Your dying may give you exceptional power over those around you who are grieving and working hard to save you. But you may find yourself in the clutches of "control freaks." You become *their* patient. They take possession of you. Is it any wonder that occasionally you behave like one "possessed"?

Relatives formerly under your control suddenly find power over your life thrust upon them. You're their responsibility now. Besides, they need to feel control over your disease. In fairness, they're giving up time on the job, coping with spouses turned grumpy, and incurring expenses they can ill afford. To their credit, most persons with this power are upset by it and decline to abuse it. They want to help you do what *you* want to do. Make clear to them what this is while your communication abilities are still intact.

More complex is the contest of wills among relatives over your care. Often, it has little to do with you; it's old business between them, and you're merely an excuse—the battleground not the stake. If they appeal to you against each other, remain removed whenever possible. Don't be drawn into the quicksand of family politics.

PSYCHOLOGICAL CONTROL

We lose some psychological control, but new forms of it arise to strengthen us. For example, we may lose our ability to *think*, to make *decisions* that control what becomes of us or to *communicate* them; thus we are at the mercy of others, no matter how well-meaning. This is a major reason we fear such diseases as Alzheimer's and stroke, and why we need advance directives.

But your mind is also the area of your life where you have the greatest control. Remember that your environment shapes your thoughts and feelings. Much of dying is machine and antiseptic smells, metal clangor, beeps, whirring, footsteps and voices of those who are more alive than you are (or so they imagine). Augment these sounds and smells with those that comfort you.

As far as possible, surround yourself with the positive, the beautiful, the well-loved. Here are a few examples:

1. Read favorite books if you're still strong enough; otherwise, listen to them on tapes. Religious, spiritual, and philosophical writings, even books on NDEs (near-death experiences) com-

fort us. Herb Kramer, dying of cancer, and his wonderfully wise wife, who is also a therapist with the dying, wrote in their book *Conversations at Midnight* that Herb filled his life with favorite poetry at the end.[6]

2. Listen to music that resonates to your depths—jazz, New Age, classical, religious.
3. Be sure the flowers people bring you are near enough to smell and to meditate on. You do not need any special technique for this; simply stare at them, immersing yourself in every shade of difference in the petals until they seem to move. Scented candles are also nice.
4. Have your bed placed by the window. A view of sky, trees, flowers, birds, and butterflies will raise your spirits.
5. Perhaps, like Herb Kramer, you too can have "conversations at midnight," deep and truthful and heartfelt exchanges with ones you love; they can enrich your life (and theirs) most of all.

GAINING CONTROL BY LETTING GO

Deliberately try to let go of details in your daily life, one by one. Allow someone else to make a decision, and then another. Think of these as exercises in trust. Even say to yourself, "I trust you to make this decision." Say it to them! If they feel it's *your* decision, not theirs, they'll turn it back. Try not to use this exercise to abnegate responsibility you *should* take.

Maintain control by being flexible and adaptive. Some days are good, some bad, unpredictably so. New symptoms warrant new modes of care. People snap at you under the stress, then ask your forgiveness. At least you're not time-bound. They are.

Another way to begin this process of letting go is through imagery. I'm going to suggest several images that might be helpful to you, but you might explore others with your counselor. Choose any that appeal to you. There are marvelous others.[7]

First, be sure that you are in a relaxed position. If you engage in relaxation or breathing exercises, now is a good time to use them.

1. You are standing on the edge of a cliff high in the Rockies, Himalayas, or Alps. The mists thicken and part to reveal other jagged, snowcapped mountaintops, a waterfall to your left, and below are foothills, valleys, perhaps the light green squares of farms. An eagle wheels through the sky. You raise your arms and fall forward. Time slows, then stops altogether as you float down through blue light.

   Float like a leaf. If the passivity is distasteful, recall how you longed for a vacation, to float in a pool's blue waters.

2. You are watching a toy boat float down a river. The boat is like one you played with as a child. You watch the boat, and then you are on it, bobbing up and down, going wherever the water takes you. Know that you'll end up where you need to be.

3. You are on a surfboard, riding the waves in from the sea, but there is no shore in sight. You will surf for eternity. A wave lifts you incredibly high, then lets you down, then lifts you up again.

You might prefer your ride on a swing, or even a roller coaster. These are activities during which you lost control in the past, yielding great pleasure.

Meditation, listening to music, daydreaming—all these are pleasurable practice for relinquishing control.

Finally, remember that it is not you who is out of control. It is your disease. Ultimately, you are moving *beyond* control.

16

SIXTEEN

RETAINING

YOUR IDENTITY

ALL your life you've struggled to become yourself. As an infant, you communicated your needs with cries and smiles. As you grew, your words made your needs more specific. As an adolescent, you rebelled against limits imposed on change and growth, against attempts to make you go into the family business or give up your sailing dream. You progressed from dependence to prideful independence. After you married, adjustments between you and your spouse were a minefield of identity control issues that you both had to work out. As you've matured, your values, opinions, votes, beliefs, attitudes, charities, and activities have defined who you are.

Suddenly, all you have ever been or done—your success at softball, your compassionate parenting, your chairmanship of the hunger drive, your heading your own business—all these recede into unimportance and your identity is a bundle of symptoms. Who you feel you are becomes past and irrelevant to those taking over your life. You are defined by the treatments you need to survive. You must move, eat, approach, avoid, until your every action is regulated and becomes a topic of comment, condemnation, or approval. You feel infantilized. Meanwhile, as the role aspects of your identity are dropping away, your illness assumes an ever-increasing presence. You join a group based not on a mutual love of books or bridge or your child's education or mountain-climbing, not a health club or a charitable organization. Your group is based on a negative, a deficiency—which is your disease.

Your identity is at risk, in danger of death. But who are you, anyway, and how can you remain you?

WHO AM I? AN EXERCISE

The identity of each of us is made up of thousands of beliefs, attitudes, experiences, opinions, and feelings—atoms of the self. Usually, if someone asks, you define yourself by a major role, such as "engineer." But if you lost your job tomorrow, you would still be you. You might feel loss, but any change in your identity would be gradual, depending on whether you obtained a similar job, became a consultant, or even chose to transform loss into the opportunity and become the entrepreneur you've always yearned to be. Gradually, "engineer" would become part of your past identity, still an aspect of who you are but with less susceptibility to change and growth in comparison to your new role.

Who are you, really? For this exercise, grab a fistful of three-by-five cards. To begin, on each card jot down a major role, such as "I am a dental hygienist," and on another card, "I am treasurer of my club," and on still another, "I am the mother of Jason and Chloe." When you have jotted down all your roles, shift to things you love and hate; and then to religious, philosophical, and political beliefs; and then even hair and clothing styles: "Short red hair is *me*." "Stripes are not." Add your favorite possessions and your best and worst experiences: "I am the father who lost (a child, a job, a house, to fire)." "I have contributed (to the arts . . . my time to fighting for . . .)." Add personality characteristics: "I'm quick to anger," "slow to decide," "kind to dogs." Or "People say I'm attractive," "give in too easily," "judgmental," "enthusiastic."

You can see that these only begin to define who you are. Now organize them, placing the most important aspects of who you are in front. No need to be compulsive about exact positioning—unless that's one of your personality traits!

These Identity Cards will be useful to us for a number of developmental tasks during this latter stage of life, so keep them handy. And by all means feel free to add. Loved ones can help as well, even where you disagree: "My spouse says I'm easygoing, but I'm not." As you progress through your end-time, you may reorganize the cards as different aspects of yourself drop back and others come to the fore. In this way, you informally measure your growth in this last developmental stage.

Now, do you really believe that anyone else would come up with the same collection of Identity Cards as you?

Each of us is a snowflake.

IDENTITY AT RISK

The identity we've defined above is now at risk in a number of ways:

1. We are less capable of fulfilling our usual roles. Our illness strips us of the ability to perform certain tasks. Our disease perverts our role as family member.
2. Illness changes our appearance, which many perceive as who we are. We feel different, disoriented, not ourselves.
3. Illness adds the role of patient.
4. Others perceive us as different from what we were; painfully, this tells us that we are becoming someone else.
5. By the same token, we find ourselves less restricted, with time enough for thought and the chance to cultivate other aspects long dormant.
6. We actually undergo transformation.

Let's examine these changes more closely.

First, illness strips us of some aspects of our identity. We are no longer able to carry on our job. Someone else does it. The story is, at first, that it's only temporary. It may not be.

In the hospital with cancer, Shelley heard how wonderfully her mother-in-law, Joan, had taken over. Her children visited her in clothes bought by their grandmother, so even *their* identity was subtly changed, as well as Shelley's relationship with them. She returned home to find "improvements," different foods in the cupboard, dinosaurs from their museum visit on the mantel. Already, part of the home she had created was past, but she was obliged to be grateful. Gifts? To Shelley, they felt like intrusions. And she was one of the lucky ones; Joan really was a caring friend, who encouraged her and "had a life."

Illness shapes us by adding something different to our lives—our role as patient. Our thoughts cluster around new information regarding our disease, new people in our lives, new modes of healing. These, together with new emotions and even medications, change us. Meanwhile, we adjust our clothing to accommodate a swelling, lost breast or hair. We adjust our food to health, nausea, and bowels. Our deteriorated appearance is received by others as changed identity. Now what defines us most is not our job but the name of our illness. One patient, who developed testicular cancer at age forty, overheard himself referred to as "the seminoma in [room] fifty-three."[1] We are *becoming* our disease. Perhaps this is one of your front cards now!

When others tell us the difference they see, they add to our sense of loss. "You haven't changed a bit" is a compliment between old, long-distant friends (you're no nearer dying than you were years ago)—but you *have* changed. We combat loss by talking about past roles, a job or a community service, as if they were still part of our lives; we give directions about our home, which kindly relatives attend to, promising you still know best. You accept their kindness. But the change is in their eyes. They have identities and preferences, too; they have to live with them.

Yet as our losses progress, we discover advantages. After all, the old roles were restrictive, weren't they? They compelled you to think certain thoughts, move in certain ways, interact with some people and not others, push feelings aside, ignore much that you loved. Now, if your pain and fear are controlled, your mind is free to roam. You can read mysteries, both thrilling and spiritual, instead of technical reports; you are released from earning a living, and from much pretense as well. Respect for your expertise and pleasure in your competence were things for which you paid a price; you no longer have to.

Relatives, friends, and medical staff still feel such restrictions. Unconsciously, they may envy your freedom.

This freedom can lead to transformation, a revision of your identity, as more important values bob to the surface. You may find that who you were was never who you *really* were. You took the first job out of school or college. You followed the path of least resistance, financial reward, or success. A celebrity mystery writer friend of mine insists that he's really a stand-up comedian—he just never had much success at it. In short, we now find ourselves becoming more of who we are than we ever were.

UNMAKING THE IDENTITY AS "PATIENT"

Psychologists have long since switched from the term "patient" to "client," implying a more equal status between service provider and purchaser. A client is more active; a patient is passive, helpless, weak, infirm, perhaps incompetent, one who sits or lies and waits to be done to. The term "patient" is a misnomer, no longer reflecting the real world.

Patience may still be a virtue, but patients no longer wait patiently, nor are they, as my dictionary says, "capable of bearing delay [and] affliction with calmness." Patients are as active as their conditions permit, informing themselves about treatments, questioning, and making decisions. Many physicians welcome them into a healing partnership. They believe that an informed and active client is likely to (1) know more, (2) understand more, (3) follow instructions because he understands them, (4) mobilize his own detection skills regarding symptom changes, (5) be more optimistic because he feels more in control, and (6) live longer—to the credit of the physician!

Doesn't "client" make you feel better? After all, you've been a client many times—of an accountant, a business, a lawyer, even the

IRS. Probably, you survived. As a client, you're no longer merely a Hodgkins or a diabetic. Many physicians take pleasure in relating to a whole, more interesting person, rather than to a disease only. Finally, in this age of skyrocketing medical costs, an informed and active patient saves money by taking better care of herself.

While we're on the subject, in the usual client-professional relationship, you are on either a first- or a last-name basis, which you *both* decide. If your lawyer calls you Jerry, you don't call her Ms. Yeager. Physicians, nurses, aides, housekeepers, and pipsqueak medical students on rounds, still wet behind the ears, often need an education in manners. I recall one older women who coolly informed the doctor's office nurse on her first visit that she was Mrs. Blake, not Amelia. "We're not friends yet," she said. They may object that your last name's too hard to pronounce. But if they can say neuroblastoma or hemagglutinatin or gamma-aminobutyric acid, or cytocysticiatroplasminuria (I made that one up), they can pronounce your name. Would they walk into a CEO's office for the first time and call him Ron? You're the CEO of your case.

A SPECIAL CASE OF LOST IDENTITY: ALZHEIMER'S

As we become more ill, often losing control over excretory functions and needing to be fed, it is commonly said that we are in our "second childhood." The comparison is both demeaning and false. We've lived our lives, as children have not. We've gained much experience, knowledge, and wisdom since we were young.

You're not becoming your daughter's child, and you never will, although she may care for you superficially in similar ways. You've had a life and made contributions to the world, doing much your daughter has not yet done, and you're still you.

If we were really children again, they'd be holding Easter egg hunts for us, wouldn't they?

Even in the most extreme case of Alzheimer's disease, where all your past eventually escapes your mind, you leave behind your imprint on the world, and it is not that of someone who never grew up! Senility is the result of *disease*, often associated with old age, but it is not a reversion to infancy.

In fact, Alzheimer's is used as an example of proof that we do not continue after death. Normally, when a person dies aware and still who he is, it is easy to imagine his soul passing from his body to somewhere else. But the Alzheimer's patient gradually loses much semblance of himself, although in early stages he seems to know this at some level. How can we account for the fact that so much of him is gone, yet something of him remains?

I think it is helpful to conceive of the Alzheimer's victim as very much in transition from here to there. Much of him has already gone, and the shell remains. Our grief over this shell is a constant reminder of who he was when he was all here.

TWELVE STEPS TO MAINTAINING IDENTITY

Some of these steps are small indeed, but they add up.

1. If you prefer, call everyone by their *last* name until you know them better, and insist that they do the same. Then *you* invite *them* to a first-name basis. Insist on your correct title: Mr., Ms., Dr., Judge, Captain. Don't let them change your marital or professional status. If enough of us insist now, it will become common practice. And try calling yourself a "client" instead of a patient. Names *do* hurt us.

2. Don't allow yourself to become a "teaching case" unless this is what you want to do. Physicians are paid to teach; so should you be, via a hospital cost deduction, perhaps. Doctors should at least ask your permission, and not perfunctorily as they walk in the door. If you agree to perform this service (most frequently in teaching hospitals, which are some of the best), state your terms.

3. If you have doubts or questions, ask. Ask about the purpose, side effects, and alternatives of each test or treatment, and if

there will be pain. You have rights to know and to refuse. Exercise them judiciously. "Informed consumer" is part of your identity; don't let them take it from you. This goes double for medications, which may change your personality or libido with little benefit. You also have the right to see your chart (if you have the stomach for it), and to complain if things are not going as expected.

4. When you enter the hospital, you will probably be asked to sign a consent form agreeing to any and all treatment, should it become necessary. Physician Jody Heymann had to sign one when, at age twenty-nine and fresh out of medical school, she had sudden seizures.[2] To her shock and amazement, the form required blanket consent to any and all diagnostic tests, surgeries including anesthesia, and treatments, performed by any hospital employee! Legally, you are entitled to "informed consent" for every single medication and procedure; that is, you are entitled to have each explained to you, including why it is necessary in your case, possible side effects, alternatives, and the like. Heymann's form was typical in that no one explained any of these. The message to her was: Sign or get out.

Ask to see such forms in advance if possible, and ask for explanations of all items. Hospitals are afraid of malpractice suits, understandably, but you may decide that the risks or consequences of some procedures are not worth the possible gains. Very likely, you'll see value in some and not in others. Deliberately decide whether you'll sign. Perhaps you'll choose a different hospital, doctor, or kind of medicine.

I really think we need a "patient-consumer movement" in this country; perhaps a union. You wouldn't walk into a used-car lot and say, "I trust you. Give me anything." Unfortunately, you may be too sick for activism now, but your caregivers can be your ombudsmen.

5. Maintain as many of your interests as seem relevant and important to you now, enjoying them as actively as you can. Refer to your Identity Cards (see pages 163–164).

6. Do as much as you can for yourself. This maintains your self-esteem and often strengthens you. When in doubt, try.

7. Resist being stereotyped, particularly regarding what you can and cannot do. Do the unexpected. Be helpful instead of needing help. Show that you can take charge of your illness. You may need to assert yourself to do this. ("It's true I have difficulty walking, but I still see and hear well.")[3]

8. Recognize the fact that people may equate your physical state with your mental state, and *vice versa*. For example, they may think that because you're in a wheelchair, you can't hear well or carry on a conversation. Recognize and deal with it.

9. Remember that being a patient or client doesn't automatically make you wrong or stupid.

10. Some errors are not worth fighting over, even minor medical errors. Name it to yourself, and then say, "I agree to this. It's okay."

11. Have an advocate with you if you possibly can; she can help you fight for your needs in case you're too weak to do so.[4]

12. Remember that you are *not* your disease. You are whoever you define yourself to be, a person struggling with it. As we have seen, this both challenges and rewards you.

Most important of all, remember how easily you have been able to reorganize your Identity Cards, switching some to the back, rewriting others, originating still others. This should impress on you how adaptable you are, and that no matter how many cards and attributes and traits and roles and values and beliefs and feelings you have let go, there is still a central core to who you are, apparently untouched.

17
SEVENTEEN

WHEN YOU

DON'T WANT

TO FORGIVE

WHEN Rudy's mother died, he was about to celebrate his fortieth birthday. Instead, he gasped great heartrending sobs for days into weeks, while his perplexed children, ages eight and eleven, asked their mom, "Why's Daddy crying? He hated Grandma."

That, of course, was the problem. He'd never forgiven her for favoring his younger brother, Carl, slipping Carl extra cash when he needed it (although she claimed she'd do the same for Rudy), gabbing with Carl on the phone every Sunday. Each time she praised Carl—he was so generous, so helpful, so much fun—it was a knife to Rudy's belly. They'd stopped speaking long ago, although Rudy didn't recall the incident; his wife claimed there wasn't any, just the gradual hardening of boundaries into rock. But deep inside himself, Rudy was his mother's loving little boy.

When Carl phoned to say their mother was in the hospital, Rudy refused to go. Time enough to reconcile when she called him herself. Now she was gone, and both brothers shared equally in the estate. It might have been easier on Rudy if their mom had carried the feud beyond the grave. Instead, her will read, "To my beloved son Rudy . . ." In the end he found himself standing over her grave, begging forgiveness.

Rudy learned what all of us know intellectually but so few of us act on: Death ends it, at least in this life.

FORGIVING THE UNFORGIVABLE

And forgive us our trespasses, as we forgive those who trespass against us.

—The Book of Common Prayer

This prayer enjoins us to forgive others just as we pray God forgives us. But can you really forgive your brother's heinous crime against your child? Can you forgive the parent who ravaged your mind? The boss who destroyed your career and livelihood? The husband who took another to your bed? The enemy who tortured you?

What's more to the point, *should* you? Should you in any way remove guilt and responsibility for evil from the perpetrator? If you forgive your brother, don't you deny or lessen the severity of your child's injury? Will he restrain himself with another child? If you forgive infidelity, don't you create a society that tolerates it? If we forget the Holocaust, aren't we in danger of repeating it?

You are the one who defines the unforgivable. What is important is to define it now. Is there an act or a person you have not forgiven? Do you want to forgive? Do you think you can?

If you cannot, there are ways to ease your anger's corrosiveness:

One way is to *accept* that this is an act or person you cannot forgive. Summarize the injury and then affirm to yourself or to another person, "I honestly, in my soul, cannot forgive this." And then clearly state why you cannot. You are refusing to engage in the superficial type of "forgiveness" that others deem holy.

If there is something I cannot forgive, and I need to let it go, I've found it helpful to *send it to the universe*. This is my way of holding the other person accountable, by drawing the universe's attention to it. This is not sweetness and light; it is revenge! One caveat: Think twice before calling on the universe as witness: You, too, might be held accountable for any part you may have had in the wrongdoing. For some, the notion of karma works equally well.

Another way: Turn it over *prayerfully to God*, acknowledging that He is more capable of the great forgiveness needed than you are.

Susan Smith allegedly confessed that she pushed her car into a South Carolina lake with her two young sons strapped in their seats, then stood there and watched them sink. For those of us who have dashed into burning buildings or dived into wild waters to save our children, or even the children of others, for those others of us who routinely perform less heroic parenting deeds every day, this act is beyond our comprehension. The horrific image of the drowning boys haunts us. Would any of us be capable of forgiving it? Perhaps. But if we can't, God can.

It is common to hear the rationale "Each of us is capable of any and every act," including the most evil. This becomes the reason for tolerance and forgiveness. Or it can be an excuse.

But I think there *are* differences among people, including our capacity for cruelty. Not everyone joined the Nazi cause; some, at great personal risk, saved lives. Some of us *are* less evil, and less capable of horrendous acts, perhaps because of better life circumstances, training, genes, or grace. And I don't think it's good for us to believe that, even in the greatest depths of despair, we are capable of pushing a car with two children in it into a lake. I think such an idea can cripple our belief in ourselves and deflect us from the kinder path.

FORGIVING YOUR FAMILY

Most often, family members and close friends need our forgiveness. Conflicts degenerate into a morass of accusations and petty acts of vengeance. Hurt piles on hurt until we withdraw like turtles into shells, snapping from the sidelines.

Sarah's daughter disowned her years ago. A successful professional, she's ashamed of her mother's unconventional ways—roaming the country, settling in a New Age community and earning a living by massage. Says Sarah, "Now I'm dying, and my brother says I should forgive her. No, she hasn't asked, but she called once when I wasn't home. I didn't call her back. I'm not up for it. I could have forgiven her earlier, but it's like a last-minute demand on me, and I refuse."

Is this wrong?

Look at it this way. By not reuniting with her daughter before the end, Sarah teaches the painful cost of rejecting others that her daughter needs to learn. On the other hand, Sarah's daughter may become embittered by what she sees as her mother's ultimate rejection of her. We cannot escape the fact that we continue to teach our children throughout our days, even during our end-time!

More unexpected are the last-minute revelations we may be called on to forgive. As if you didn't have enough to deal with, a friend or family member suddenly confesses a terrible secret to you, a betrayal, either of you or someone close, that calls into question your relationship with the offender. Now you're supposed to be "wise." What do you do?

Your heightened sense of moving on may give you the ability to see beyond your own hurt to the tragedy of the person who has betrayed you. In fact, you may feel sorrier for him than for yourself. You may see that it is worse for him as the perpetrator of the deed than for you as the victim of it. The damage is on his soul, not yours. If you are having difficulty, try the steps to forgiveness that I outline below.

If the betrayal is of someone else, by all means have the perpetrator seek the advice of a religious or psychological counselor. But I would not advise you to tell him to confess to the person he wronged until he has clarified all his motives and reasons with a professional. Confession sometimes does more harm than the deed confessed; does he want this? His secret obviously causes him pain. He knows the deed must be rectified in some manner, and the fact that he's exposed his distress to you is proof of that. Yet he can't face the loss that confession would cause, or he doesn't know how to go about it. He needs professional help.

SEEKING FORGIVENESS FOR YOUR
OWN DARK SECRETS

Just as your friends and intimates are tempted to unburden themselves to you and receive your forgiveness, you may be tempted to confess a dark secret to someone you have wronged.

In his last year of life battling ALS, Bill yearned to tell Peg about the extended affair he'd had with an associate on Los Angeles business trips. It troubled him that the lie stayed coiled between them. Instead, he confided to his minister, who asked, "Would you be telling Peg for her sake or your own?"

"Mine, I guess."

"And how would she feel about it?"

"Devastated."

"Then, do you think it's wise?"

"I'd be punishing her for my own wrongdoing, wouldn't I?"

He told his minister at length instead.

A few months before Bill died, Peg sat down beside him on his bed and said, "There's something I've been meaning to tell you. I'm grateful for our life together."

"So am I," Bill whispered.

"I'm trying to say, if anything's bothering you, I forgive you."

Stunned, Bill could only gape at her in tear-filled gratitude. She'd known all along.

What is your secret? Money squirreled away? A child by another man? Secret sexual practices? Who else knows? What are the chances of your spouse's finding out? If they are high, would it hurt him more to learn the truth now, or later? Some believe concealment is far more painful than the truth, especially when it involves children.[1] Or that even if a person does not know consciously, he knows at some deeper level. Strange signs hint at the hidden.

Ask yourself if revealing your secret will do harm or good, and be very specific about what that may be. Remember, you're telling him that a relationship he cared about isn't what he thought it was. Is this kindness or cruelty, no matter how unintentional?

WHY DOES IT HURT SO MUCH?

The greatest damage torture inflicts is the "unmaking" of a person, compelling his shameful regression back through developmental stages, with loss of control over life and body processes as well as the loss of language, because language can no longer convey what is happening to him.[2] In similar fashion, trusted friends and relatives have the power to unmake us, to destroy who we thought we were and transform us into something alien. Rudy never felt wholly his mother's son. The woman betrayed by her husband never had the marriage she thought she had. Sarah's daughter disconfirms all Sarah's years of working as a single mother to support them—all the chats, games, holidays, trips, struggles, and school conferences. They are denied, and so is Sarah.

In each case of conflict that needs forgiveness, the unforgiven has disconfirmed our identity in some way. He has killed off a part of ourselves as surely as if he had taken a sword and sliced off a limb. It is this soul-murder we find so difficult to forgive. Further, the betrayal has come at the hands of those who "made" us in the first place, who gave us life by praise, support, love, respect, and validation of our thoughts, beliefs, and actions.

But it gets worse. Eventually, as one aspect of our identity is destroyed, another springs forth. Rudy *is*, in part, the rejected son and brother. Sarah *is*, in part, the disowned mother, even bonding with other mothers who have experienced such rejection. It's her *story*, her *myth*, with love and sympathy extended to her on this account. How can she relinquish rejection?

Forgiveness and reconciliation destroy our identity as victim, and the death of any part of us, no matter how undesirable, is painful. This is one reason people cling to the injuries done them, and why forgiving is so hard. But the love and rejoicing we gain when we reconcile is usually worth the pain.

WHY FORGIVE?

There are a number of reasons why it may be a good idea to forgive:

- An unforgiven injury is ballast, holding us down from destined flight. When we let go, we soar.
- An injury is just that; the real harm is our response to others in the context of our hurt, distrust, or anger. Harm is rarely done to one person only; its effects ripple out to others. The same is true of forgiveness.
- We forgive at the end of life because it's our last chance.
- Unforgiveness is an unwritten codicil of our last will and testament, an unanticipated lien on our estate.
- In the midst of His agony, Jesus said, "Father, forgive them; for they know not what they do." He is our model.
- We forgive others so that God can forgive us. Even if the harm done us is far worse than any *we've* done (we can't be sure), we will still need forgiveness ourselves.
- Forgiveness is an "act of self-preservation."[3]
- Forgiving can lead to a resurrection of love.
- It is "spiritual surgery"[4] on the soul, cutting away the rotten parts so the healthy can grow.

PRELIMINARY STEPS TO FORGIVENESS

At lunch with her mother one day, Mary Anne, a school counselor, recalled her dead father's abuse. It was a progressive process of acknowledgment between the two women. But Mary Anne was shocked to learn of her mother's own violent abuse at his hands.

"He was sick," she said, shaking her head. "So generous one minute—remember how he tipped everyone twenty-dollar bills?—so depressed or furious the next."

"Remember when he used to think we were whispering about him?" her mother asked.

"Manic depression, that's what it was!" The insight shot into

Mary Anne's head like a laser beam, and with it, the beginning of forgiveness. Mary Anne had just *reframed* her father's behavior by recognizing it for what it was, a mental illness. It was a first step to forgiving him.

Sometimes we can *make excuses* for behavior, which lessens the offender's responsibility for it. We excuse, in part, according to how much injury we have sustained. We may not be so hard on the destroyer-boss if we have created a new and even more rewarding career. Sometimes we can *let the memory of the injury fade* as other things become more important. We may *explain* it or *justify* it in some way, humanizing it. We may focus on the *person* in all her pathetic humanity, immerse ourselves in who she is, and ask ourselves, "Would I want to be her?" She may seem so much more damaged than we are. Alternatively, we may simply *accept* that the injury was horrible and move on. Thus, preliminary steps to forgiveness may *make the injury less harmful or the injurer less responsible*.

None of this is actual forgiveness, which holds the injury severe and permanent and the perpetrator responsible, but which releases her from future obligation and ourselves from resentment.

HOW TO FORGIVE

Social worker Beverly Flanigan provides us with a helpful set of steps to follow:[5]

1. *Name the injury*. Assess the damage done to you and examine how it has changed you and your belief system. Talk both to others and to the injurer.
2. *Claim the injury*. That is, stop denying that it hurt, and stop defending yourself against it. Acknowledge that the injury has permanently changed you for better or worse, and accept this.
3. *Blame the injurer, not yourself*. Hold *her* accountable.
4. *Balance the scales* either by punishing the injurer or by replacing what she has taken, lest you inflict the same injury on someone else as a way of getting back.

5. *Make the decision to forgive.* You, not she, are responsible for your own life.

6. *Re-create yourself* with new core beliefs, dreams, and myths.

BEING FORGIVEN—FORGIVING YOURSELF

When "killer" Republican political strategist Lee Atwater was suddenly diagnosed with a brain tumor at age thirty-nine, he apologized for his "naked cruelty" during the 1988 Presidential campaign, seeking forgiveness from those he had hurt.[6] This act reaffirmed the faith of many others in what constitutes right and wrong. Again, the effects of our harm or forgiveness are not restricted to just one person.

Sometimes we cannot forgive others, because there is something we have not forgiven in ourselves. Perhaps it was our own part in the unforgiven act that we do not want to recognize. We have met nasty gossip on the job with nasty gossip of our own. Or we cannot forgive ourselves for how we reacted to an injury. Or we are forgiven but still feel guilty.[7]

If you find it difficult to forgive others, instead of concentrating on the injury, call to mind your own regrets. Often, your lack of self-forgiveness will appear as if it had been written in invisible ink.

How can you forgive yourself? You haven't much time.

One way is to ask forgiveness from others, as Atwater did. People are ready to forgive the dying, knowing that some day they'll need to be forgiven, too. If the injured is dead, write him a letter. Engage in a forgiveness ritual with candles and prayers.

If you remain unforgiven, remember that *he cannot forgive you for what he has done to you.* It is a paradox that the injurer blames his victim for his own viciousness. Otherwise, he'd need forgiveness himself! Furthermore, it becomes the *victim's* fault that the injurer can forgive neither her nor himself!

Finally, confess your sin to a minister, rabbi, or priest and receive absolution. If God forgives you, isn't it rank hubris not to forgive yourself?

FORGIVING GOD

Theologian Lewis Smedes reminds us that we may also need to forgive God for allowing our child to die, for the pain we endure, or for
the violence in our country.[8] If God is all-powerful, He could have
prevented these; if not, He allows us the freedom to act and take the
consequences in a universe where anything can happen. Biblical justice collides with biblical mercy. Rabbi Kushner's answer is that
God, while not powerful enough to prevent tragedy, can help us deal
with it.[9]

HOW DO YOU KNOW YOU HAVE FORGIVEN?

You know you've forgiven when

- You ask yourself if you have.
- You no longer obsess on the injury or the injurer.
- You feel more distance from both.
- You are compassionate toward yourself.
- Your faith in God is renewed.
- You're free of resentment and anger.
- You've gotten on with your living and dying.

Forgiveness is a spiral weaving inward, outward, and upward.

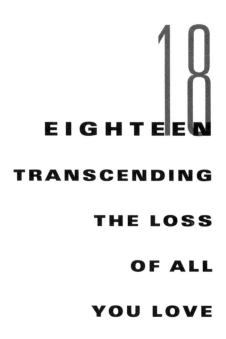

EIGHTEEN

TRANSCENDING

THE LOSS

OF ALL

YOU LOVE

CALL to memory a time you lost a loved one to death. Remember how relatives, friends, and neighbors gathered around to hold you up, figuratively and perhaps literally? In all likelihood, they brought time-honored gifts such as chicken and casseroles. Their meaning was that you were still worth nourishing, body and soul, even though the dead beloved—who fed you or whom you fed those many years—was beyond nourishment. When you could not bear to eat without her they insisted that you do, perhaps taking on her role.

Or perhaps other life losses gathered friends to you—loss of a job or physical ability, a mate to unfaithfulness or divorce, an opportunity, a well-earned prize or reward—all the small deaths of life that we endure. Perhaps with these went losses of dreams, hopes, respect, loyalty, and identity. People sent cards and flowers, took you shopping, offered alternative scenarios for your future, and reassured you that you still had what you had lost (respect), or that it wasn't worth keeping. (Your job? Look at what it was doing to you! Your wife? She was never the person you thought she was. Get a new one!)

Thus love, distraction, reframing, replacement, and hope for the future helped us transcend losses in the past. The problem is that many of these methods aren't going to work for us now. We can't make a new plan, at least not the kind we would have made before. Not only that, but also, if there are any unresolved losses from the past, any grief we got stuck in and never overcame, our present losses bring it back. New losses remind us of the old; in fact, the old begin to haunt us.

When we transcend a loss, we (1) overcome it in some fashion and (2) integrate it into our identity, re-creating who we are. How we have transcended loss in the past points the way to how we approach the multiple losses that we face in the end-time.[1] How can we transcend the loss of *everything* we love?

WHAT YOU ARE LOSING DURING THE END-TIME

To me, it is extraordinary how few people recognize the bereavement that the dying face—including all of the following:

1. Not just one loved person, but *every loved person* in your life: your spouse or partner, children, parents, brothers and sisters, close friends, co-workers, fellow volunteers, even casual acquaintances. You are losing all their long companionship, the touching, words, intimacies, exchange of opinions, sharing, and ways of honoring each other and being together.
2. Your *work* or life project, and your sense of contributing to the community.
3. Your hobbies, arts, and favorite *activities*, from cycling to walking the world, photography, jewelry-making, tutoring.
4. The sense of *purpose* that all those activities gave you.
5. The *distraction* from death they also provided.
6. The many *pleasures* that cheered you in the past, the delights of the occasional gin and tonic, perhaps chocolate, and, most important of all, sex in all its variety and possibility.
   Once you are declared ill, even if the ravages of your body

do not make sex impossible, concerns about attractiveness, fears of killing oneself (as the heart patient experiences), lack of privacy, and, finally, our puritanical society that simply cannot couple sex and death and shames *you* for wanting to do so—all these make sex more furtive than when you were a teen! And during some stages of illness, perhaps due to medications, the libido may disappear—another loss.

7. You lose your *future*, with all its plans, hopes, expectations, and possibilities. You will not be at your grandson's wedding, or see "how it all turned out": the trial, the war, the new discovery. In the past, you studied the future through a telescope. Now it's across the room.

   Worst of all, it gradually dawns on you that you will not be there at the deathbed of your own child, to love and console him when his time comes.

8. You lose such *illusions* as certainty, changelessness, and the ability of you and your loved ones to protect each other.

9. You are bereaved of the *worldview* that you and your mate shared. It is shaken now.

10. No longer can you *revise the past* together. Now, life as you lived it is being cast in granite.

11. You lose the mutual *validation* of each other's thoughts, feelings, opinions, values, and assurances. Now, she must go on, and you cannot.

12. You are also suffering from the *grief of your loved ones*. In the past you comforted each other, but how can you do so now? True, they're not losing as much as you are, but they feel the limitations on their ability to comfort as keenly as you do. And they recognize that one day *they'll* lose it all, too. They *do* have, however, the old transcendence tools of replacement and distraction, for example, which are only minimally available to you now.

13. As you grew older, your *dreams* changed. You redefined success at work, as well as romance. You settled for a trip to Hawaii instead of around the world. "A room of my own" underwent metamorphosis from escaping Mom and Dad to a place for the two of you, to space for growing children, and then to a

smaller, more manageable retirement abode. Now you can't even transform the dream. It's over. You suffer from the loss of what never happened.

14. You are also bereaved of your *sense of self* as growing and developing.

15. In the past, you *learned* from loss, if not immediately, then after a time. But what can you learn from the loss of your entire self? And who is left inside to do the learning?

In Chapter 12, "Riding the Emotional Roller Coaster," I suggested that dying people who were depressed should be diagnosed as suffering from bereavement rather than from a mental illness, Major Depression. If all of the fifteen losses listed above don't constitute bereavement, then what does?

I list your losses at length partly to help you recognize them, partly to show you that someone else does. Most people, and most of the books and articles in the field, recognize the losses of caregivers and those left behind, but do not recognize the bereavement of the dying themselves.

Your modes of transcending such losses in the past are less available to you now. You cannot distract yourself with pleasure or replace one job with another (although you can substitute activities such as meditation); you cannot plan a future you do not have. How, then, *can* you transcend the loss of everything you love? In the next section I suggest some of the more helpful methods still available to you.

RE-VALUING

When you went to work for the company, you were indoctrinated in the value of the product, the reverence due top management (whose portraits hung in the halls), attitudes toward competitors, and your own place in the system. If you worked for a Fortune 500 company, the culture was very different from what you encountered when you worked for a small, family-run business. You accepted this indoctrination in order to function successfully and put food on the table. You needed to believe in your corporate culture so you could justify to yourself and others your acceptance of it.

But when you were laid off, the scales dropped from your eyes. Contradictions that had whispered through your brain became shouts, and you saw things "as they really were." Your boss was a pompous, dictatorial ass, workers had lost their souls, and the product had fleas.

This reevaluation proved to be a major method of transcendence over the loss of your job and made the circumstances of your leaving less painful. It helped you overcome your loss with analysis and replacement, then integrate it into your new identity as an employee elsewhere with a new culture to honor and believe in. Thus, you re-created yourself.

Melanie's company informed her that unless she returned from her health leave by a certain date, she'd be replaced. After six years of loyal work, suddenly she was no longer part of the company, nor they of her. How else could she cope with the hurt except by devaluing them, as apparently they had her? They could "disown"—so could she!

This re-valuing, or reevaluation, of the important and significant in your life is also good for friends who fall away during the end-time. A superb defense against previous losses, it now becomes more radical and spread over a wider area of your life.

IDEALIZING

In many ways, the positive side of re-valuing is idealizing, for example, our relationships and our past. Idealization makes our lives more meaningful by perfecting them.

We are the ones who enjoyed an extraordinary relationship with this mate, child, or friend, as well as our great popularity within the club, on the volunteer board, or in local community government. Crisis sands imperfections smooth.

A widow of fifteen years whom I counseled told me her husband was nearly perfect. "He had only one fault," she said with a laugh. "He loved smelly cheese." This marriage was now perfect and complete in death, as it had not been in life.

Just as the bereaved have the drive to perfect their relationships with those they've loved, so do the dying. Loving relatives compassionately rewrite the family's history, a healing conspiracy of idealization.

DROPPING AWAY

Our lives are crammed with important details, none dispensable. During the end-time many of these drop away, and we are surprised at how easy it is to let them go.

Some we no longer need. Our fetishes for exercise and eating right in order to stay healthy are no longer necessary. Now, both movement and food are circumscribed by our physical condition, illness, and appetite.

Some duties we are excused from, because we simply can no longer perform them. The dust balls may gather under the furniture, our caregivers being more tolerant than we are. While it's important to do what we can, for both physical and psychological benefits, it is also important to let go of what we absolutely cannot do.

Visitors bring with them the fresh air of our church or group, with their provocatively odd people and events. We can wish we were still there, often remembering more enjoyment than we really had. We let our visitor know how worthwhile his work is; but it isn't the *most* worthwhile thing in the world, is it? We let it go.

What would the most worthwhile be? Answers are wriggling like tadpoles just at the edges of our minds. (Shhh! What was that?)

Many of the drop-aways were distractions from life's losses, from time pressing, from the gathering cloud of death on the horizon (with its silvery gold strip of sunlight beneath it, signaling another sunrise on a distant shore—can that be?). Distractions drop away.

If this distresses you, remember that the supports for a rocket fall away just before liftoff!

CONSOLING OTHERS

You'll recall how Mark, the graduate student afflicted with a brain tumor, consoled us and helped us through his death. By consoling others we console ourselves as well. When we transcend others' losses, we feel transcendent ourselves. Some of the most important things you can do for your bereaving loved ones are:

1. Tell them how wonderful they have been to you and how grateful you are for their help.
2. Let them know the benefits you are experiencing now, the re-valuing, the new priorities, and the unexpected revelations. (Be honest, though. Emphasize the *truly* positive.)
3. Offer your investment in their future. Look ahead into it with them—their coming marriage, their son's Little League performance, their reward of rest and relaxation, which they'll need when this is over. This helps relieve the guilt that relatives almost always have (and that is almost always unmerited). They are feeling that they could do more, could even save your life.
4. Share with them the story of your life.
5. Hear them out, just as they are hearing you out.
6. Assure them they can go on, and that if you can you'll visit them in spirit and lend them strength. Many of the dear departed have done so in dreams or even in person.
7. Share with them any glimpses you may have into the world beyond, however subjective. Especially share NDEs (near-death experiences) or visions, if they want to hear them.
8. Let them know how highly you value them.
9. Make them presents of small gifts.

GIVING IT AWAY

Why wait until your will is read? You may enjoy the pleasure of giving Chloe that bone china now, and Michael that antique table.

There is, however, one situation in which you might want to wait.

Sometimes a relative turns greedy, trying to make off with the stereo before the others can. Your executor or even your lawyer can protect you in such circumstances. Refer such squabbling to someone else. You don't deserve to hear it.

REPLACEMENT

Always before in your life when you lost something, you replaced it with something else. Usually, the replacement was similar to what was lost, such as a lover or a job or a home. Now your replacements are different. You replace previous life activities with new ones, such as

- Relieving pain
- Meditating
- Audiotaping the story of your life
- Writing a journal of your experience
- Recording dreams as they become more vivid and significant
- Listening to favorite music
- Focusing on the life of the spirit
- Getting a friend to take you on a nature "field trip" to the beach or mountains
- Doing something—usually creative—that you've always wanted to do but never had the time

You can lead quite a satisfying life with these new activities.

GRATITUDE

If you are grieving the loss of a particular aspect of your life, it is because you were fortunate enough to have it in the first place. The homeless person does not grieve the destruction of his house in flood or earthquake. Nor does the schizoid grieve the loss of an intimate.

Alfred Lord Tennyson said, "'Tis better to have loved and lost /

Than never to have loved at all." Don't you feel that what you mourn now was worth having?

Instead of concentrating on the loss, focus on the gratitude you feel for all that has been good in your life.

LOVE

Love has always been the greatest form of transcendence, and it will be throughout your dying time. Now is an opportunity to bring everything you love into your life if you haven't done so before. Bring

- A kitten
- A circulating art exhibit from the library
- Birds to a feeder outside your window (watch the cat!)
- Friends with problems for you to help
- Music, poetry, and meaningful short stories
- Long intimate talks with those you love
- An indoor garden—plant everything you ever wanted to grow
- God, a guardian angel, or a divine spirit
- What else?

Love has a wonderful way of begetting itself. As you incorporate increasing love into your life, you see with new, loving eyes. You love the commonplace more. One person I knew experienced a radical conversion into love and told me, "It was as if I stared into a blinding white light, yet I could see."

THE SENSE OF JOURNEY

If you were leaving your loved one at the airport to go on a business trip, you'd kiss her good-bye and maybe mention again that the yard needs watering, and that your plane gets in at seven Sunday night. You certainly wouldn't hang on each other, crying hysterically and carrying on. Imagine an airport like that! And yet, when we begin to leave each other at death, we grieve exactly in that way, as if we were never going to see each other again.

How do we know?

Everywhere we hear that the purpose of life is love. Then why is the system rigged to rip love apart, wife from husband, parent from child, friend from friend, beloved leader from nation? Perhaps it isn't. Perhaps we only think it is. Perhaps *perfect* love would be perfect faith—that we and our loved ones are *not* ripped apart.

If this is so, then we are, indeed, beginning a new stage in our journey, and we will be reunited at a stopping point down the road. What would be the point of believing otherwise?

NINETEEN

IT DOESN'T

HAVE TO BE YOURS

(AND IT NEVER WAS)

A few years ago, I stored my belongings; packed up my Honda with camping equipment, multiseason clothing, an old typewriter, two briefcases (my "desks"—one for business and one for writing); armed myself with a youth hostel pass; and set off on an odyssey across the country. I didn't think of it as a quest, but in the course of the following year I was unexpectedly healed of six major life losses in absolutely extraordinary ways. I was also blessed with many revelations, one of which, I believe, will help us during our dying time.

That revelation was simply this: It doesn't have to be yours (and it never was).

NOT YOUR PRECIOUS POSSESSIONS

Throughout our lives, the things we own define us. As infants and toddlers we learned which toys were ours, which not ours. As we grew, our possessions extended us out and away from the borders of our bodies. Our clothing signified to which group we belonged, just as it does today, most obviously in private schools or gangs. Or it communicated how we were different, significant, and worthy. Our corner of the attic, then our room, office, and home, also enlarged our identity, endowing us with their meaning and significance. Our taste was judged exquisite, good, or bizarre, and thus so were we.

As we grow, our relationship to our possessions changes. The acquisition years of our twenties and thirties, with new homes, furnishings, and children, yield to the middle years, when there may be more money for a luxury or two. Thus, whatever is *ours* is also *us*. This is why we feel personally violated by whoever steals, destroys, or defaces our possessions.

Our "things" have meaning far beyond their appearance or utility. The crystal vase bequeathed to us by a loving and long-passed grandmother recalls family gatherings with her and other long-gone relatives disappearing into the haze of memory. It may be all we have left of them. Thus, possessions preserve what we have lost. Your athletic trophy or the gavel you received when you stepped down as president of your organization carry the meaning of the entire experience.

Possessions transcend loss by reviving the lost experience. The wedding ring once meant love and marriage (after the divorce, you secreted it in the bottom drawer). If you have transcended the loss, it is easier to give up the ring. If not, you must work to do so now.

No wonder it's so hard to release these tangible memories when our time comes to die! The son who receives your World's Fair souvenir may not understand its significance to you, yet he may grieve that this is a part of you he did not know. You can tell him now, of course, but it will be your story of it, your myth, not the experience as it happened. Perhaps that is better, perhaps not.

You'll need to develop a different frame of mind to make it easier to let go of the things you love.

First, in passing them to someone else, you preserve them.

Second, think of your belongings as a Kwakiutl potlatch of canoes, button blankets, and exquisite carved bone or wood soul-catchers along the misty British Columbia coast—a show of wealth to be divided among your heirs.

Third, know that what you think is yours originally "belonged" to someone else. Or, if the item is new, recognize that the materials once belonged to the earth. The wood, the cotton, the oil in the plastic—all basic elements formed into a product within the mind of someone else, tempered, carved, stamped, or woven and then sold to you, perhaps through another. Eventually, it will all return.

In this sense, whatever possession you believe to be "yours" has been so only temporarily; only borrowed, really. Now it passes on to those you select, and they in turn must eventually release it back to the earth.

NOT YOUR CHILD

Sarah, the mother disowned by her more conservative daughter, had a kind of premonition many years before when that daughter was six. Sarah had walked the girl from their home out to the street one morning to see her off to school. Long chestnut hair swinging at the waist of her frock, skirt swaying, the little figure's sturdy white-stockinged legs marched into a mist blown in from the sea. And, as Sarah watched, the mist wreathed about her daughter like the arms of a stranger, and her child, never looking back, disappeared. Sarah wanted to run after her but stood paralyzed by the comprehension that her child was already on her way into her own future, which Sarah, with all her love, could not enter. Her child was not really hers: "She was just on loan. She belonged to herself, her future husband, her own child perhaps. Maybe the world. Not to me."

Admittedly, Sarah had a harder separation from her child than most of the rest of us do. But her experience was a stunning metaphor of the truth that none of us belongs to another. We love to speak of "my" husband, "my" granddaughter, "my" patient, "my" customer, even. It enlarges us, anchoring us in a much greater, less vulnerable, family and community than our single selves. It is an affectionate illusion.

Our children are gifts, but only for a while. We are honored with the responsibility of raising them, or blessed (and some days we're cursed). Ultimately, they belong to the universe, and we can pray and trust that it will do as well by them as it does by us.

NOT YOUR CAUSE

For over thirty years, Helen worked for the women's movement in small ways. Concerned with jobs and equal pay, she read Betty Friedan and later Gloria Steinem, got out the vote, and spoke up at meetings. Then a series of heart attacks left her weak and dying in her sixties. How could she relinquish a cause in which she believed so deeply?

At first she grieved for that part of her life that was no longer hers. She believed that women were in trouble again in spite of advances in employment, that there were forces in motion to blame society's ills on women who were in the workplace instead of in the home "where they belonged." Then Helen began to recognize the great contributions of younger women: Susan Faludi, author of *Backlash*, and Naomi Wolf, who expressed Helen's own experiences in *The Beauty Myth*, among others.

Not merely pressing the cause forward, Helen felt, they did it better than she and her generation. In a moment of inspiration, Helen *willed* it to them, consciously bequeathing "her" movement to these leaders. She still contributed, by *receiving* their message. Without Helen and millions like her, Faludi and Wolf and the rest were nothing. Their message needed to be heard and acted upon. With the movement in their capable hands, Helen was confident of women's future.

If you have a cause about which you care deeply, you can do as Helen did. You can *bequeath* it to those who carry on. Write them a letter, outlining specifically your charge to them. Put it in your last will and testament, thereby *testifying* to your belief in the rightness of your cause.

As long as it flourishes, so do you. This is the hidden reason behind passionate espousal of wilderness preservation, for example. The wilderness continues you.

EXERCISE: YOU'RE NOT LEAVING IT BEHIND, YOU'RE LEAVING IT *TO*

Make a list of the things, people, or causes that are the most painful for you to leave. Then place a notation beside each item, bequeathing it to someone or something else. Here are some suggestions:

- A favorite possession (or several)
- A much-loved person, maybe even one you've never met
- The sunset or sunrise
- A poem or a piece of music
- The store or business you founded (consider "leaving" it to a competitor, thereby incorporating forgiveness)
- New Mexico's desert skies or Pennsylvania's history
- An old theater scheduled for demolition by myopic developers in cahoots with stone-blind city councilors
- The Democratic or Republican Party
- Your library
- Your church

Bequeathing what we love extends our lives, at least spiritually. If you can, bequeath a sum of money, even a small one.

There is another advantage. These things, people, places, and actions are where those who love you can find you. They *are* you—much more so than your pots and pans (unless you're a master cook), your jewelry (unless you fashioned it), or any of the thousand things you simply *own* and had to allocate in your will.

These "possessions" are you, and bequeathing them regenerates you in the same way a baby is conceived.

WE CAN BECOME MORE THAN WHAT IS OURS

As we were growing up, we extended our identity through our possessions. But now we can become so much greater than anything we ever owned! This was shown to me on my yearlong journey.

Most of my belongings, the very ones I've willed to my family and friends, were in storage, and I was far away. I rented other people's hostel bunks or tenting land. Along the way, I worked in libraries, and occasionally found computers to use—a university's, a friend's—somehow they appeared. Whatever else I needed appeared, too, sometimes just before I needed it.

But the frightening part was that I did not miss any of that great roomful of things I'd stored! What was wrong with me that I no longer cared about my things? Their *meanings* lived inside me, yes, even the photographs, and I could not give those meanings away. Of course, I knew they still existed. My things had not been consumed by fire, as had some of my friends'.

On the road, I didn't own much, and I didn't need to.

Instead, I took possession of other things far greater than anyone could store. For example, I lived for hours on great Southern plantations, wandering the grounds. Perhaps you long to wander through Carlsbad Caverns, or roam the world until each rocky outcropping of Machu Picchu, each twisty street of Paris, each koala or kangaroo or emu of the Australian outback, each play of light and shadow on Mount Kilimanjaro is as familiar to you as the lines in your hand. Or surround yourself with the priceless ormolu clocks, majolica plates, Limoges china, and regency furniture at the Prince Albert Museum in London. Whatever you're passionate about, you might long to linger near, and it could take many lifetimes to do just that. But as you take it in, you see, you contain it, it becomes part of you, and yet it remains long after you are gone.

I was admiring a swan-shaped tureen in the Shelburne Museum in Vermont. Along came a little girl, who asked her mother, "What's that? What's it for?"

"It's for swan soup," came the grisly reply.

Her humor shook me from my immersion into the realization that I contained it, and that I had grown larger and extended myself to everything else I took in on this trip, just as my possessions had once extended me. The tureen did not possess me. Nor did my belongings in storage, although they would have if the thought of doing without them had held me back. You will no longer be owned by your house, your yard, your machines that need fixing.

It's like being turned inside out, isn't it? What we own belongs to the universe, and what we are passionate about is ours: Alaska's blue glaciers, Canada's night-silvered lakes, Venice's ornate stone bridges, Australia's Great Barrier Reef, Mexico's Copper Canyon. We wind up with *more* than we ever thought we had. And if what is ours belongs to the universe, then the universe is ours as well, and, by extension, ourselves!

TWENTY

WHAT'S LEFT

UNDONE

JEFF, the thirty-two-year-old computer programmer savaged by AIDS, suffered profound regret that intensified the pain of his illness; he had not spent his brief life in the art of photography, which he so loved. At eighteen, newly emancipated from an impoverished family, he had been too anxious for financial security, accomplishment, and acquisition to follow his dream. So he entered a field where there was great demand and reward for his technical prowess. Now in his last year (as they told him), computers, money, accomplishments even, all dropped away, and only his partner, Doug, their close friends, and his love of photography were left.

This is what we face when we are dying—the family, friends, and lovers we never had, the success we never attained, the art we left undone. Maybe we've taken a meaningless job to pay the rent, then the pediatrician, then the kids' college bills—always knowing we were capable of more. Years lengthen into decades, while death stands at our shoulder, perhaps in the shifting shape of a crow, whispering, "Do it NOW!" If we heed it, we have fewer regrets.[1]

If the life-threatening illness you battle still allows you time, and if, as one schizophrenic but gifted young student of mine once observed, you've been in the "wrong rain" all your life, you can still DO IT NOW. You won't have as much time to get as much done as you would have if you'd begun earlier, but if it's something you love, like Jeff's photography, it's the *process* that counts, not the end result. If you don't have time, there are still ways of dealing with regret that can ease the pain.

EXERCISE: WHAT HAVE I ACCOMPLISHED

With a close relative or friend, list all the accomplishments of your life.

- How proud of them are you?
- What were the major blocks to these accomplishments? What did you have to overcome?
- Do you think you've done pretty well, or poorly?
- What does your friend think?

I'm wagering you haven't given yourself enough credit. How so? Your list contains only action items, things you did, nothing passive, nothing you received from others. It's all very well to say of our lives, "I accomplished." It's just as important to say, "I received," bringing to fruition *someone else's* accomplishments. It may be a source of satisfaction to say "I supervised" or "I originated" or "I influenced." But consider also that you *were* supervised, giving someone else the chance to work through you. Further, as you were influenced, for example, by someone on the City Council or the board who convinced you of a right action that you subsequently voted for, so you also created—the law, the progress, the enhanced community.

So, let's add to your list. As a member of your various communities, to whom and to what have you contributed? How has your receptiveness helped shape the better forces of your company, city, state, nation, and world?

EXERCISE: WHAT WOULD I HAVE ACCOMPLISHED IF I'D LIVED LONGER?

Don't censor yourself as you make this list. Write down everything that comes to mind, even if you think it's silly, because some of the less important items are also the easier, one-shot possibilities if time is short. You can probably take that brief local trip you've promised yourself for fifteen years, call up that old friend, even push a peanut up Broadway with your nose.

One or two major regrets may emerge. In fact, some of you didn't even need a list to ferret out long-buried dreams and desires. You know instantly, just as Jeff knew.

If you still have time, you can do as Jeff did. The week he was diagnosed, he dropped in at the local community college and signed up for a photography course. Through the instructor, he got himself invited to a professional group that met at sunrise on Wednesday mornings. When he became too weak and nonmobile, he spent his remaining months poring over great photographs. Doug brought home tomes from the library and fixed up a bed-tray to hold them. Then there were all the back issues of *Life* and *National Geographic*, the tapes to view, the great photographers to listen to, and their biographies to experience. Thus he was developing into the photographer he'd always dreamed of being. Although he didn't have time to become Ansel Adams, Annie Liebowitz, Edward Steichen, or Galen Rowell, he contributed to the entire existential project of photography by learning about and appreciating the work of others.

Jeff and Doug had a strong circle of friends to help them, as well as the support of such organizations as Hospice, Shanti, the Northwest AIDS Foundation, and the Chicken Soup Brigade. As Jeff progressed down the road he was meant to travel, many others watched and thought about their own lives. There was a message for them here. They began making changes as well, incorporating more of what they were meant to do and be.

A funny thing happens when you do this. Once you make a beginning, the universe conspires to smooth the way, providing opportunities to assist you. Strange synchronicities arise. You see a meeting notice on the bulletin board, someone just ahead of you in line at the library returns an important book suggesting new vistas, an old friend phones and mentions a resource.

Goethe wrote:

> Whatever you can do, or dream you can, begin it.
> Boldness has genius, power and magic in it.

As Jeff showed his friends, it's never too late until it is.

OTHER REGRETS: FAME, MONEY, SUCCESS

Above, we plumbed regrets over what we could have done and did not. But some of us skate for the gold and don't even make the team.

As a practitioner in an art highly susceptible to this problem, I'm well acquainted with the dilemma of freelance writers who end each month rent-challenged. Meanwhile, sleaze, scam, and instant books by nonwriters top the bestseller lists. The June 27/July 4, 1994, issue of *The New Yorker* detailed the struggles of a critically acclaimed literary novelist who when interviewed had been living on a bucket of chicken (eighteen pieces) for three days. Sympathetic to his plight, one of my author friends wanted to write and tell him how to lower his laundry bill, but she couldn't spare the stamp.

None of this is fair, of course, but then it never would have been, no matter how rich and famous he—or you—became.

You were never good enough to qualify, or beat out the competition, or satisfy your dad, or be approved by all—even if you were number one. And if you *were* number one, it was only temporary. You couldn't last a season beyond Martina Navratilova's nine Wimbledon wins; she couldn't either.

Now you're leaving all that behind, the visions of success, the unfairness of limitation. Your visions weren't realistic; your limitations were human. Furthermore, superiority is culturally defined; look at Andy Warhol's Campbell's soup cans.

One revelation on my journey took place in the Washington, D.C., youth hostel. I was standing in the common room (hostel-speak for living room), watching people from all over the world milling about, each carrying a very different world inside his head; in the days or weeks to come, these worlds would cross-fertilize and pollinate, breeding new understandings, new alliances. Each person came bearing gifts of the uniqueness that lay inside him. For a disoriented instant, it seemed to me that the whole world was in this room, unity in diversity. I could not write about the world of this Taiwanese nurse or that Greek teacher, but *they* could, and what precious gifts they offered. How could I be jealous?

It's hard to watch sleaze succeed. But as others' "good stuff" flourishes, we can take a longer view. Think of something that has succeeded in your field—an invention, perhaps. Isn't the world richer for that gift? Is it really something you could have done? Isn't it better, objectively, that that invention be in the world rather than your own failed one?

I think of novels by Gabriel García Márquez, Alice Walker, John Irving, Toni Morrison, Jane Smiley, Ruth Rendell, P. D. James, and Margaret Atwood (to name a few), of breathtaking stories by John Cheever, Tim O'Brien, and Amy Bloom. I couldn't have written those, because my vision simply is not theirs (nor my craft). How impoverished our culture would be without them!

The problem, of course, is the "I" in accomplishment. But *the importance lies in the work, not in who does it.*

Now, of course, no one can do quite what you can—you're a snowflake, remember. But enough people can do some of it, so that you need not feel it will never exist.

REASONS WHY WE WANT TO ACCOMPLISH

- I wanted to swim around the world so my parents would love me.
- I wanted to be a star, because success is the best revenge, and an Oscar or an Emmy would *show* the classmates who rejected me, the ex-wife who ran out on me, and the boss who made my best years a living hell and deserves to die.

- I wanted to get stinking rich, because then everyone would approve of me, and if they're not going to love me, that's a good substitute.
- I wanted to (fill in your own), because then I'd be okay.

Our longings for accomplishment are bribes: "See me." "Hear me." "Respect me." "Love me." This is what they say.

When school counselor Mary Anne was a child, her manic-depressive dad dispensed twenty-dollar bills to everyone who served him. The waiter, the taxi driver, the porter at the airport, the personnel at his club—all were recipients of his largesse. "They love me," he used to say. Did they?

COMING TO TERMS WITH WHAT'S LEFT UNDONE

There are eleven major ways in which you can come to terms with not having accomplished what you set out to do, not succeeding at it, or not following your dream:

1. Recognize that the task was unrealistic, that no one has ever turned paper into gold or flown to the moon on a bicycle, although admittedly a cancer cure would have been nice.
2. Concede that your standards were inhuman. Perfect parenting is a goal attained by few, mostly men and women over sixty.
3. Realize that many of your criteria for the success of your life were probably laid on you by loving parents during your brilliant babyhood.
4. If someone else did it better, he was more talented, or luckier, or less plagued by obstacles, or more in tune with the culture (that is, more "common," if it makes you feel better). Millions of sperm swim for the egg, and usually only one makes it. But *none* would have if they hadn't given it a try.
5. Distinguish between (1) what you've accomplished and (2) the recognition of it by others. Take a good look at your contribution list. No one can take these from you. If you feel

proud of what you've done, often in the face of terrific odds, that's got to be enough, because others can't see it from your vantage point. Besides, they're too busy being concerned about *your* recognizing *them*.

6. Just as Helen willed her cause to other feminists, you can will what you've left undone to others. Perhaps you can leave some money to it or write support letters. Write a fan letter to Mother Teresa, Whitney Houston, Bill Gates, Jimmy and Rosalynn Carter, Billy Graham, Oprah Winfrey, Bernie Siegel, Bill Moyers, Marianne Williamson, or Jane Smiley.

7. Rejoice in the accomplishments and successes of others. Obviously, the world needed them, and if we love the world, we're glad.

8. Confess to yourself the rewards of failure. If a particular life disaster still haunts you, think of any unexpected benefit it had for your life. Be honest!

9. If you were an also-ran, you were still part of the field, and without the field, there would be no race, and without the race, there would be no "giant step" for humankind.

10. Rejoice in the realization that you and I are part of the larger accomplishment—the world—and it survives.

11. HONOR YOURSELF for small kindnesses and great attempts.

Now, some snide people are going to call the above "rationalizations," but that doesn't make them any less true.

NEW GOALS

When we were children, our parents and teachers taught us that the great tasks of life were to grow healthy, get an education—both for a good job and for our personal development—marry, have children who do the same, then get out of the way (retire, travel, shut up). We're not taught that dying is one of the great developmental tasks, the culmination, the transition from body to spirit. We're learning much of this on our own.

Or perhaps, like Jeff, you didn't follow your dream. Or you over-worked and had no time for a dog or a trip to the mountains or a concert or enough sleep or dreams or any of the hundreds of other things you love.

We think that we get love only *from* people, and if we don't have enough, it seems out of control and we feel deprived. But there's an-other source of love, and that's ourselves. Being loved isn't always under our control, but *loving* is.

In the time left, if you feel that you have not been loved enough, resolve to love more. There's very little difference between the sub-jective feelings of being loved and of loving; in fact, they both feel the same—warm, fuzzy, joyous, and full. You have time and opportu-nity now. The more you incorporate what you love into your life, the less "what's left undone" will matter.

In the past we lived with such goals as caring for family, getting a raise or promotion, finishing chores, and not wasting time. What other goals have been an important part of your life? We may hang on to these for a while—they're a good distraction—but eventually they fall away.

Now we may even think we're goal-less, but this isn't true.

Among our goals are the following:

1. To manage our illness in the best ways possible, minimizing pain and increasing control
2. To live as long as we can while still maintaining an acceptable quality of life, so that we can continue our loving relationships
3. To develop ourselves spiritually, in preparation for the transition from here to there. This development includes
   - Reconciliation
   - Teaching others by how we die
   - Learning from the everyday as well as the occasional revelation we may experience
   - Meditation or other spiritual practices
   - Making provision for the loves we leave behind
   - Incorporating more of what we love into our lives
   - Opening ourselves to the unusual experiences we may begin to have as our earthly lives shut down (of which much more in the later chapters).

ACCOMPLISHMENT AND LOVE

Once again, consider your regret over what's left undone. So often, what we set ourselves to do is based on a deficiency of love. Think about it. Perhaps your parents didn't love you unconditionally; perhaps the condition was success. Or they fussed over you and rewarded you more for Bs than for Cs, and this reward seemed like an outpouring of love to you.

Perhaps you had a tough time finding a lover. You felt you needed success or money or power or beauty to attract one; our culture teaches us that attraction is based on consumerism.

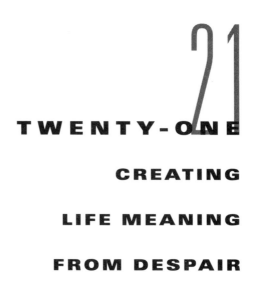

TWENTY-ONE

CREATING

LIFE MEANING

FROM DESPAIR

IS there anything you'd die for? Can you say, I'd die for my country? for freedom? for my family? for God? to save others?

Members of the armed services, police, and fire departments put their lives on the line for a cause. Perhaps you're one of them. Dying for country, freedom, family, God, or to save others gives meaning to both our lives and our deaths. It enlarges us, making us one with something greater than ourselves. We do not say, "Life at any cost!" Some things are more important than life itself. And some *deaths* are more meaningful than others, especially when they make our *lives* more meaningful.

If you are experiencing despair over your life's ending, that is only natural. Pain, physical deterioration, and the prospect of losing all you love intensify despair.

Yet if you can make your life and death meaning*ful* rather than meaning*less*, you will ease your despair. There are ways to do this, even during your dying time.

THE MEANING OF MEANINGFULNESS

Listen to the words of men and women I interviewed as they grappled with issues of death and meaning:[1]

Della, age thirty-nine, a Mormon mother: "The meaning of life is to become like our Father in heaven." He has a plan for all of us, and we must follow it. Della's two little girls are adopted. When she and her husband went to an orphanage to adopt another baby, they were left alone with it "to feel its little spirit," but the experience was different from the other two. They felt "awful." After praying for guidance, they concluded that this baby was meant for someone else.

Luke, age seventy, a white-haired, bearded mystic, defines life meaning as "spiritual evolution, the evolution of consciousness. We're all in the process of moving from the physical to the spiritual."

"The here and now," argues Marty, age thirty, a guitarist suffering from cirrhosis. "The past is gone, the future—who knows? Good booze, good lovin', good times." He grins slyly. "Where it's at."

Gwen, age fifty-five: "I see a pattern in my life. There were so many sudden losses. Even when I was little, the beatings from my parents were always so sudden and random, capricious. Deaths were always unexpected—my husband and children. But then, so were my psychic experiences—visits from the dead, out-of-body experiences. Those spiritual times helped me overcome . . ." Gwen's life was so hard that we could almost expect occasional breaks with reality, psychic or psychotic. This is how she created meaning.

For Sam and Nina, dedication to a cause greater than themselves gives them life meaning: "We're all part of the environment," Nina says. "Sam and I feel it when we're saving oil-soaked birds, or trekking through the Olympic rain forest."

Thus, "life meaning" can be a purpose, a reason for our existence, a goal or aim toward which our lives are driven. Or it can be a pattern in which we see major events and relationships repeated throughout the whole, a tapestry of unique design.

For some, the greatest terror is the possibility that there is no meaning, that our decisions do not matter, that our choices are absurd, that our suffering, pain, and sacrifice are for nothing, that it doesn't matter if you climb the ladder of success, get that appointment or promotion or sale, marry this person rather than the other. For some, the greatest terror is that there is no life plan written in the sky or the stars, that the beautiful sculpture you created or bought is insignificant. The death of your son or daughter in Vietnam, the triumph of evil over good, what if it doesn't matter? This is the "sickness unto death" of which Sartre wrote.[2] If there is no meaning, then we can only rage.

Some believe that they *search* for meaning, and that either they will find it or they will not. I believe we *create* it by transcending loss. A loss transcended makes life meaningful, because loss means death to us, and death untranscended makes so much meaningless. Transcendence means life, rebirth, immortality, or resurrection.

Although it is better to create life meaning before your end-time, perhaps you are too young, or have been too preoccupied with the business of living. There is still time. I offer a number of methods below. Try one or two that feel comfortable.

METHOD 1. LIFE MEANING AS PURPOSE: HEAVEN

Imagine you're in heaven before your birth-time. Luminous blue sky surrounds you, and doric columns rise into the heights above. You and your companion souls are awaiting assignments. A great angel moves down the line, dispensing slips of paper like communion wafers to each, offering subdued words of congratulation and explanation. As he approaches, you have mixed feelings. It's hard to leave this gloriously beautiful and exciting place with so many loved ones and abilities that you won't have "down there"; you'll have to learn the earthly nuisance laws of gravity, motion, time, and multiplicity of everything all over again. But human life is a gift, its purpose to evolve you and the universe in some way. Gazing into the clear gray eyes of the angel, you accept your assignment.

On the slip of paper is written the following (your choice of script or font):

"The purpose of your life on earth is to _____ (Fill in the blank.)

"You are being sent to learn _____.

"You are being sent to _____.

What was the original purpose of your life? Did you accomplish it? If not, why? If there is still time, can you? If not, this is a loss. Have you transcended it? Can you?

Now imagine that you can return to that before-birth-time. Would you accept this assignment? Turn it down? Why?

If the imagery of heaven and angels is uncomfortable, visualize yourself in a classroom with the same assignment.

METHOD 2. LIFE MEANING AS CHOICE

If something awful has happened to you, imagine that you *chose* it to be a condition of your life. Visualize yourself saying, "Yes." Why would you do this? What did it teach you or someone else? Whom? Why? Sometimes you can come up with reasons after the fact. Was there anything positive about it? A blessing in disguise? Bad things are meaningless in proportion to our inability to explain them.

METHOD 3: LIFE MEANING AS PATTERN: THE QUILT

Pretend that your entire life is a quilt you've pieced together. Instead of leftover material from your other projects, you use whatever you find in a box of scraps you stumbled on under the stairs when you were a child. Imagine, further, that the darker colors—black, navy, and brown—are tragedies, losses, or sorrows you've endured, as well as dark emotions of anger, envy, and depression. Perhaps the reds, golds, and oranges are more positive feelings, such as sexual attraction, caring, warmth; the medium blues and greens are the positive, stable events and relationships in your life; and, finally, the pastels, yellows, and whites are joys and spiritual experiences.

What does your quilt look like? Sketch it with colored pencils, crayons, or paints, if you can. Is it predominantly dark, medium, or light? The top is your childhood, and your life periods progress down the quilt's length. Is there one dark square from your childhood, perhaps a death, that repeats throughout your life? Or a relationship in your youth that colors the rest of your quilt—a good marriage, perhaps?

Analyze one life period at a time. What were your major losses in childhood, adolescence, youth, middle, and old age? How did you transcend them? That is, (1) overcome, and (2) integrate them into your life, re-creating it and yourself as well? Did you gain something from these experiences? What? Are the gains by any chance silver, gold, or even jeweled?

YOUR LOSS AND TRANSCENDENCE LIFE THEME

Do your losses and transcendences form a pattern, just like that of a quilt? That is, do you see that types of losses are *repeated*, as well as modes of overcoming and integrating them?

This pattern of loss and transcendence is your *life theme*.

For example, throughout her history, Sarah could trace such experiences of powerlessness as her daughter's disownment.

During her childhood in a religious school, she was picked on because she wore thick glasses and talked "like an encyclopedia, they told me. I didn't think so." Her teachers relieved her misery in small ways, with bit parts in school plays and a place on the softball team. In return, she performed "favors," cleaning blackboards and erasers, running errands, even grading the math papers. She felt powerless, both at school and at home, where her brothers ruled. She transcended with an overactive imagination that zipped her to far-off places around the galaxies, as well as by riding her bike everywhere. On rainy days she had her nose in a science fiction book.

Marriage brought no respite from powerlessness. On the contrary, her husband insisted that she give up her science ambitions. Wives should be kept "barefoot and pregnant in the kitchen." In return, he supported and protected her, just as her teachers had. Further, as she realized years later, she could not fail at a science she never attempted; this is the reward of untried dreams—that they remain untarnished as well. Meanwhile, her daughter succeeded where Sarah had not dared, and held her in contempt. When Sarah turned forty, her husband left her for a beautiful younger woman who shone as hostess, gardener, and home decorator. After years of raising children on small support payments, she lost one son in Vietnam, and another married a French woman, moving abroad to raise their family. Too old to be hired by anyone for anything, Sarah stumbled on massage, became proficient, moved out of her apartment, and toured the country for several years, finally settling in a New Age Arizona community. Here she built up her business, accepted tourists into her modest new home, and became a power in the local chamber of commerce.

What patterns does she see? "I was always 'done to.' I overcame by doing for myself and escaping to places where I didn't need anyone's approval. I've done a lot of traveling, a lot of reading. I'm even writing science fiction stories."

In Sarah's own words, her core life theme is "Being done to versus escape through independence, travel, and reading."

Now, perhaps in her last year of life, death is "doing it to her" again, continuing her pattern of powerlessness. But she transcends through her community activities, New Age beliefs, reading, and writing. She can strengthen the transcendent aspects of her life in several ways—by recognizing factors beyond her control in her losses and increasing the positive factors within her control. If she has not completely transcended these losses (her daughter's disownment, for example), she may yet do so—by forgiving, by reconciling herself to it, or by releasing her daughter to God.

Was there a purpose to her life, an assignment? She isn't sure. "I think it was to strengthen myself, just as I've done."

Do you see a pattern or theme in your life? It's easy to determine. List major losses on one side of a sheet of paper; on the other, major strengths, defenses, or other methods you have used to overcome your losses. You may find repetitions, many approximate rather than exact. Sum them up as bipolar—losses on one side, transcendences on the other—as we did for Sarah above. (If your life seems disorganized, that may be part of the theme!)

METHOD 4. LIFE MEANING AS RESULT

A simple way to create life meaning is to ask at the end of your life, "What's happened in the world because I lived? What difference have I made to anyone or anything?" You may have done something individually or as part of a group.

A major trauma often creates life meaning that lasts. A prisoner of war sees the subsequent peace as part of a grand design, a justification for his life. Monuments, tributes, and medals decree this significance. The AIDS quilt and the Vietnam Veterans Memorial preserve individuals, extending them in a kind of immortality and affirmation of their worth.

Try the following brief exercise.

"_____ never would have happened if I had not lived." (My children would not have been born, for example).

"If I had not (fought for our country), the result would have been _____."

Don't overlook negative events! Be on the lookout for what I call the silver lining effect.

"If this (betrayal or injustice) hadn't happened to me, I never would have had the opportunity to _____." What did it force (or free) you to do? Whom did you meet as a result? What relationships or peak experiences came out of it? A criminal caught and convicted of violating your house is stopped from violating others.

Does this make your life more meaningful?

METHOD 5. LIFE REVIEW/LIFE STORY

Review your life, recounting the ups and downs, the various relationships and events. Either write it or audio- or videotape it to hand down to the family. Tell or write it as a *story*, with a beginning, middle, and end. A local professional biographer might help.

You may be asked to relate a memorial history, more likely if you come from a prominent family, led a life in public service, or were present at historical events. The history might be local or national, part of an oral history project.

ANOTHER WAY OF CREATING LIFE MEANING

Lawrence LeShan suggests revisiting places that had meaning to you in the past.[3] He cites the beautiful film *The Trip to Bountiful*. To what places would you return?

On my one-year journey, I returned to a huge house I'd lived in as a very young child in upper New York State. Amazingly, I found it with no difficulty. Now a bed-and-breakfast, it had been a place where I experienced four years of violence and trauma, a strange place of dreams and protective ghosts that had been my own psychic defense against what was happening to me. Now, on the dresser in each room sat a journal filled with the happy experiences of many visitors. The ghosts were gone, the house no longer "remembered," and a darkness in my heart lightened.

22

TWENTY-TWO

OUR GREAT VALUE

AS DYING PEOPLE:

TEACHING OTHERS

BY HOW WE DIE

UNTIL you became ill, your social value was as a purveyor and consumer of goods and services. The media reported your accomplishments and pandered to your tastes—clothes to wear for impeccable performance; tools to succeed; places to work, raise a family, and recuperate. Omnipresent advertising flattered you, told you that your worth lay in what you bought. In sum, your ability to sell and buy made you worthy of respect.

But the day came when you were no longer "attractive." You could not get and spend as you had. If female, you could not breed. Society might flatter you as "still active" (not yet dependent)—you volunteer, play golf, travel, have hobbies, so you still consume and you still "count."

You cannot, however, move as quickly or easily, you grow weaker and do less for yourself. You become dependent on others to drive you to the hospital, prepare food, clean your room. Others select your medical equipment and pharmaceuticals.

You used to be the one who cared—someone's parent, someone else's child, a volunteer who tended others. Now you must be tended. The message is that you are "less" in the eyes of society. The media pass you over and report the tribulations of your caregivers. Even the patronizing "still active" (won't always be) no longer applies. Many indicate, simply by not looking at you as they speak, speaking *across* you to others, that your usefulness is past. If you are not demented or in a coma, you feel dead before you die. Is there anything beyond usefulness?

The shock steals over you like the plunging cold before an arctic storm. Not only is your worth no longer in how much you sell and consume—*it never was!* The realization is disorienting. You were everything you were, but also so much more. You didn't know this until now. Now, all you are left with is the ineffable "so much more," but this seems to cancel out your lifelong struggle, accomplishment, and worth.

What is that "so much more"? How are we of value now?

We are worthy of respect because we are living human beings, with all the gathered wisdom of our lives. We are of great value in that we teach the meaning of life and death by how we die.

TEACHING OTHERS BY HOW WE DIE

As parents, we inculcate our children with skills they need to survive: "Share toys in school," "Do your homework," "Dance with everyone, even nerds." Implicit are beliefs about honesty, responsibility, helpfulness, justice, and compassion. We teach by word and deed. If we are lucky, our children grow up to have children of their own, passing a few of our values on to them.

At some point we think our teaching is over. We may feel less valued, supernumeraries whose advice is not required. We've done our work well, our children are grown, they don't need us. It is precisely at this point that, unknowingly, we begin to teach the most valuable lessons of all: how to age positively and lead a rich life even when afflicted with physical disabilities, progressive unattractiveness, and perhaps poverty—all of which the young look upon with horror. (We did, too.)

Finally, we teach them how to die. We don't set out to, but, make no mistake, they're watching and learning as they did when they were children. And just as they saw us take a drink or return that extra quarter to the check-out clerk, just as they accompanied us to the voting booth or the church and hung out with our diverse friends, so, unaware, they're watching and learning now. What are we teaching?

Mark, the brilliant graduate student dying of a brain tumor, conveyed to us all the kindness and consideration of which he was still capable; he showed us that, in death, he was becoming *more* of who he was; he taught us that we need not feel guilty, that we did well by him and by ourselves; he helped us honor the fact that, finally, we were facing our own death in his.

Sarah taught her daughter a bitterer lesson, the painful consequences of disowning her mother. She believes her daughter will never reject anyone again.

OTHER LESSONS WE TEACH

Handling Fear: We show those around us that even when we are terrified we still manage to carry on, that we survive our fears (until we don't), and also perhaps that we are not as afraid as we once were. If our lesser fear is based on glimpses of a future life or a willingness to be done with the pain of the present one, we communicate that. We are honest and forthright; if we conceal, those we love imagine the worst.

"Musts": We teach that there are fewer of these "musts" and "shoulds" than we thought, just as a busy parent finds that the cleaning doesn't need doing so often. We encourage those we love to honor their own longings as they honor those of others; to live more richly in the present. We help them rejoice in the moment. Oddly, such emotions as gratitude and joy in prayerfulness may heal. Thus, even if we don't cure ourselves, we may help *heal* ourselves and those we love.[1]

Last Crusades: The fact that we are dying does not rob us of opportunities to better our own lives and the lives of others. For Sue Rodriguez in Canada, the cause was aid-in-dying; for writer Paul

Monette and others afflicted with AIDS, it was compassion, honesty, openness, and insistence on medical progress; for Gilda Radner, it was humor and help for those afflicted like herself; for Helen, the feminist, it was continuation of a cause she believed in.

Life Review: We teach our children what our life was like and help them understand its meaning, so they can treasure it as part of their own.

Belief in Afterlife: If we believe in an afterlife, we share this with them. Even though they may reject our credulity as a pitiful defense against the horrible thing that is happening to us, our faith will help them when we are gone, and also when their own time comes.

In our last days, some of us are fortunate enough to "leave" our bodies, travel to "another place," and then return. We have near-death experiences, or enjoy visits by entities from the other side who are ready to guide us over. Accounts of such altered states are common. They are "experiences," and, like all others, not necessarily "true" in the sense of literal reality, but they *happen* to us. Later I will discuss them in detail, but suffice it now to suggest that you communicate them to those at your bedside. They will choose to believe or not, but they cannot help but take comfort in your own belief.

Impermanence: We teach them that everything is in transition, nothing lasts. They may know it with their minds; we help them know it in their hearts. "This, too, shall pass" can be said of sorrow, but must be said as well of joy. We encourage them to love in the present, and not wait for death.

Forgiveness: By our examples of forgiving others and ourselves—if this is our decision—we teach them to forgive or ask forgiveness *before* the end. Why live in guilt?

Ritual: If we devise a ritual for our dying, we encourage them to do the same, thus making their passing easier. Likewise, we teach them to make their practical arrangements well in advance.

Death as the Final Stage of Development: While few of us actually look forward to our death, there are myriad rewards, as we have seen. Growth and development do not end until the last breath. Our children may think they are grown at fifteen, twenty-one, thirty, forty, and even sixty-five. But there is always more—more knowledge to assimilate, more understanding of others to enrich our lives, more startling revelation.

Some people assume that dying is a waste of time. When we are closer to death we may see our *lives* as wasted and our *dying* as profound. Also, it seems unwise to assume that we end with death. We don't *know* that.

Elisabeth Kübler-Ross is eloquent on her discovery of how much the dying have to teach us.[2] Whether from compassion, a yearning for surcease of fear, or a desire to know, others listen. Dying may indeed bring us renewed reflection and wisdom that we can share (although it may not), such as being present in the here and now. You have nowhere else to go! They do, but you may make them stop awhile.

Not long ago I received a card from a dear, very practical psychologist friend of many years. His mother had died. I recalled how ambivalent about her he had been, how his face had clouded when he spoke of her. Naturally, I expected that "unfinished business" would have made her dying an ordeal for him. Instead he wrote, "I was fortunate to be with her during her final days. I really don't know what 'transcendent' means, but I went through it—beauty, pain, love, hope, and despair, all wrapped up together. Dying is so fundamentally a spiritual experience—such growth!" His mother's death was her last, most valuable, teaching to him, through which he grew far beyond the friend I had known.[3]

It may seem a lot to ask that, in our final hours, we remain aware of how our teaching continues. For those we love, we perform a service the results of which we will not live to see.

Some of your teaching is a simple by-product of your journey. But others may ask questions and hang on your reply. Volunteer to teach, by all means, but do not let it be another demand on you, especially if it feels voyeuristic.

COMPELLING OTHERS TO LOVE AND CARE

As we've seen, your dying may seem a waste of time since it doesn't *produce* anything. Yet the preservation of your life by the medical staff is not a waste of *their* time. *Your* time is now valueless and irrelevant. There's no place you have to go, no one you have to see. They keep you waiting with impunity. But *their* time is still important, because it extends your valueless life. How can that be? This is one of the greatest contradictions in our schizophrenic view of life and death. Remember, for their time and life to be of value, yours must be as well. You are their livelihood. Without you, what would they do?

You are of value not only to the medical establishment but also to the health-care industries—products, medical drugs, and insurance.

But there is another reason that you are invaluable to health professionals, family members, friends, and volunteers: *by the very nature of your helplessness, you teach them caring.* You compel them to the hard work of kindness and compassion. You teach them accountability, lest they abandon you. If by chance they do—if they isolate you and leave you alone in your final agony and do not do all in their power to ease it—then you teach them the terrible wrong of it. You offer yourself up as an admittedly unwilling sacrifice, a series of spiritual lessons. You allow them an opportunity to work out, through caring for you (or not), the growth of their very souls—if you believe in souls. You bequeath to them a heroism that they cannot obtain in any other way.

Who, then, is more valuable than you are?

In times of grief or crisis, we are accustomed to ask, "What am I supposed to learn from this experience?" It's an appropriate question, and often the answers are illuminating, as was the answer Ruby received when she employed the gestalt therapy technique of talking to her breast.

But another appropriate question to ask is "What am I supposed to teach? What are others learning from me in this crisis?" We may teach that our body is an old Columbo overcoat, wrinkled, stained, and finally falling away from the soul. Or that death is the hell reserved for all of us at the end of life. Or that dying (like birth) is tough, but life is worth it. Or that death is a cloak of invisibility over the universe, concealing a gift ultimately of far greater value than earthly life.

TWENTY-THREE

RITUALS AND MYTHS

FOR THE END

OF LIFE

AS a child, you made a wish and blew out your birthday candles in one breath to be sure the wish would come true. Or you and your friends whacked at the suspended piñata until it broke, showering you with candies; squealing with laughter, you scrambled after them under the furniture. During Hanukkah's eight days, you spun your dreidls and stood by your parents as they lit a new menorah candle each evening; guests brought "gelt," small bags of gold-foiled chocolate coins. Christmas was a season of midnight mass, decorating the crèche and tree, and opening gifts. At Easter, in your best finery, you hunted for colored eggs while your Jewish friends ate matzohs, gefilte fish, potato latkes, and macaroons at the Passover family seder. Christenings, confirmations, bar and bas mitzvahs, graduations, and weddings brought additional rituals, feasting, and celebration.

In all of the above you were a participant, often a focus of the ceremony. These rituals helped you affirm the spiritual aspect of your existence, and, more significantly, assisted you through a passage from one season of life to the next. But, with your dying, the focus shifts away from you, the "central character," the "hero of the play," to the supporting cast. The rites are funeral, memorial, and wake, all after you are dead; they are for your loved ones, not for you. If you are fortunate, your religion provides you with some brief sacrament. But shouldn't your dying, your last passage from this life to who knows where, be an occasion of ritual celebration and assistance to you, similar to birthdays and graduations?

WOULD YOU LIKE A RITUAL FOR YOUR DYING?

Some people think a dying ritual is a pretty radical idea. One of my friends expects that he'll feel too awful toward the end to be bothered or even concerned with a ritual. You may not believe there's anything to celebrate. How can you predict exactly when to do it, anyway? You may want to think of yourself as living up to the last minute, too frightened to turn down that long passageway even temporarily (you may recover). Even if you are peering down the hall, your caregivers may pull you back; some might be aghast: "Don't even talk that way!" they may say. "You're going to be fine." Rituals may seem unimportant to you, occasions you attend politely for the sake of others, even when they are for you.

On the other hand, you may decide that the various features of a ritual, the lighting of incense and candles, the prayer, the wearing of special clothing perhaps, are appropriate over a fairly long period of time, a comforting way of beginning your existence on a spiritual plane.

How might a dying ritual help you? First, it may ease your passage from one season to another just as other rituals have done; this specific transition is from body to spirit. As with those others, it could be a time of recognition and marking by the people who are important to you. It may help you bridge the chasm from here to there, providing you with a sense of continuity and connection to the greater whole. Many details of dying can by ugly—the decay, the stench—but incense, flowers, music, and the like add beauty to the process. Why not? Ritual gives you company along the way, for as far as those who love you can go. It can provide your loved ones with a promise for their own passing. Finally, it will help you recognize that, just as birthdays and weddings were transitions from one stage to another, so is this one. You *feel* you are headed for the light rather than the void.

The notion of a ritual for dying is not an unusual one. Centuries ago, people died in public, surrounded by relatives, friends, and neighbors. Dying was neither secret nor shameful. Now, new practices are unfolding. The tragic advent of AIDS has challenged families and friends to endow the lives and premature deaths of young men and women with meaning in the form of simple new ceremonies including candle-lighting, readings, flowers, and music. While these are funeral practices as well, the crucial difference is that these rituals are performed while the dying person is *still alive*, an active participant in both their planning and their execution. Typically, since no one can predict the exact day of death, rituals may take place over a number of days, weeks, or even months for some practices such as the wearing of special jewelry.

PLANNING A RITUAL FOR YOUR DYING

You may find it helpful to start the planning by answering the following questions:

- Will you include others, or is this something that, like praying or a personal retreat, you'd rather do alone?
- If you do include others, who will they be? Family members? Friends? A healing circle? All who enter your room?
- Will your ritual take place each day, over a number of days or weeks, or will you restrict it to one?
- How will you ask others to help? Will you do it directly yourself? Ask a few to inform the rest? Send out announcements?
- Will you plan your dying ritual by yourself, or will you form a "committee" to help?
- Between daily rituals, if you choose them, will you put away all items, or leave them out, perhaps on a little "altar" table?
- How long will your ritual be? Twenty minutes? Half an hour? Your physical condition may interrupt; be flexible.

The following are guidelines to possible ritual features for both your dying and your funeral or memorial service.[1] They are decisions you will want to make either alone or with other participants. You may want to begin when you are still feeling comparatively well, as you do with advance directives. Many of the suggestions require some experimenting, comparing types of incense and pieces of music, for example. If you recover, you can always save your plans for the future.

1. Incense? What scent? Sandalwood? Frangipani? If you're unsure, ask a friend to let you smell samples.
2. Music? Which piece or pieces? Cassette? CD? Do you want to play opera one day and jazz the next? For how long? All twenty minutes? Will everyone sit quietly and listen, or will it be background to the rest of the proceedings?
3. Stories? At your funeral, friends tell stories about you. Wouldn't it be nice if they did so now? If you're strong enough, you can reciprocate, enriching your relationships.
4. Eulogy? You may be able to float above your whole funeral proceedings and hear them, but you can't be sure. Hear them now! Your friends can think of it as a rehearsal.
5. Live music? Do you have a friend with a guitar whom you'd like to invite to play a song or two? (Feel free to *disinvite* some brash volunteer, or ask your advocate to do so for you. A simple "She prefers the piano" or "She prefers Gilbert and Sullivan"—whatever the volunteer doesn't play—should do it.)
6. Drumming or chanting? They may actually change your brain waves, making it easier to enter an alternate reality.[2] You can create your own drum or mantra.[3]
7. Poems? Poems you choose, to be read by friends and family? Or should each bring a favorite? (Limit the length.)
8. Bestowal of possessions? Now might be a nice time if you plan to give favorite things away. Even small gifts, such as a book from your personal library or a piece of costume jewelry, are meaningful.
9. Flowers? Probably many people are sending or bringing them, but if you long for lilacs or forsythia, ask.

10. Special clothing? Are there special gowns, shirts, or jewelry you'd like to wear? One woman I knew in Santa Cruz went about in her wheelchair in a long white gown and a rosary of beads she'd fashioned herself, different kinds and colors for different major events and people in her life.[4]

11. Touch? The dying are touch-starved. Everyone's afraid of catching "it," no matter how noncontagious it is. Or they fear transmitting their own germs. Suggest kinds of touch: embraces, kisses, hugs, strokes, massages, hand-holding.

12. Prayers? They not only comfort, they *heal,* if not in this life, into the next; if not the body, the soul. Ask your friends to form a prayer circle around you and pray for you and for each other as well.[5] You will probably all feel better.

13. Imagery? Those attending you in your last hours can help with whatever imagery you'd like to "die into." This might be taped from a previous session with a therapist or facilitator, or it might be something you and your caregiver have practiced. Or you might want to be told to "let go" or "go to the light."

14. Family rituals? Think of your last moments as baptism into a new life, and use meaningful aspects of other family rituals. Blow out the candles on your final birthday as a symbol of this life going out; light one for your birth into another. Sing special songs together. If you are too weak, ask others to do so.

15. Tales of the dead? If your family hands down inspirational stories of how members have died, retell them now.

Many cultures have myths of dying, handed down as stories from parent to child. The dying person in those cultures feels that she *knows* what will happen next (and that something *will* happen)—a canoe trip down the river, a crossing. She even takes along precious personal belongings so she will have them in the next world.

But our culture is fragmented, and while some segments may carry on their own religious traditions, as a whole we do not have myths to assist us through the passage, so it is reasonable to devise our own. Family stories of dying may help us do this.

Remember that a dying ritual is a way of transforming a physical event into a spiritual one.

CREATING YOUR MYTH

Your ritual for dying is one way of mythologizing how your life and death connect, the heroism you show, and the gifts you may bestow. According to Joseph Campbell, a myth is the story of a hero who "ventures forth from the world of common day into a region of supernatural wonder: fabulous forces are there encountered and a decisive victory is won: the hero comes back from this mysterious adventure with the power to bestow boons on his fellow man."[6] Great religious leaders such as the Buddha, Jesus, Lao-tse, Mohammed, and Zoroaster accomplished such missions; so did Native American shamans and mythological Greek and Roman heroes like Hercules. Heroes descend into darkness and death, fight evil in many guises, and return with "light" for their communities.[7] The entire cycle is one of birth (separation from the eternal soul), life (initiation into knowledge), death (return to God and love), and rebirth.

Your personal myth is the story you tell yourself and others of how you lived your life and what it means. How do you create it? You have already, in part. When you tell a new friend how your marriage broke up, or how you ran the marathon (wonderful metaphor!), you are mythologizing.

Are you happy with your myth? Is it too much victim and not enough growth? Does it ring true? Sometimes our myth is defensive—to explain or justify mistakes. Now is the time to perfect it. What darkness in your life have you gone down into and traveled through? What have you brought back for your family, community, or world? Now in the "valley of the shadow of death," what battles do you fight? What return do you look forward to?

There are several major methods of myth creation. You can do it in your mind alone, write it out in a journal or type it on a computer, tape it, record it in a scrapbook or photo album, or simply tell it to a trusted friend. Any one—or all—of the following may help:

1. *The linear method:* Begin with your birth and continue on from there, telling the story of your infancy and toddler years, childhood, preteen, teen, youth, middle age, and elder time. If it is written down somewhere, you can always add, delete, or cor-

rect. You decide what to include and what to omit. Remember to describe your feelings, reactions, choices, and decisions. Your myth is not just a set of facts.

2. *The highlight method:* Describe one important person or event in your life. How did he or she affect you, for good or ill? Where and how were you wounded? Why? How did you heal? Now you move on to other important people and incidents.

3. *The summary metaphor method:* You can create a far briefer and simpler myth. Choose the one(s) truest to you.

   - "I am a person who has always _____. Even during my toughest times, when _____. I had a lot of friends, who _____. And some enemies, who _____. To sum it all up, _____."
   - "My life has been a journey _____." Was it along a road? Through a town? Did it begin in a special place? End in one? Are you still on it? Did you/Do you ride, walk, or fly?
   - "I followed the rainbow, looking for that pot of gold. My special difficulties have been _____. The mileposts were _____. There were people along the way who _____. Now I'm at the top, and my view is of _____."
   - "I was inspired by (a movie, novel, play, or biography, or a person such as Mother Teresa, E.T., or *Field of Dreams*). I felt like the hero (or other character). This story is heroic to me because _____. In some ways, I and my life have been like them because _____."
   - "All my life I've been a warrior fighting for _____."
   - "My life has been a garden in which I cultivated _____."

   Was there a darkness in your life that you traveled through? A great loss you transcended? Did you learn something special and bring it back as a gift to others? What was that?

   Ask a friend to paint a rainbow, mandala, or talisman representing your myth.

4. *The recipe method:* Related to the others, you may want to include some or all of the following in your myth:

- Important places. What did they say or mean to you?
- Homes.
- Sanctuaries.
- Sacred or dearly loved spaces.
- Enemies. How did they destroy you? How did you rise from your own ashes like the phoenix and become immortal?
- Lovers. How did they hurt you? Make you grow? Heal you?
- Work. How was the unmeaningful valuable? How did the best create you?
- Family. What were your deepest sorrows? How did you transcend them? What have been your deepest sources of joy?
- Money. What have been the seasons of poverty and wealth?
- Sex. What was the best, and what was the worst?
- Family rituals. Were birthdays and other holidays sources of tension or joy? What did they say to you about your place in the family? How did this change?

You've always had a myth, although it was mainly unconscious. And you've usually acted in accordance with it. If you believe you are the black sheep of the family, your actions may be quite different from what they would be if you feel you were the hero. Thus, your myth is self-perpetuating. Are you happy with it? Do you want to change it?

What story do you want people to tell about you? Do you think they'll tell your true story, or a different one?

In families, particularly, stories get told about each other, perpetuated until the truth is lost and fiction replaces it. Sometimes these story changes are benign; Bill's suggestion at the company board meeting resulted in an invitation to the president's office, a grand success that grew in the retelling.

Sometimes the *family* myth of who you are can be cruelly different from your own. This happens because if your own myth were acknowledged, it might contradict the personal myths that other family members cherish. They might have to revise. So the extent to which you can or cannot preserve your own myth within your family is a matter of your status within it, your power. If you have less power, your myth and identity are transformed.

For example, Sarah's daughter has, without intending to (and with the subtle collusion of her father—Sarah's remarried ex), created an exaggerated and twisted version of Sarah's myth over the years, even filling in parts of it herself, until disowning Sarah became a reasonable response to the person they made, rather than a daughter's ingratitude. Since Sarah isn't even on the scene and is also poor, she has little power. This is typical of a dysfunctional family; individual members will preserve their own personal myths at the expense of the myths of others. The entire *family* myth changes. And may the best myth win!

If you are in this position, there are several ways to rehabilitate your myth:

1. Leave a record of it with a trusted family member or friend.
2. Request family counseling to work out your myths so that you don't metaphorically destroy each other.
3. Make sure your friends know your true myth.
4. Challenge family members individually, if you have the energy.
5. Recognize false myths as part of the "life isn't fair" syndrome; if your conscience is reasonably clear, you, and no one else, are the author of your journey.
6. Order your own epitaph and thus "set in stone" your version of your own myth: "A talented artist" or "A loving father."
7. If you are religiously or spiritually inclined, leave your myth to God, in Whom all truth resides.

TWENTY-FOUR

BELIEF IN

AN AFTERLIFE

IS A CHOICE

AS a Vietnam medic, Bill saw too much carnage strewn about the killing fields to believe in an afterlife. Stomachs eviscerated, arms and legs blown off, eyes rolled back, breath stopped—no souls rising. Peg argues, "It would be so much easier for you if you believed. Look at the great religions, the people who came back." "Their imagination!" he scoffs. "I'm not going to say I believe when I don't. I'd be selling out." Besides, it's not manly; it's cowardly, in fact, he might add. Heroes go to their deaths whether from war or ALS, without the comfort of false hope.

Marian's daughter Carrie bought her Raymond Moody's *Life After Death*, a physician's account of patients' near-death experiences (NDEs).[1] Marian, in the last stages of kidney disease, refuses to read it. She's afraid she'll go to hell for all she's done, most of which Carrie doesn't know. She abused her own wheelchair-bound mother during that last dying year—"tit for tat," Marian claimed—twisting a wrist, smearing oozed white cereal over her face, in her eyes, leaving her in her own stench. Then there were more distant sins: stepping out on her husband, beating Carrie. Nor did she confess half of what she'd done to her priest, although she accepted absolution readily enough. No, an afterlife was not in Marian's best interest.

As Agnes's heart fails, she begins to believe in an afterlife. She didn't always. One morning out of the blue she awakened breathless, and she knew. It was a grace. She hadn't even prayed.

Charles often smells his dead wife's rose perfume in the living room, and a few months after she died, the radio suddenly flicked on one night with her favorite tune, "Anniversary Waltz." He isn't fool enough to tell anyone about these experiences. He hugs them to himself as treasures. His son thinks he's irrational at times, and wants him to come live with his family during these last Parkinson's years: "It's not good for you to be alone. Davy'd love having you around." "I'm not alone," Charles says. "I'm not afraid. Death isn't the end," he adds, responding to his son's unspoken fears. His son gives him a pitying look. Not to fear death is simply additional proof of his father's failing mind.

Jeff, dying of AIDS at thirty-two, wants to believe. An afterlife would make up for the unfair brevity of this one. But the faith and comfort of his friends seem mindless. Safer by far to have a definite negative answer rather than live on within confusing realms of possibility.

Is your attitude toward an afterlife like Bill's, Marian's, Agnes's, Charles's, or Jeff's? This chapter helps you decide. We'll examine evidence for and against an afterlife, then show how each belief is a choice that you can make, with pros and cons.

THE EVIDENCE AGAINST AN AFTERLIFE

Bill's argument against the possibility that we die into another existence is by far the most persuasive. We see with our own eyes that a body is dead. No movement or sound, no slight rise and fall of breath. The machines show us no movement inside, either, no electrical activity in the brain, no twitching nerves or beating heart. The skin grows cold to the touch and grays without coursing blood beneath it, limbs stiffen, blood congeals in pools at the body's lowest gravitational points. Odors of gaseous body bloat and decay may assail us.

With a surgeon's razor skill, Sherwin Nuland details how the various body systems break down, depending on the disease.[2] It is all so undeniable. As children, we see it in our pets, and as adults, in those we love. Benignly, we're oblivious to much of it in ourselves, unless we hold up a constant mirror, but our loved ones see, and we can imagine. Our minds blur over final decay until only the bones of all our gifts and loves remain. The "I" is not there to watch or feel it.

But the argument for our sensory evidence—everything dies and decays, and that's that—has a more powerful corollary. It is the *mind* that processes this sensory information, and science shows us that the mind is a function of the *physical* brain. Scientists can stimulate different sectors of the brain to elicit anger, pleasure, and memory, and even trigger out-of-body experiences! For example, emotions are partly based in the amygdala region, and when this goes, so do the emotions. In the 1940s and 1950s, prefrontal lobotomies eliminated anger in patients but also made them different people. The anencephalic infant receives the same sensory stimuli as other babies but cannot process them. Further still, hormones (glandular secretions) such as melatonin and serotonin, as well as chemical agents such as lithium and antidepressants, regulate emotions and even thought processes. Although therapy can modify them, too, it may do so by affecting the biochemical systems. Finally, our sense of spirit or soul may be a form of (body-based) emotion, merely a dyspepsia of the mind.

It's all very mechanistic cause and effect, concrete and physical. We're urged not to "romanticize" the illness and the breakdown of these systems that leads to death, not to assign meaning, or shroud it with poetry, or pretend dignity. (I'm not sure why. Where's the harm?)

The evidence of our senses over long years of experience, validated by scientific research, tells us that dead is dead.

THE EVIDENCE FOR AN AFTERLIFE

Such sensory evidence is too restrictive for the great religions of the world. Faith is the bedrock on which an afterlife is built. We are adjured to believe in the nonsensory. But we're given a little help—the sensory experiences of those who have gone before us, enshrined in religious works such as the Bible, the Koran, the Bhagavadgita, the Torah, the Tibetan Book of the Dead, as well as the oral traditions of African and Native American societies. The ancients heard the voice in the burning bush, met Raven or Coyote on the forest path, witnessed the risen Jesus. These experiences constitute evidence from sensory experiences once removed! And they tell us that we rise from the dead, or that we must reincarnate, or that the land of the dead lies beyond the river Styx, across which Charon ferries us.

There is, however, other evidence for the possibility that something exists beyond the physical (which itself diffuses into atoms, waves, and electricity), and therefore that we might continue after life. Oddly, it arises from the very senses that tell us death is the end; most of us experience but discard this evidence, or push it to the backs of our minds, or pass it on only to family members from generation to generation, and to close friends who will not use it against us. A multitude of "bizarre," "inexplicable" physical manifestations do not conform to the rules of physics, gravity, and other scientific principles, so we reject them. The wilder the experiences, the more secretive we are. They are beyond the senses, or extrasensory, in whole or in part.

The following could be construed as evidence for life beyond the physical:

1. *The Experiences of the Bereaved:* Charlie's vision of his dead wife is typical. The appearance of the dead to the living, in reality or in dreams, is so common that psychiatrists and psychologists accept it as normal. According to a Gallup poll in 1987, 15 percent of us claim to have seen ghosts. The clock that stopped "never to run again, when the old man died" is an old, well-loved song. The dead relative who appears in a dream to divulge the whereabouts of missing papers and jew-

elry is a banality. We tell ourselves that, at some level, the dreamer really knew where the items were. Recently, a friend related that many of her mother's electrical appliances had broken down since her father died a month ago, and that the electrically operated garage door keeps opening and shutting of its own accord. I've heard innumerable such stories. Supposedly, because the dead are on another plane, they can communicate only by influencing electricity. Another explanation is that this is all poltergeist phenomena, generated by the upset mind of the survivor, but then, that's unscientific, too.

2. *Angel Visits:* People used to ask why in biblical times so many people saw angels but almost no one does today. That's changed. Angels are all the rage; 32 percent of us claim to have seen them or felt their presence, and 50 percent believe in them.[3] I'll admit to some skepticism here. I think some of these angel-viewers have overactive imaginations, some have a pathological craving for attention, and a few are out-and-out liars. But all 32 percent? Folie à millions? I don't think so. More people are simply admitting they have seen them, and others are paying attention. Those who've told me personally about their angel(s) are not exhibitionists; some experienced them before their popularity; angel-viewers are careful to confide only in those they trust, and they're sane enough to avoid giving the appearance of being nuts—especially to a psychologist!

3. *Precognitive Dreams:* While 24 percent of us believe in precognition, precognitive dreams are usually dismissed as unproven unless the dreamer tells a friend *before* the event.[4] The fortune-telling field is so rife with fraud that we don't believe anyone or anything—unless we ourselves had the dream, wrote it down, showed it to a friend, and then disbelievingly watched it come true.

4. *Déjà vu:* Meaning "already seen," this is the most common extrasensory experience of all, a feeling of familiarity with a place you've never before visited, for example. Scientists have all kinds of explanations for these memory tricks, but let's be logical: If you've never even been in this part of the world,

how did you know about the tulip tree hanging over a stone bench behind the house?

5. *Clairvoyance and Clairaudience:* We're schizophrenic in our judgments here. If it's a saint or a group of peasant children hearing voices or seeing visions, we say they're holy. Otherwise, they're psychotic. Joan of Arc was a saint. Luckily for her there were no psychiatrists around; unluckily for her, there were priests who branded her a heretic; history is kinder. Hardened police detectives claim that psychics solve tough murder cases for them. What are we to make of that? Were you on the scene when the psychic "saw" two men with distinctive body features beating a third to death? Did she fool the detective? Perhaps she only "intuited" one logical detail, based on her research in local newspapers, and it got expanded to a dozen during successive retellings. Or are we reaching?

6. *Other Unexplained Phenomena:* What about the miracles at Lourdes? Were they all misdiagnosed or psychosomatic? What about chance-in-a-billion synchronicities (that coincidentally increase when you pay attention to them)? You run into someone you haven't seen in years, the only person who can answer a vital question. What about vision quests? Past-life regressions? Earth lights and Marian visions? Oceanic and other mystical experiences? Healing by touch? Bigfoot and the Loch Ness monster? Witches? What about satanic possession, UFO abductions, and other "experienced anomalous traumas" such as kundalini? For that matter, what about my mother? She knows who's calling before she picks up the phone. When I was a child, I saw nothing unusual in dialing home unexpectedly in the middle of a school day and my mother answering with alarm, "Yes, honey, what is it?" ("Banal," you say. "Corny." But that's the point!)

Very likely, you can fill in your own unusual experiences. One man told me that, as a child, he saw himself grown up and in a canoe with a young boy—who later was born his son.

If we restrict "reality" to our physical, sensory experience, well and good. But then, it's only fair and logical to include *all* sensory experiences, those we can explain and those we can't. It's cheating to reject those that don't follow our "rules."

Now, just because we can't figure out how and why something happened doesn't mean it's *extra*sensory. It may just mean we haven't discovered the physical principles. But then, where does physical leave off and extraphysical begin? With atoms? Electromagnetic waves? Energy? Further, even if we all agreed that there is something beyond the physical, that doesn't mean we have souls that live forever. It means only that there's a possibility, and that the great religions may be based on logic—science, even—as well as faith.

A SPECIAL CASE: THE ARGUMENTS FOR AND AGAINST NDES

The near-death experience (NDE) is a special case of extrasensory perception. You are probably familiar with it. In 1975, Dr. Raymond Moody published a group of unusual accounts that his patients had confided in him.[5] He was struck by the commonalities. All of the patients had (1) been declared clinically dead, and (2) reported experiences with many of the following features: a sense of being out-of-body and looking down from above, feelings of warmth and serenity, a tunnel, a buzzing, dead relatives and pets beckoning, a brilliant white light within which some described a being, a life review, a decision to return for some purpose, a positive life revision, transformed values, and lessened fear of death or none at all. Moody's work is enhanced by other credible scientists, Kenneth Ring, Bruce Greyson, Karlis Osis and Erlendur Haraldsson, and Melvin Morse.[6] Tom Harpur, a Canadian Anglican priest, concludes that NDEs have been reported throughout human history, and that they are spontaneous occurrences, convincing people of afterlife, rather than being created to fulfill a need.[7]

A number of other scientists were quick to claim, however, that the NDE was not evidence of an afterlife; rather, it was simply a hallucination, the last gasp of the dying brain, purely biological in origin and nature. The controversy rages.

Before I proceed with an analysis, and in all fairness to you, the reader, I have a confession. There are two kinds of people in this world: those who've had a *genuine* NDE and those who haven't. Those who've had them have had them. No one can convince them otherwise.

Many years ago at the age of twenty, long before the term "NDE" was even coined, and certainly long before they became fashionable, I had one. If NDEs are a garden, mine was a weed. Healing from post-op pneumonia, I awakened one morning unable to breathe, that is, to expand and contract my diaphragm. I popped out of my body and looked down at it on the bed. Aware that I had a choice—to float out over the New York skyline or to get back in—I understood that this was because I was so damaged that I could not fulfill my purpose in this life. So I could stay on as a kind of "freebie" or move out, presumably returning at some other date to do it all again. Thinking of my parents, I decided to stay. The sudden lead weight of my body felt like someone had clapped an X-ray shield around my shoulders. Naturally, I changed my mind and wanted out again. No deal![8]

That's it. No tunnel, no light (that came later, in another "dream-vision," a sort of continuation of this one), no bells and whistles. I did experience the lessened fear, the transformation, and the revised priorities. But the problem is this:

Let us say that, right now, you are lying in your bed reading this book. Perhaps you have a drip in your arm or a catheter, and the TV's on, and trays are banging in the hall. Then again, maybe you're reading this over a sandwich at work, or on the redwood bench outside your RV in a national park.

Now, suppose a scientist walks up to you and informs you that you're hallucinating. Right now! Do you believe her? Of course not. No one is going to tell you, or me, that we're not where we are, doing what we're doing. If we believed her, we'd have to question all our other experiences as well. An NDE is every bit as real as other life events, and no one can tell NDEers that we're hallucinating.

Susan Blackmore, a British scientist, has explored NDEs.[9] She doesn't deny they happen; they are not, however, proof of afterlife or even of being out-of-body. Rather, all human brains go through similar processes as they shut down. Similarity in people of different countries and religions is reasonable because the phenomenon is biological.

Blackmore suggests that the characteristics of the NDE can be explained by brain physiology. The "tunnel" and "light" form because the center of the visual cortex has many more cells than the areas farther out. Oxygen deprivation resulting from the dying process would free the cells from their normal regulation. They could start firing randomly. Light from the many cells in the center fading to the dark from the few cells on the sides might resemble a tunnel.

I find this explanation truly extraordinary. Here we have spent our entire lives without the capacity to see directly into our bodies (without X rays), but at the very end of our lives, we can suddenly see our brain cells going off in a spectacular fireworks display, a "Fantastic Voyage" through our own heads.[10] Mind you, we are not talking about dreams, thoughts, feelings, and fantasies, all (supposedly) encoded in different parts of the brain. We're talking about actual physiological and electrochemical processes within the brain! Why we don't see our blood coursing through our veins (maybe we could represent it as the River Styx) remains unexplained.

Dr. Blackmore and other researchers have more persuasive explanations for the warmth, beauty, and joy NDEers report: they're due to natural opiates or endorphins in the brain. That is a reasonable theory until you recall that these same opiates have worked overtime in many patients for months already, all without noticeable NDEs. Perhaps they increase at death as at no other time—a peculiarly nonadaptive mechanism. One would think such increases would occur when there was still a chance of preserving life by lessening pain. Perhaps nature is kind at the end.

The researchers add that endorphins can cause seizures in the temporal lobes, and that seizures can stimulate memories, hallucinations, and out-of-body experiences (OOBEs). Years ago, I witnessed a demonstration of such temporal-lobe stimulation, the subject reporting an OOBE. The scientist argued that he'd proved the NDE was merely a physiological phenomenon. But the subject was hardly convincing. He was out of his body—but that was it. OOBEs are not NDEs. NDEs are much more. People who meditate or take such drugs as LSD or mescaline report OOBEs, floating above the body without any of the other NDE aspects such as the choice, the sense of purpose, the light, the life review, and transformation. Finally, even though stimulation of the temporal lobe can produce OOBEs, that does not prove the OOBE is a *physical* phenomenon. It may be that the temporal lobes are the seat of the spirit's attachment to the body, and that such stimulation facilitates their separation. In fact, Kenneth Ring theorizes that the temporal lobes may be sixth-sense organs (possibly sensitized by childhood trauma) that can detect alternate realities.[11]

Blackmore reminds us that stimulation of the temporal lobes induces memories, suggesting that a life review might be a logical final memory. But why would a life review be more logical than, say, recollection of a wedding scene?

There are, of course, the unexplained phenomena of NDEs, particularly among those who report, for example, seeing objects on high shelves of emergency rooms, objects they couldn't have seen from their beds; or hearing conversations in the halls; or even watching specific activities by relatives in their homes, later confirmed. Scientists who favor the physiological nonextrasensory explanations of NDEs tend to lump these into exaggerations, rumors, delusions, wishful thinking, and outright lies. Here I must agree to an extent. Attempts to track down an NDE in a blind person have failed.[12] As with the current rage for angels, I think misperceptions and misstatements abound, and personal knowledge leads me to believe that at least one case is outright fraud. But are *all* of them delusions and lies?

IS A RADICAL NEW HUMAN CONSCIOUSNESS EVOLVING?

Coincidence is God's way of remaining anonymous.

—BERNIE SIEGEL, M.D.[13]

Some thinkers offer provocative belief in a new evolution of human consciousness based on the evidence above. Kenneth Ring believes NDEs show that humanity is attaining a "higher level of spiritual awareness and physical functioning."[14] Neuroscientists are leaving the door open to the possibility that alternate realities are realms that "truly exist outside time and space," and are not fantasies. In his book *The Future of the Body*, Michael Murphy offers a brilliant compilation of evidence from history. He cites athletic feats, the paranormal, psychosomatic abilities, stigmata, multiple personality, placebos, spiritual healing, hypnosis, biofeedback, imagery, bodily disciplines, and martial arts, as well as creative individuals, religious adepts, saints, and mystics. Murphy suggests that we are in a process of evolution beyond what we think of as our limits, and, further, that we may continue this development beyond bodily death, that transformation of consciousness is the next evolutionary step.[15] Another writer terms this transformation "a new paradigm of reality," an "alternate worldview, with its . . . alternate realities, spirits, mystical journeying, and ideas of the unity of all things."[16] In this context, still another suggests that true healing "always involves a death and transformation of some aspect of the person," that is, a hero's journey, and that death can be a healing.[17]

If any or all of the above is so, then death is truly life-saving!

HOW DO YOU DECIDE IF THERE IS AN AFTERLIFE?

We have reviewed *logical* and compelling evidence on both sides of the question. Neither side can prove the other is wrong, nor do we expect such proof in our lifetimes. Therefore, belief in an afterlife is a *choice* that we make, one way or the other. Like Bill and Marian, we may choose not to believe for powerful reasons. Like Peg, who believes the NDE evidence, and Charles, who senses another presence, and Agnes, who is "graced," we may look to an afterlife. Like Jeff, we may struggle. According to our own preferences, we give more weight to one possibility or the other.

Many years ago, James Pike, beloved and brilliant Episcopalian dean of St. John's Cathedral in New York City (he was originally trained as a lawyer), was speaking to a group of Columbia University students about faith. He said something like this: We have no scientific proof that smoking causes cancer. We only have evidence pointing in that direction. So, when you have a lot of evidence but you don't have the final proof, *a leap of faith is logical*. Considering all the evidence pro and con, as well as your own intuition and desire, a leap of faith regarding existence of an afterlife may be a next *logical* step.

As with so many life issues, you will be most comfortable if you choose a position and stick with it.

Benjamin Franklin declared his own choice in his epitaph:[18]

The body of
Benjamin Franklin, Printer
(Like the cover of an old book,
Its contents worn out
And stript of its lettering and gilding)
Lies here, food for worms!
Yet the work itself shall not be lost,
For it will, as he believed, appear once more
In a new and more beautiful edition
Corrected and amended
By the Author

TWENTY-FIVE

PLANNING YOUR

ETERNAL FUTURE

I hope with all my heart there will be painting in heaven.

— CAMILLE COROT

WHEN you die, will cherubs with strategically draped body-parts fly your soul to heaven? Quill in hand, will white-bearded St. Peter check off your name in his big fat Akashic Record? As the pearly gates swing wide to streets of gold, will long-dead loved ones in rainbow gowns beckon? Will you spend eternity on a fluffy cloud, playing your harp—not your guitar, not your kettle drums, not even your piano—to the voices of angelic choirs?

Even the negative visions of afterlife are static. Like Tantalus, you snatch at a bunch of grapes that moves forever beyond your reach, or, like Sisyphus, you roll a boulder uphill only to have it roll back just as it reaches the top. You haunt the house of your childhood, take possession of another's body, or scream forever in hellfires. At the blast of a trumpet, you, and all who have ever lived, are called forth from the blackness of your graves and, your bodies once more whole, you submit to the Last Judgment. Alternatively, to pay a karmic debt, you reincarnate in a strange land as a baby—or a toad.

Your own concept of afterlife may take any of these forms. But then what?

Just as you have a choice to believe that an afterlife exists, you also have some foreknowledge of its nature, and even some control. Hard to believe? The scenarios above are other people's, not necessarily either your own or objective truth.

Seventy-one percent of us believe in an afterlife and 16 percent do not. Presumably, 13 percent are unsure.[1] This means that almost three quarters of us have a future to plan. Isn't it amazing that most of us don't think to do so? We may be under the mistaken impression that we can't, but simple logic tells us that, if we *do* continue, we have choices and decisions to make.

Unless you're the spontaneous type, you wouldn't be caught dead without a plan.

Let's first review the advantages of futurelessness for the 16 percent of you headed in that direction, then prepare for the future of those who continue. Even financial and retirement planners among us will agree that this is wise.

THE PAST AS PRISON:
DEATH AS YOUR "GET-OUT-OF-JAIL-FREE" CARD

Those of you who don't believe in life after death can look forward (at least, temporarily) to the following advantages:

1. You won't have to worry about dying again.
2. Psychotic bosses, unfaithful lovers, treacherous friends, wars, earthquakes, traffic jams, Republicans, and panhandlers are other people's worries, not yours.
3. You're no longer a prisoner of appetites; food leaves you cold, and as for alcohol, you're on the wagon.
4. There's no need to control, achieve, impose order, make friends, and lead the pack (it's going nowhere).
5. Memories of past disaster that made you too timid to try paragliding no longer constrain you.
6. You have no regrets. Death is a purgative, cleansing you of all guilt and failure, a kind of high-colonic. The on-living may remember, but you don't, and they can't remind you.

7. You're beyond the reach of your enemies. Living well may be the best revenge, but dying's better.

8. The meaning of life, revealed to your on-living brothers and sisters, is irrelevant.

9. True, you'll never reunite with those you love, but you won't know it. This brings tears now, but the dead don't cry.

10. Dying releases you from the need to earn a living, be socially useful, and fight for or against anything. So you might as well start living your death right now.

11. You have no need to read the rest of this book.

Of course, you realize that denying afterlife can be as great an illusion as affirming it. But that's your own business.

I leave you with what I believe to be the most eloquent, authentic statement for the alternative to an afterlife that I have seen. Susan Blackmore, the anti-NDEer writes, "We are biological organisms, evolved in fascinating ways for no purpose at all and with no end in any mind. We are simply here and this is how it is. I have no self and 'I' own nothing. There is no one to die. There is just this moment, and now this and now this."[2]

Now to those of you who plan to continue.

WHAT WILL YOUR LIFE AFTER DEATH BE LIKE? AN EXERCISE

Your first reasonable assumption is that life after death has a purpose. If your present life does, you may logically conclude that it does not stop dead unless you do.

Keeping this in mind, answer the following questions. You already know most of the answers. You just don't know you do.

1. When you die, what relatives and friends will greet you on the other side? List those you hope to see. Perhaps there is someone you dread?

2. After you reunite, is there something they want to show you?

What might it be? Might there be gardens, a library, a commune, a musical group, other worlds? Describe them. Why are they showing you these?

3. If you meet a Being of Light or angelic presences, who are they? What is their message? Is it similar to those from your loved ones, or do they have something different to say to you and show you?

4. Will you experience the kinds of adjustments to the next world that you did when you were born into this one, that is, new relationships to space, motion, time, and your abilities? Will you have to learn to fly and contact the "living," or will you just know, perhaps because you've done it before?

5. If you undergo a life review, what are its highlights? What do you rejoice in? What makes you proud? What do you regret? What fills you with shame?

6. You are told that you lived your life on earth to learn certain lessons. What were they? Did you learn them? What is their importance to both yourself and to God or the universe?

7. Will your body be resurrected? How will that work? Will you undergo a Last Judgment? Will all your sins be forgiven? Then what do you think will happen?

8. If there is such a thing as reincarnation, is it something to which you are "sentenced" or is it "permitted"? If you have a choice, will you choose it?

9. If you do, who will you be? What will be the purpose of your new life? Will you be with those you love, or with different persons entirely? What tasks will you return to perform? Will you marry? Have children? What will you change from this life?

10. Are there other lessons you must learn? What are they? Lessons of kindness, assertiveness, appreciation of beauty? Skills, nonviolence, love of earth, truthfulness to yourself, faith—in yourself or something else? How will you learn them? If karma exists, what karma will you need to work through?

11. What are your most troubling faults? What faults will others say you have? What corrections must you make, and how hard

will you have to work at them? Or does your death eliminate the circumstances and therefore the flaws?

12. Some believe we reincarnate into circumstances best for what we need to learn and for contributing what we can. What circumstances would help you learn? Poverty? Fame? A position of social responsibility? Disability? Life in a war-torn country? Life with an abusive parent? What experiences might help? Complete the following: "I don't think I could learn anything from _____."

13. Much of our emotional suffering in dying results from the belief that we cultivate our skills, talents, and abilities to such a height, only to have them end. Why would we choose to believe that? Why suffer needlessly? Will you grow the talents and abilities you've had in this life? Which will you keep?

14. Do you have undeveloped talents? What are they? "I would have been a good (salesman, peacemaker) _____."

15. Will you pursue these abilities? To what extent? How important are they? "In my next life, I am going to (be a jazz pianist, climb Mount McKinley) _____."

    This may arouse regrets you did not know you had, but regrets are also promises.

16. Do you have a soul mate? Did you meet him or her in this life? If not, will you be together when you die? What is he or she like? More spiritually developed than yourself, less, about the same, or on a different plane entirely?

17. Speaking of soul, is there sex on the other side? (I've heard there is.) What will you do after the orgy?

18. Will you seek out persons you have never met? What do you have to offer each other? A soul connection?

19. You finally receive the answers to your life questions: Why did this person die? Why is there loss and pain? Reflect on the most important questions. What answers do you expect to hear? Did anything good come from your trauma? For you or for someone else? Tap in to this wisdom now, instead of later.

20. Finally, if there is a purpose to the universe, what might it be? How have you contributed to it? How can you continue to do so?

You see, we really do know a lot of the answers to life's most pressing questions, if we only ask!

Of course, some will say your afterlife plan is pure fantasy. Tell them that your present life is, too—yours and theirs. After all, our lives, our health, our feelings, our dreams and longings, are all products of our thoughts. Even sexual arousal and satisfaction are functions of the mind. We don't call them unreal, or say they don't exist!

THE ADVANTAGES OF PLANNING YOUR AFTERLIFE

First, you alter your entire perspective on life and death in a positive direction. You see more possibilities for this life as well as for the next one, and, therefore, you have more hope.

Second, where death may have looked like a concrete wall in your future, or a clanging jail cell door, your view of yourself stretches all the way from this life to the next.

Third, your new afterlife perspective helps you solve some of this life's problems. Some seem less serious; others don't have the deadline you thought they had.

Fourth, if you are living, with a long-term life-threatening illness, such as cancer, and if you still have time, it makes sense to begin some of your afterlife now. For example, why not improve activities you plan to continue, and if you're going to start something new, say, switch from government work to travel writing or glass-blowing or something else you know nothing about, why not get started? Why not at least begin the research? You have nothing to lose and joy to gain.

Fifth, you may find renewed self-confidence and a sense of purpose and continuity in your life, giving joy to yourself and comfort to those around you.

Death is the original second chance, the time-out for good or bad behavior. If we can start over on one side of death or the other, having learned from our mistakes, we may continue our personal and universal evolution.

TWENTY-SIX

ENHANCING

YOUR

SPIRITUAL

DEVELOPMENT

I'M not religious, but I'm very spiritual."

This statement, made to me by dozens of people, perfectly expresses what I perceive as a widening rift in the soul of our culture. A recent Gallup poll indicates that 94 percent of Americans believe in God. And yet: "I'm not a practicing Catholic (or Jew or Episcopalian)." "Too much sin and hellfire." "I prefer a more positive, joyous spirit."

Some people attend religious services out of love for God. Religious fervor grips the "born-again." For good Mormons, life revolves around their church. Many people hold fast to the old-fashioned traditional values, trying to revive them in the face of increasing family breakdown, violence, and lost children.

Others view religion as a kind of "afterlife insurance." If there is a God, He'll see them in church and won't send them to the "other place." An occasional twinge of fervor relieves their boredom. Church is an opportunity to socialize with the like-minded, or sit and mull over the direction of their lives. It is good exposure for the kids, a rest while doing something useful, virtuous even, briefer than the vacation they have no time for.

Currently, traditional religion is undergoing a spectacular challenge by alternative religious beliefs and practices that stress transcendent, mystical experience.[1] One would think that ministers, priests, and rabbis would be delighted with the rise of New Age spirituality, signaling as it does a turning away from decades of materialism to matters of the soul. Not quite.

Typical of attacks by traditional religion is that of Douglas Groothuis, writing in the evangelical *Christianity Today*. He singles out Betty Eadie's best-selling *Embraced by the Light* as an example of much that's wrong with the New Age.[2] Eadie's NDE Being of Light is "unbiblical"; her humans are not born to sin; on the contrary, they are basically good. Thus, one needs no confession, Act of Contrition, and holy forgiveness to achieve salvation. In fact, not even repentance is required—a view some Catholics call "cheap grace." You get it for nothing. No pain, all gain. As for evil, according to Groothuis, Eadie maintains that the Jews chose the Holocaust in a precarnate life; Groothuis attacks this as both blaming the victims and whitewashing sin. Finally, Betty Eadie claims to have been embraced by Jesus; while he does not come right out and say so, Groothuis and others imply that this is extraordinarily presumptuous.

Other supporters of traditional church values object to the sudden omnipresence of angels; they are not "personal servants," available at will to do one's bidding. Another concern is that New Agers do not need the mediation of church and trained clergy; they have direct contact with their higher selves, beings of light, angels, and loved ones from the other side. Finally, Groothuis warns against the biblical "demonic deception"; he, along with many other members of the traditional clergy, believes that these New Age "fantasies" are precisely that.

Many of these views have merit; however, the widening rift between traditional and "new" religions may indicate another modern democratic emancipation, entailing the transfer of religious power from the church to the people. For example, traditional religions are largely patriarchal; in the new (much of it old) spirituality, women gain a much larger place for their own special intuitive talents.

Power is always partly economic. Traditional churches may be alarmed at lighter offering plates. A lot of money is being made on NDEs, angels, healings, shamanism, and other trappings of the New Age. The clergy may call such activities "cheap grace," but I have to say there's nothing cheap about the books, seminars, workshops, healings, retreats, and the like. Plenty of money is changing hands. When money is involved, truth is often a casualty.

How can you decide who, of all the New Age gurus, is telling the "truth" as they perceive it, and who is flat-out lying for money? One way is to use your God-given mind. Analyze what is being said. Is the channeler or the medium uttering banalities or saying something meaningful? Another way is to pay attention to your gut reaction, to take what is valuable to you and leave the rest behind, no matter the source. Not long ago, some friends and I attended a talk by one of these speakers. We emerged, silent at first, then abashed and appalled that we'd believed her before. Finally, we were angry that she'd defiled spirituality. Each of us knew separately, then together. There are now plenty of New Age defilers out there, but the fact is that there have been con artists in traditional religions as well. We know that many New Age phenomena are true in our own lives. Our gut reaction will not always discriminate truth from fiction (it didn't for the followers of Jim Jones), but it can caution us.

It is probably too early to tell if New Age spirituality is a fad that will pass, leaving church and temple in their accustomed supremacy over all things religious; or if the New Age represents a fundamental paradigm shift.[3] I suspect that (1) the new sense of immediacy in the spiritual relationship, (2) the long-denied recognition and acceptance of unusual experiences and alternate realities, (3) the resumption by women of their rightful place in spiritual guidance (a move that traditional religions have resisted), (4) the honoring and union of diversity in peoples and religions, (5) the oneness with nature and resulting practical earth stewardship necessary for human survival, (6) the accessibility of the transcendent, the mystical, and the rapturous, (7) the alternative healing that is not necessarily cure, and (8) the infusion into daily life of spiritual meaning and mindfulness will survive. Perhaps they will be incorporated into traditional religions where the mystical has flourished. They will survive because, once found, they are too precious to sacrifice to an institution that, in some respects, suffers from hardening of the arteries.

Reciprocally, the New Age itself must guard against institutionalization, and must remain fluid and permeable enough to grow.

What does all of this mean for you in your dying time? Until now, you may have been too busy for spiritual practice. "When I'm at death's door, then I'll have time to meditate, go to church, read my Bible," many say. Yet this postponement does not make sense. If you plan to perform any physical feat, you train for it. To run a marathon, you run gradually longer distances. To ski, you do conditioning exercises. To act, you rehearse. In the spiritual life, the rules of training and practice also apply. See Michael Murphy's book *The Future of the Body* for some valuable suggestions.[4]

Daily or weekly practice of your faith will stand you in good stead, because you will have a chance to grow with it and inside it. At the end-time, during the roller-coaster ride of strange and sometimes terrifying experiences, your religion will be familiar to you, a rock or a life preserver or a lighthouse beacon, and you will trust it. Your religious or spiritual practice comforts you. It elicits your best, so that you die at your highest. It often promises you an afterlife, whether the bardos of *The Tibetan Book of the Dead* or Christian resurrection or Hindu reincarnation or the NDE of the New Age.

Is there any place where New Age and traditional religions meet? I believe so. They meet in prayer.

PRAYER

More tears are shed over answered prayers than unanswered ones.

—St. Teresa of Avila

I write not from the perspective of a professional theologian or minister; rather, my perspective is that of a lay pray-er who has made the momentous personal discovery that *prayer works!*

In *Healing Words*, Larry Dossey cites a platoon of research studies showing that intercessory prayer (IP) affects bacteria, plants, animals, and humans.[5] For example, prayed-for bacteria and plants grow more rapidly than the nonprayed-for. Many of these studies are double-blind, randomized, and controlled, thus meeting rigorous scientific requirements.

A cardiologist designed a study to find out whether or not IP affected patients in a coronary care unit.[6] The IP group did not know they were being prayed for, nor did those praying know the patients. The pray-ers were church members in prayer circles, and were informed only of the first name and the disease of each patient.

The results? Compared to controls, the IP group needed less intubation or ventilation, fewer antibiotics, and fewer diuretics. They suffered fewer episodes of cardiac arrest, pneumonia, and congestive heart failure.

As Dossey points out, this research is not without flaws.[7] Researchers did not ascertain that the intercessors prayed; there was no measure of how they prayed or how well they did so; relatives of the controls probably prayed for them; and, most important, the IP group did not live any longer. Although the differences between the IP and the control groups were small, prayer did get measurable results. It is possible that, with more practice and training, prayer could become a powerful healing technique. Further, I think it important that there was no measure of *inner* healing in the two groups; symptoms alone were assessed.

With regard to *how* we pray, Dossey makes a major distinction between praying for something specific and an attitude of prayerfulness that includes thankfulness.

Traditional prayer follows religious instruction—a formula recited by rote or a specific request such as the healing of a loved one or even winning the lottery. In contrast, prayerfulness is meditative; you do not tell God what to do, for example, to cure the patient. Rather, you pray for her, focusing on your love and gratitude, asking for her welfare but not with a specific outcome. You have confidence that whatever happens is right. This type of "nondirected" prayer is more effective than "directed" prayer according to the research.

If you pray for a specific outcome, you may not get it. Then you feel that your prayers are either unanswered or denied. I've found, however, that if you examine the results of prayer a little more closely, especially over a period of time, you may be astonished to find answers far different from anything you could have conjured up, but *in the best interests of the person you prayed for.* We don't always know the best outcome. Healing may take a form other than what we expect. Further, your prayer is answered, in that *you* recognize that different result as positive. If you pray to win the lottery, you may receive whatever is *behind* your prayer, for example, the opportunity to travel, be loved, devote your life to art.

A mother I know was enduring the experience most of us recognize as the very worst, the suffering and dying of her child. She prayed for him to be cured, of course, to live a long, good life, and implicit in this was how she imagined his life—attendance at college like his older brother and sister, a job he loved, marriage and children—a whole litany of what parents expect and hope for. His recovery was within God's power, she was sure. Instead, he died; and this was an answer, of course. At first she was bitter. Why should there be divine intervention for other children but not for hers?

The child's suffering, however, was lightened with visions at the end, and he seemed to die into his mother's love for him. His life and death influenced many people around him; she never felt it was pointless. Further, her prayer partly assuaged her own grief, and she found that it was not quite so sharp for as long as she thought it might be. One of the gifts of prayer is to transform the inner lives of those who pray.[8] Rabbi Kushner, who suffered a similar experience, found strength in a God not omnipotent but compassionate.[9]

You may pray to live forever, but you know that that prayer won't be granted—not in this life nor in your present form. But isn't there something more important than eternal human life, something you can't quite grasp about love, beauty, gratitude, and upwardness? I stumbled on this power of prayer on my journey, when I found myself in an almost constant state of thankfulness.

As you disconnect from this world, prayer provides you with a sense of connectedness to the next.

My point is simply this: If you have enough faith to pray for a miracle, then *have faith in no miracle!*

IS DEATH NECESSARILY BAD?

In our culture, we approach serious illness and death with terror, dread, and grief at leaving all we love. But Bernie Siegel reminds us that the ancient Greeks believed illness had a purpose, to compel a renewed relationship to the gods.[10] Freud postulated a death instinct he termed *thanatos,* and Jung believed we are drawn to death as rest. The small deaths of life turn out to be creative acts of transformation.[11] Why not the final one?

I wonder, as I listen to all the grieving around dying, if it's not possible to have the opposite reaction, if both the dying and the bereaving cannot view themselves as making a transition from one form to another, one life to the next. Can they not view their separation as temporary?

Some will regain their health, and some will die. Skeptics like to point out that you have as much chance of a cure at Lourdes as of winning the lottery. But is cure all there is? Perhaps the pilgrimage is more important than the goal. The very act of faith, of surrounding oneself with prayer, might not have transpired without your illness. Faith rests not in bodily cure but in the rise of spirit, the pilgrimage of consciousness, and in your own affirmation of what is right, beautiful, and good.

Many speak of how much they have learned from their illness, how much it's given them. But I'm not sure it's the illness. I think they have learned from the side effects, the positive spiritual experiences.

Our dying creates in us the search for harmony, meaning, and spiritual altitude.

It bestows on us time away from the distractions of daily things.

It enhances opportunities for love and reconciliation with family, friends, and even strangers—our caregivers—whom we did not have time for before. Graciously remember that there may be a reason why these particular people have joined the ending of our lives.

Lack of energy evokes in us the passivity to watch the birds outside our window, smell the lilacs, listen to music, be grateful for the breath of life, enjoy quiet moments of contemplation, reflect on what is happening to us, anticipate our transformation, and meditate prayerfully.

Once experienced, the spiritual is more important than anything else—and is the place we journey to.

27

TWENTY-SEVEN

WHAT IS IT

LIKE TO DIE?

WILL your death be painfully dragged out and dreary, or will it be mercifully swift? A technomedical emergency, or serene?

Will you drift off into a coma and breathe your last without even realizing it? Or will you be agitated and cry out near the end, trying to communicate what you see to those you love while they assume you're hallucinating?

Will death bandage your eyes and forbear and bid you creep past—a notion Robert Browning hated—or will you "taste the whole of it . . . in a minute pay glad life's arrears of pain, darkness and cold," until your reunion with light and love?[1]

The evidence shows that we have more control over these final moments than we think, but we cannot guard against the unforeseen. We may be able to postpone death until after our daughter's wedding or our grandson's graduation. We can insist on more medication. We may even struggle to live longer, worried about how those we leave behind will fare. But we cannot predict or direct everything. It's easy to forget that we never could!

Each of us is unique, and each will perceive our own last moments in the context of all our lives, feelings, thoughts, and beliefs. Each of us will die our own death.

A hundred years ago, death happened in the home or out on the prairie, among relatives who cared for their own. Death was often quick and unexpected—plagues, infections, childbirth, and pneumonia carrying people off by their forties.[2] Gradually, dying moved into the hospitals; emerging sanitary practices and medical technology virtually doubled life spans, often at the cost of extended suffering. Dying became unfamiliar, an unknown, shrouded in terror. During the last two decades, with the advent of both hospice and AIDS, loved ones are reclaiming the intimacies of compassionate care.

For the dying, the process is different from what witnesses imagine. You may have watched a loved one die a difficult death or an easy one; you may have read books on bereavement. But the actual experience remains secondhand. If you've nearly died yourself, you believe you "know" more, but you are still alive. Just as birthings may vary dramatically in the same mother, so may "deathings," that is, each "almost" death differs from the last, as well as from the final one. To your own experiences you can add the anecdotal accounts of others who have nearly died as well as those accounts of nurses who have been present at many passings. But even these filter through the values, feelings, and beliefs of the witnesses.

Until now, you've been on the outside looking in; now you are on the inside. The following are reasonable expectations.

UNEXPECTED CHANGES

Dying is a process of being taken by surprise. Your persistently robust appetite fades, even without nauseating treatments. Of course, being much less active, you need less food; but wasting away may be part of your disease process. You may not thirst as you used to, and yet you may not become dehydrated. Much of the time, a sip of water, ice chips, or a moist sponge suffices.

New symptoms also take you by surprise, new pains or numbness signaling disease progression, inability to do things, weakness, paralysis. Your doctor informs you gloomily that your "numbers" are bad. You find yourself alternately fighting these changes and resigning yourself; hopes are raised then dashed; signs of healing are trailed by omens of increased debilitation. Myriad other changes toward death are happening inside your body, but you don't need to know what they are specifically. Then, one day, you awaken to a craving for ice cream, champagne, and a visit to the zoo!

You live between worlds, and that's a tough place to be: no longer at home in this one, not yet secure in the next. Your interests change. Friends bring you popular magazines featuring celebrities, fashions, and sports, but you yearn for something else. They feel you withdrawing; you don't intend to and you certainly don't intend to hurt them. Emotionally, you career from irritability, to denial, to acceptance, with an occasional dash of élan, even joy. Medications plunge you into the abyss, float you high, or plague you with hallucinations.

To make matters worse, your loved ones, in the throes of anticipatory grieving, are out of synch, ready to accept your death just as you get angry or depressed again. To cheer you and comfort themselves, they "see" improvement in your condition. They urge you to stay while you're packing to leave. They reconcile themselves to losing you so that their own ordeal will end, while you hope anew. You're torn between hanging on and letting go. If you're lucky, a shrewdly compassionate person like Sister Anne Munley perceives the problem and steps forward to mediate.

Sister Munley reassures hospice patients that what was once abnormal becomes normal during the dying time, and is nothing to worry about.[3] You may sleep longer and longer, especially during the day. Many of the natural body functions you took for granted are suddenly "on strike," replaced by incontinence, diarrhea, constipation, difficulty breathing. You may find it hard to think, reason, and remember because of dementia, medication, or simply the illness's exigencies and consequent exhaustion. Even Reynolds Price could hardly read and write (except for short poems) during his long battle with a spinal cord tumor.[4] (He recovered enough to finish *Kate Vaiden*!) Progressive weakness may frustrate you; the spirit is willing but the body uncooperative.

Toward the culmination of your dying time, you will probably become less emotional, less fearful, more peaceful. In the end, your long sleep may simply deepen into coma, your breathing slow, stop, restart, and stop again.

When I was a young mother, I entered a hospital for unexpected surgery. My pain intensified over the postoperative week, along with requests for relief. My physician scolded me and discontinued the pain medication, then discovered the problem and rushed me back to surgery, after which I went downhill rapidly.

One Friday, with tubes in every orifice including several new ones, I was taken completely by surprise with the realization that I would not survive. My mind split, a great chasm running down the center of it, a kind of continental divide. Now my concern was for my husband and small children. I would not be there to raise them. I told my husband to send for his mother. "She'll care for the children and comfort you," I said.

Now, I deplore our culture's scapegoating of mothers-in-law—I'm one myself—but I really couldn't stand mine. So when I said, "Send for her," my husband knew it was serious. He swallowed tears, but didn't argue. The doctor had told him.

And then I managed to let them all go—children, husband, everyone and everything I loved. Perhaps my NDE ten years before had prepared me. In any event, I was headed "out."

That weekend, dedicated nurses never left my side; they fought a heroic battle to save my life with every weapon at their command, forcing me to survive.

By Monday, the crisis was past. Suddenly, I ached for my husband, home, and children. I wanted to read them ghost stories again, prune roses, mix lemonade, fold laundry, yes, even attend a parent-teacher conference. But I was deeply troubled. How could I have been ready to let go so easily of all I loved?

A crusty old Catholic nun named Sister Patricia was in charge of the ward and visited periodically. She could make "How are you feeling?" sound like a challenge (maybe my perception, not being Catholic). But that day I confessed my distress: "I love my children. How could I be so ready to leave them?"

Her answer? "You've been very ill."

When we are fully alive, we have passionate loves, commitments, terrors, loathings, and goals. But on the brink of dying, these fall away, not simply because they must or because they are impractical, but also because our love is no longer restricted. We are becoming less individuated, more universal.

GOING TO LIVE IN YOUR DREAMS

When you first become ill, you may have troubled dreams, even nightmares. Often, they prepare you for death, quite brutally if you are not ready (so they are not wish-fulfillment), but they do indicate that you are being born into another life.[5] Toward the end, the dreams of the dying often become transformative, another gift to ease the passage. Dreams may help you create the meaning and significance of your life, encode a summing up or life review, and transmit a wisdom beyond your own.

Cancer patient Herb Kramer dreamed of being in Tibet with monks in saffron-colored robes. Here, his "mantra" came to him. It was "Nothing dies."[6] Although he was not originally a spiritual person, toward the end of his life his dreams, visions, and mystical experiences multiplied. Buddhists believe that when we die, we go to live in a dream that does not end.[7] That is why it is important to work with our dreams in *this* life.

The following tips from dream experts will help you do this:

- When you awaken from a dream, immediately tell it to yourself, just as if you were recounting it to a friend. That fixes the dream in your mind before it slips away.
- Record it in a dream journal or on a tape.
- Rely on your own interpretation rather than a dictionary of meanings. Different dream objects mean different things to different people within the context of their experience.
- Ask yourself, "How do I feel about this person or element of my dream?" Your anxiety, envy, elation, or desire can guide your waking life.

- Often, the meaning of your dream hovers just on the edge of your mind. One way of grasping it is to use the gestalt method. In a state of relaxation, ask each element of your dream what it has to say to you—even the bus that carries you or the water that buoys you. They can be quite talkative!

- Allow the various elements of the dream to have a dialogue with each other by writing out the dream, then underlining the important words and making up a true statement about yourself using each word. This can be a playful, imaginative, and creative process.

- Another way to understand the meaning of your dream is to lie back, close your eyes, and free-associate. "The man with the feather reminds me of . . ."

- Try viewing your dreams in terms of polar dimensions such as safety/danger, good/evil, powerful/weak, rich/poor, and young/old.[8] Dimensions recur over several dreams, cueing you to conflicts or concerns in your life.

- Another technique is to draw the dream.

- Don't ignore nightmares; they contain valuable information. You may be able to transform a negative dream, altering its direction and ending, either within the dream itself or after you awaken. Recognize, however, the message of the original terror. Some experts believe that you can change reality by changing your dreams, instead of the more common notion that when reality changes, your dreams change as well.

- Discuss your dreams with a friend or counselor who'll lead you in your interpretation without imposing his own. A dream interpretation group can be helpful.

- If you have trouble remembering your dreams, before you go to sleep at night say to yourself several times, "I am remembering my dreams" (not simply, "I will remember my dreams").

- You might like to attempt "lucid dreaming," that is, changing the course or action of your dream while it is still going on.[9] Use the books in the Notes and Resources section of this chapter to help you and/or join a dream group.

- One dream expert believes you can use your dreams to recognize or re-create your own myth.[10]

VISUALIZATION AND FANTASY

It is possible that you have used visualization to attempt self-healing, to relieve your pain, and to practice letting go. Now, as you become less physical and more spiritual, you can use it to release yourself into the next reality.

Many years ago a wonderful therapist, who considered "deathing" analogous to birthing, told me how he helped clients envision their favorite places in their last moments. One woman wanted to climb a mountain, a favorite place for her and her husband while he was still alive. She and the therapist practiced this imagery, and it helped her in the end.

As your outer, physical life becomes less active, you may become a fantasy athlete. Herb Kramer's wife, Kay, a therapist, puts it beautifully: "The eyes of the mind turn in another direction."[11] Your body cannot walk, but your mind soars. You cannot get to the corner market, but you can get beyond it. One patient told a caregiver that she'd been flying through the hospital cafeteria, concerned because her relatives there were too upset to eat!

Visualization practice will help you now. Choose visions to which you resonate.[12] Die toward a vision of something you love. Say, for example, "I give myself to the sunrise," and practice doing exactly that.

MOVING IN, MOVING OUT, MOVING BEYOND

As your external experience constricts, inner freedom blossoms. Like a toddler, you explore farther and farther beyond your mother's knee, not quite trusting what you see out there, gradually becoming acclimated to it but still hovering between the security of what you know and the freedom of the strange. The process of dying seems to be one of moving from this world to the inner one, and then beyond into space and other worlds. Our culture denigrates fantasy, dreams, and "imaginary" places as the stuff of children, so you may have difficulty adjusting to the "facts" of alternate realities.

Between waking and sleeping, you may feel you are "on a journey" and try to communicate this to those around you, but your language seems symbolic to them and they cannot understand it. You see a real presence or visit a real other world, but they respond within the limits of what our culture defines as real; they say you're hallucinating, or "merely" dreaming, and you get upset. You want them to know there's hope. It's one of your "final gifts" to them, as Maggie Callanan and Patricia Kelly attest in their splendidly reassuring book.[13] They have nursed hundreds of dying patients. According to them, you will become aware that you are nearing death, and you will try to communicate what you see, and what you need in order to die, perhaps someone's permission.

You are on a threshold between worlds, and one of your final gifts to those you love is a vision of the passage, if they will only listen. I like to call this a "threshold experience." You are still in this world, but the other superimposes.

A typical threshold experience is a visitation, perhaps repeated over several days, of loved ones from the other side who are present to ease your passage. You address them across the room or at the foot of the bed. Your sons and daughters get upset that you're saying crazy things again; perhaps the doctors should cut your medication. It's not a function of medication. You're probably aware that your loved ones can't see these others; you react with excited persuasion, and when this fails, secrecy. In any event, you have your hands full communicating with both worlds. Such visitations have been documented across cultures and down the ages.[14]

The new, enlightened attitude of psychology and medicine toward NDEs and deathbed visions recognizes that they are real to the client, whether or not the caregiver accepts them as such. If you're lucky, someone like Sister Munley or Nurses Callanan and Kelly will invite you to talk about your experiences and ask, "How does that make you feel?"

POSITIVE DYING INTO ALTERNATE REALITIES

Gone are the ups and downs of treatments, the new hopes for a cure. They are replaced by devastating symptoms and dysfunctions. Your favorite rituals soothe you—meditation, massage, music, candles, flowers, visualization, religious rites or practices—especially if you have forgone frantic efforts and codes to keep you alive. Dreams beatify, and you spend more time in them. Visions of others may crowd your bed, and you may look forward to an NDE. You are serene. You may become telepathic. Hope now is for a good death, and, beyond that, no longer of this world.

Some people fear abandonment until these last hours. Gradually you'll become aware that you are not alone, never have been, never will be. Love surrounds you with light.

The battle is fought. Some may say it is lost. As you fade in and out, you hear a loved one say, "She's going downhill."

By now, you know better. You are moving out, from body to spirit, from this reality to an alternate one, your consciousness rapidly evolving into union with the greater.

Try to realize that you are a divine traveler. You are here for only a little while, then depart for a dissimilar and fascinating world. Do not limit your thought to one brief life and one small earth. Remember the vastness of the spirit that dwells within you.

—PARAMAHANSA YOGANANDA[1]

NOTES AND RESOURCES

INTRODUCTION
1. American Medical Association, *Family Medical Guide*, 3rd ed. (New York: Random House, 1994).
2. Sheldon Kopp, *If You Meet the Buddha on the Road, Kill Him! The Pilgrimage of Psychotherapy Patients* (New York: Bantam Books, 1976).

CHAPTER 1: PREPARING FOR DEATH
CAN TRANSFORM YOUR LIFE
1. Robert Browning, *Prospice*.
2. Carlos Castaneda, *The Teachings of Don Juan* (New York: Pocket Books, 1976).

CHAPTER 2: CUTTING DEATH DOWN TO SIZE
1. Hannelore Wass and Robert Neimeyer, eds., *Dying: Facing the Facts*, 3rd ed., Series in Death Education, Aging, and Health Care (Washington, D.C.: Taylor and Francis, 1995).
2. Robert A. Neimeyer, *Death Anxiety Handbook: Research, Instrumentation and Application* (Washington, D.C.: Taylor and Francis, 1994).
3. Personal communication, 1988.
4. Wass and Neimeyer, *Dying*.

CHAPTER 3: ARE YOU LIVING OR DYING?

1. Robert Ader and Nicholas Cohen, *Psychoneuroimmunology* (New York: Academic Press, 1981; updated with David Felten, New York: Harcourt Brace Jovanovich, 1991). Seminal work in the field.
2. Ibid.
3. Candace Pert, "The Chemical Communicators," in Bill Moyers's *Healing and the Mind*, ed. Betty Sue Flowers (New York: Doubleday, 1993).
4. Martin Seligman, *Helplessness: On Depression, Development, and Death* (San Francisco: Freeman, 1975).
5. Lawrence LeShan, *Cancer as a Turning Point* (New York: E. P. Dutton, 1989). Wisdom applicable to other diseases as well.
6. Lydia Temoshok and Henry Dreher, *The Type C Connection: The Behavioral Links to Cancer and Your Health* (New York: Random House, 1992).
7. Daniel Goleman and Joel Guerin, *Mind Body Medicine: How to Use Your Mind for Better Health* (Yonkers, N.Y.: Consumer Reports Books, 1993). Recommended as an overview of the field.
8. "Anger Doubles Risk of Attack for Heart Disease Patients," Harvard University Medical School research presented at American Heart Association annual meeting, *The New York Times*, March 19, 1994, p. 7.
9. Dean Ornish, *Dr. Dean Ornish's Program for Reversing Heart Disease* (New York: Ballantine, 1991).
10. Thomas Delbanco, "The Healing Roles of Doctor and Patient," in Bill Moyers's *Healing and the Mind*, p. 15.
11. Bruce Bower, "Questions of Mind Over Immunity: Scientists Rethink the Link Between Psychology and Immune Function," *Science News*, 139 (April 6, 1991): 216.
12. Bernie Siegel, *Love, Medicine and Miracles* (New York: Harper & Row, 1986). Required reading!
13. Marc Ian Barasch, *The Healing Path: A Soul Approach to Illness* (New York: Tarcher/Putnam, 1993). Splendid book!
14. Lawrence LeShan, *Cancer as a Turning Point*.
15. Kat Duff, *The Alchemy of Illness* (New York: Pantheon, 1993).
16. Ibid., p. 73.
17. Audre Lord, *A Burst of Light* (Ithaca, N.Y.: Firebrand Books, 1988): 124.
18. Bernie Siegel, *Peace, Love and Healing: Bodymind Communication and the Path to Self-Healing, An Exploration* (New York: Harper & Row, 1989).
19. Kat Duff, *Alchemy*.
20. Lawrence LeShan, *Cancer as a Turning Point*.
21. Bernie Siegel, *Love, Medicine and Miracles*.
22. Michael Lerner, *Choices in Healing: Integrating the Best of Conventional*

and Complementary Approaches to Cancer (Cambridge, Mass.: MIT Press, 1994).

23. Denis M. Searles, "Sham Shamans Anger Native Americans: Exorbitant Fees Paid for 'Cures' for AIDS, Cancer," *The Seattle Times*, November 13, 1994, A15.

24. Larry Dossey, *Healing Words: The Power of Prayer and the Practice of Medicine* (San Francisco: HarperSanFrancisco, 1993).

25. David P. Phillips and Daniel G. Smith, "Postponement of Death Until Symbolically Meaningful Occasions," *Journal of the American Medical Association* 263 (April 11, 1990): 1947–1951.

ADDITIONAL RESOURCES

Herbert Benson, *The Relaxation Response* (New York: Wings, 1992).

Joan Borysenko, *Minding the Body, Mending the Mind* (Reading, Mass.: Addison-Wesley, 1987). Especially good on meditation techniques, handling emotions, and interplay of mind and body.

Deepak Chopra, *Journey into Healing: Awakening the Wisdom within You* (New York: Harmony Books, 1994).

Deepak Chopra, *Quantum Healing: Exploring the Frontiers of Mind/Body Medicine* (New York: Bantam Books, 1989).

Deepak Chopra, *Body, Mind and Soul: The Mystery and The Magic* (videocassette) PBS, 1995.

Harris Dienstfrey, *Where the Mind Meets the Body* (New York: HarperCollins, 1991). Author is the editor of *Advances*, the journal on mind-body health.

Bill Moyers, *Healing and the Mind*, 6 videocassettes (New York: Ambrose Video Publishing, 1992).

Bernie Siegel, *How to Live Between Office Visits* (New York: HarperCollins, 1993).

David Spiegel, *Living Beyond Limits: New Hope and Help for Facing Life-Threatening Illness* (New York: Times Books, 1993).

Lawrence Vollhardt, "Psychoneuroimmunology: A Literature Review," *American Journal of Orthopsychiatry* 61 (January 1991): 25–47.

Andrew Weil, *Spontaneous Healing: How to Discover and Enhance Your Body's Natural Ability to Maintain and Heal Itself* (New York: Alfred A. Knopf, 1995).

CHAPTER 4: WHAT DOES YOUR ILLNESS MEAN TO YOU?

1. Susan Sontag, *Illness as Metaphor* (New York: Vintage Press, 1979).

2. Gilda Radner, *It's Always Something* (New York: Simon & Schuster, 1989).

ADDITIONAL RESOURCE

Larry Dossey, *Meaning and Medicine: A Doctor's Tales of Breakthrough and Healing* (New York: Bantam Books, 1990).

CHAPTER 5: SHOULD YOU TELL OTHERS?
HOW CAN YOU TELL YOUNGER CHILDREN?

1. Sherwin Nuland, *How We Die* (New York: Alfred A. Knopf, 1994).
2. Hannelore Wass, "Death in the Lives of Children and Adolescents," in *Dying: Facing the Facts*, p. 269.
3. Kathleen McCue, with Ron Bonn, *How to Help Children Through a Parent's Serious Illness: Supportive Practical Advice from a Leading Child Life Specialist* (New York: St. Martin's Press, 1994). Highly recommended.
4. Ibid.
5. Hannelore Wass, in *Dying: Facing the Facts*.

ADDITIONAL RESOURCES: CHILDREN'S BOOKS

Leo Buscaglia, *The Fall of Freddie the Leaf* (Thorofare, N.J., and New York: C. B. Slack, 1982).

Earl Grollman, *Talking About Death: A Dialogue Between Parent and Child* (Boston: Beacon Press, 1990).

R. Hitchcock, *Tim's Dad: A Story about a Boy Whose Father Dies* (Springfield, Ill.: Human Services, 1988).

L. D. Holden, *Gran-Gran's Best Trick: A Story for Children Who Have Lost Someone They Love* (New York: Magination, 1989).

Jill Krementz, *How It Feels When a Parent Dies* (New York: Alfred A. Knopf, 1981).

Eda LeShan, *Learning to Say Good-By: When a Parent Dies* (New York: Macmillan, 1976).

Bryan Mellonie and Robert Ingpen, *Lifetimes: The Beautiful Way to Explain Death to Children* (New York: Bantam Books, 1983).

Donna O'Toole, *Aarvy Aardvark Finds Hope* (Burnsville, N.C.: Celo Press, 1988).

J. Vigna, *Saying Good-bye to Daddy* (Morton Grove, Ill.: Albert Whitman, 1991).

E. B. White, *Charlotte's Web* (New York: Harper & Row, 1952).

ADDITIONAL RESOURCES: PARENT GUIDES

Helen Fitzgerald, *The Grieving Child: A Parent's Guide* (New York: Fireside, 1992). Highly recommended. This book and the one by Kathleen McCue (note 3 above) cover somewhat different but important material; read both.

CHAPTER 6: LEGAL, MEDICAL, AND FINANCIAL PREPARATIONS:
PSYCHOSPIRITUAL GUIDANCE

1. Patricia Anderson, *Affairs in Order* (New York: Macmillan, 1991). Highly recommended as a general overview.
2. Jane Smiley, *A Thousand Acres* (New York: Alfred A. Knopf, 1991).
3. Gerald M. Condon and Jeffrey L. Condon, *Beyond the Grave: The Right Way and Wrong Way of Leaving Money to Your Children (and Others)* (New York: HarperBusiness, 1995).
4. Kenneth Doka, *Living with Life-Threatening Illness: A Guide for Patients, Their Families, and Caregivers* (New York: Lexington, 1993).
5. Mark Dowie, *We Have a Donor: The Bold New World of Organ Transplanting* (New York: St. Martin's Press, 1988). A surprisingly lively account of both donors and recipients.
6. Guttorm Bratt Ebø, M. D., Torben Wisborg, M.D., and Nina Øyen, M.D., "Using Newly Deceased Patients in Teaching Procedures," *New England Journal of Medicine* 332 (May 25, 1995): 1445; J. P. Burns, F. E. Reardon, and R. D. Trugg, "Using Newly Deceased Patients to Teach Resuscitation Procedures," *New England Journal of Medicine* 331 (December 15, 1994): 1652.
7. Ernest Morgan, *Dealing Creatively with Death: A Manual of Death Education and Simple Burial*, 13th ed., revised and expanded (Celo Press, Zinn Communications, 35–19 215th Place, Bayside, NY 11361). Excellent practical guide.
8. AARP, 1909 K St. N.W., Washington, DC 20049, (202) 872-4700. Free publications on legal, financial, and medical aspects of health care.
9. Quoted in Charles Panati, *Panati's Extraordinary Endings of Practically Everything and Everybody* (New York: Harper & Row, 1989).
10. Ernest Morgan, *Dealing Creatively with Death*.
11. Earl C. Gottschalk, Jr., "Taking Financial Steps for Terminally Ill," *The Wall Street Journal*, July 2, 1992, C1.

ADDITIONAL RESOURCES

David Outerbridge and Alan Hersch, *Easing the Passage: A Guide for Prearranging and Ensuring a Pain-Free and Tranquil Death Via a Living Will, Personal Medical Mandate, and Other Medical, Legal, and Ethical Resources* (New York: HarperCollins, 1991).

David Owen, "Rest in Pieces," *Harper's* (June 1983): 70. A very funny article on organ donation; try to obtain it. "Most people secretly believe that thinking about death is the single surest method of shortening life expectancy."

Eugene Robin, *Matters of Life and Death: Risk Versus Benefits of Medical Care* (New York: W. H. Freeman, 1984).

Thomas and Celia Scully, *Making Medical Decisions: How to Make Difficult Medical and Ethical Choices for Yourself and Your Family* (New York: Simon & Schuster/Fireside, 1989).

Alex J. Soled, *Estate Planning: Easy Answers to Your Most Important Questions* (Yonkers, N.Y.: Consumer Reports, 1994).

Funeral and Memorial Societies of America, 6900 Lost Lake Road, Egg Harbor, WI 54209, (800) 868-3136.

United Network of Organ Sharing (UNOS), 1100 Boulders Parkway, #500, Richmond, VA 23225, (800) 24-DONOR.

CHAPTER 7: COPING POSITIVELY WITH DAILY LIFE

1. Reynolds Price, *A Whole New Life: An Illness and a Healing* (New York: Atheneum, 1994).

2. Arnold Beisser, *A Graceful Passage* (New York: Doubleday, 1990). Beisser is a UCLA psychiatry professor and a quadriplegic as a result of polio. A beautiful, moving, wise meditation on issues of life and death.

Norman Cousins, *Anatomy of an Illness as Perceived by the Patient* (New York: Norton, 1979).

Kat Duff, *The Alchemy of Illness*. Duff had chronic fatigue syndrome. Great beauty and wisdom in this insightful account of her physical, emotional, and spiritual battle. Her understanding of the *value* of illness and the sometimes unhealthfulness of health is *must* reading.

Alice Hopper Epstein, *Mind, Fantasy and Healing: One Woman's Journey from Conflict and Illness to Wholeness and Health* (New York: Delacorte, 1989). Valuable for her use of imagery (with the assistance of her therapist husband) in battling cancer.

Arthur Frank, *At the Will of the Body: Reflections on Illness* (Boston: Houghton Mifflin, 1991). Frank had a heart attack at thirty-nine, then developed testicular cancer at forty. He movingly tells of coping with stigma and changes in identity.

Joseph Heller and Speed Vogel, *No Laughing Matter* (New York: Avon, 1986). One of our major writers tells the gripping story of his bout with Guillain-Barré syndrome.

Jody Heymann, *Equal Partners: A Physician's Call for a New Spirit of Medicine* (Boston: Little, Brown, 1995). Newly graduated from medical school, Heymann was suddenly hospitalized for seizures. Don't read this alone late at night if horror stories keep you awake!

Hirshel Jaffe, James Rudin, and Marcia Rudin, *Why Me? Why Anyone?* (New York: St. Martin's Press, 1986). A rabbi and marathon runner is suddenly afflicted with leukemia in his forties. His friends, the Rudins, show how they struggle with his illness and the same spiritual issues.

The experience deepens Jaffe's rabbinical understanding and ministrations.

Leonard Kriegel, *Falling into Life (Essays)* (San Francisco: North Point Press, 1991). Polio at eleven left Kriegel "a cripple." He tells us how he coped with his rage and loss.

Audre Lorde, *The Cancer Journals* (San Francisco: Aunt Lute Books, 1980).

Paul Monette, *Borrowed Time: An AIDS Memoir* (New York: Harcourt Brace Jovanovich, 1988). A powerful testament.

Lon G. Nungesser with William D. Bullock, *Notes on Living Until We Say Goodbye* (New York: St. Martin's Press, 1988). One of the most valuable books on dealing with stigma, daily living, and emotions. Nungesser suffered from Kaposi's sarcoma, a frequent manifestation of AIDS. Broadly applicable advice.

Robert O'Boyle, *Living with AIDS* (*Seattle Times* newspaper columns, 1992). O'Boyle communicated to us his daily struggle.

Gilda Radner, *It's Always Something*. This is her heart-breaking story, told with shafts of humor, of her suffering from ovarian cancer and her stages of believing she was well, that the next treatment would work.

3. Jean Achterberg, Barbara Dossey, and Leslie Kolkmeier, *Rituals of Healing: Using Imagery for Health and Wellness* (New York: Bantam Books, 1994). Shows how to ritualize daily activities with breathing exercises and imagery for various diseases.

4. Kenneth Doka, *Living with Life-Threatening Illness*.

5. Kathy Charmaz, *Good Days, Bad Days: The Self in Chronic Illness and Time* (New Brunswick, N.J.: Rutgers University Press, 1991). Highly recommended.

6. Barney Glaser and Anselm Strauss, *Awareness of Dying* (Chicago: Aldine, 1965). A classic in the field.

7. Leslie R. Schover, *Sexuality & Cancer: For the Woman Who Has Cancer, and Her Partner* (rev. 4/94) and *Sexuality & Cancer: For the Man Who Has Cancer, and His Partner* (rev. 10/91) (New York: American Cancer Society). Both helpful for those with other diseases as well as cancer.

8. John Whitacre, *Confronting Life-Threatening Illness: Maintaining Control and Establishing Positive Objectives* (Ann Arbor: Pierian, 1992). Helpful workbook.

ADDITIONAL RESOURCES

Philippe Aries, *The Hour of Our Death* (New York: Vintage Books, 1981).

Deena Metzger, *Writing for Your Life: A Guide and Companion to the Inner Worlds* (San Francisco: HarperSanFrancisco, 1992). Working through this book could be immensely valuable to you.

CHAPTER 8: BETRAYED BY THE BODY

1. Bernie Siegel, "The Great Teacher," poem, personal communication, 1995.
2. Lon Nungesser with William D. Bullock, *Notes on Living*.
3. Gilda Radner, *It's Always Something*.
4. Julia Epstein, "AIDS, Stigma, and Narratives of Containment (AIDS and Homophobia)," *American Imago* 49 (fall 1992): 293.
5. Edward Jones et al., *Social Stigma: The Psychology of Marked Relationships* (New York: W. H. Freeman, 1984). Superb scholarly work.
6. Rod Serling, "The Eye of the Beholder," in *The Twilight Zone Companion*, ed. Mark Scott Zicree (New York: Bantam Books, 1982).
7. Susan Sontag, *Illness as Metaphor*.
8. My thanks to Joyce Figueroa for filling in these details featured on *Evening Magazine* TV show with Penny LeGate, Seattle, March 13, 1995.
9. Lucy Grealy, *Autobiography of a Face* (New York: Houghton Mifflin, 1994).
10. Lon Nungesser with William D. Bullock, *Notes on Living*.
11. Leonard Kriegel, *Falling into Life*.
12. Edward Jones et al., *Social Stigma*.

ADDITIONAL RESOURCES

Erving Goffman, *Stigma: Notes on the Management of Spoiled Identity* (Englewood Cliffs, N.J.: Prentice-Hall Press, 1963). A classic in the field.

Abraham Verghese, *My Own Country* (New York: Simon & Schuster, 1994). A doctor cares for patients with AIDS in a small Tennessee town.

CHAPTER 9: TWENTY-SEVEN RULES FOR DYING THE "RIGHT WAY"

1. Elisabeth Kübler-Ross, *On Death and Dying* (New York: Macmillan, 1971).
2. Stephen Levine, *Who Dies? An Investigation of Conscious Living and Conscious Dying* (New York: Anchor Books, 1982).
3. AARP, *Nursing Home Life: A Guide for Residents and Families*, 1987, Rev. 1993, p. 27; see the paragraph on "Fear of Retaliation."

CHAPTER 10: POWER OVER PAIN

1. Elaine Scarry, *The Body in Pain: The Making and Unmaking of the World* (New York: Oxford University Press, 1985).
2. Elliot S. Dacher, *PNI: The New Mind/Body Healing Program* (New York: Paragon House, 1991).
3. J. Jarrett Clinton, "Acute Pain Management Can Be Improved," *Journal of the American Medical Association* 267 (May 20, 1992): 2580.

4. Agency for Health Care Policy and Research (AHCPR), reported in *Facts on File* 54 (June 9, 1994): 413.
5. Robert Browning, *Prospice*.
6. My thanks to Margo McCaffery, R.N.,M.S., FAAN, for her suggestions and references in this section.
7. *Presentation of Findings*—Mayday Fund, Mellman-Lazarus-Lake, Inc., 1054 31st Street, Suite 530, Washington, D.C. 20007 (September 1993).
8. Sandol Stoddard, *The Hospice Movement: A Better Way of Caring for the Dying* (New York: Stein and Day, 1978). A classic. Updated and expanded, New York: Vintage Press, 1992.
9. Mayday Fund *Presentation*.
10. AHCPR (June 9, 1994).
11. American Cancer Society and National Cancer Institute, *Questions and Answers About Pain Control: A Guide for People with Cancer and Their Families*, (1992).
12. McCaffery, personal communication, 1995.
13. M. N. Duggleby and J. Lander, "Cognitive Status and Postoperative Pain: Older Adults," *Journal of Pain and Symptom Management* 9 (1994): 19–27.
14. AHCPR, "Managing Cancer Pain: Patient Guide," publication no. 94-0595 (March 1994): inside cover.
15. Kathleen Foley, "The treatment of cancer pain," *New England Journal of Medicine* 313 (February 1985).
16. American Cancer Society, *Questions and Answers*.
17. C. S. Cleeland, "Assessing Pain in Cancer: The Patient's Role," in *Management of Cancer Pain* (New York: Hospital Practice, 1984): 17–21.
18. Michael Lerner, *Choices in Healing*.
19. David Spiegel, *Living Beyond Limits*.
20. Norman Cousins, *Anatomy of an Illness*.
21. Mayday Fund *Presentation*.
22. S. E. Ward and D. Gordon, "Application of the American Pain Society Quality Assurance Standards," *Pain* 56 (1994): 299–306.
23. Margo McCaffery, Betty Rolling Ferrell, and Edith O'Neil, "Does Lifestyle Affect Your Pain-Control Decisions?" *Nursing* 22 (April 1992): 58.
    Margo McCaffery and Betty Rolling Ferrell, "Patient Age: Does It Affect Your Pain-Control Decisions?" *Nursing* 21 (September 1991): 44.
    Margo McCaffery and Betty Rolling Ferrell, "Does the Gender Gap Affect Your Pain-Control Decisions?" *Nursing* 22 (August 1992).
    Margo McCaffery and Betty Ferrell, "How Would You Respond to These Patients in Pain?" *Nursing* 21 (June 1991): 24.

24. Flora Johnson Skelly, "Price of Pain Control: Is This the Risk You Face by Appropriately Prescribing Narcotics for Pain?" *American Medical News* 37 (May 16, 1994): 17.

25. Gene Bylinski, "New Gains in the Fight Against Pain," *Fortune* 127 (March 22, 1993): 107.

26. Study reported in the *Journal of the American Medical Association* 272 (September 28, 1994): 912.

27. The SUPPORT Principal Investigators, "A Controlled Trial to Improve Care for Seriously Ill Hospitalized Patients: The Study to Understand Prognoses and Preferences for Outcomes and Risks of Treatment (SUPPORT)," *Journal of the American Medical Association* 274 (November 22/29, 1995): 1591.

28. L. D. Empting-Kochorke et al., "Tips on Hard-to-Manage Pain Syndromes," *Patient Care* 24 (April 30, 1990).

29. Barbara J. Logue, "When Hospice Fails: The Limits of Palliative Care," *Omega* 29 (April 1994): 291–301.

30. Ada Jacox et al., "A Guideline for the Nation: Managing Acute Pain," *American Journal of Nursing* 92 (May 1992): 49.

31. Jane Cowles, *Pain Relief: How to Say No to Acute, Chronic, and Cancer Pain* (New York: Mastermedia, 1993). Excellent overview of pain diagnosis, measurement, and treatment, both traditional and alternative.

32. Sources of information for this chart include the above works as well as Jean Achterberg et al., *Rituals of Healing*.

    Judith Ahronheim and Doron Weber, *Final Passages: Positive Choices for the Dying and Their Loved Ones* (New York, Simon & Schuster, 1992). Excellent overview of traditional pain relief.

    Jon Kabat-Zinn, *Wherever you Go, There You Are: Mindfulness Meditation in Everyday Life* (New York: Hyperion, 1994).

    Susan S. Lang and Richard B. Patt, *You Don't Have to Suffer: A Complete Guide to Relieving Cancer Pain for Patients and Their Families* (New York: Oxford University Press, 1994). Comprehensive on specific medications and side effects.

    Michael Lerner, *Choices in Healing*. Includes physical, mental, emotional, and spiritual aspects of pain relief. Helpful for many diseases, not just cancer. Annotated list of residential programs for people living with cancer..

    Bill Moyers, *Healing and the Mind*.

33. Reynolds Price, *A Whole New Life*.

34. Michelle Locke, "Marijuana Club Is Refuge for Those Who Live in Pain: Cancer, AIDS Patients Flout Law to Find Relief," *Seattle Times* (March 28, 1995): A3.

35. Elizabeth Küber-Ross, *On Death and Dying*. This goal of pain relief is

the centerpiece of the hospice movement, as set forth by Dame and Dr. Cecily Saunders in Great Britain.

36. Ada Jacox, D. B. Carr, and R. Payne, "New Clinical Practice Guidelines for the Management of Pain in Patients with Cancer," *New England Journal of Medicine* 330 (March 3, 1994): 651.
37. Jane Cowles, *Pain Relief*.
38. Bill Moyers, "Healing from Within," videocassette 3 of *Healing and the Mind*.

ADDITIONAL RESOURCES

Mary Batten, "Take Charge of Your Pain," *Modern Maturity* (January-February 1995): 35. A good brief, simple overview.

Robert G. Twycross and Sylvia A. Lack, *Oral Morphine: Information for Patients, Families, and Friends* (Bucks, England: Beaconsfield, reprinted with revision, 1995). A highly recommended booklet. Can be ordered from Roxane Laboratories, Inc., P.O. Box 16532, Columbus, OH 43216.

CHAPTER 11: HOW TO BE IN A SUPPORT GROUP

1. David Spiegel, *Living Beyond Limits*.
2. I suggest, for one, Bill Moyers, videocassette 3 of *Healing and the Mind*, "Healing from Within," showing David Spiegel's Group.
3. Joseph Campbell, *Hero with a Thousand Faces* (Princeton, N.J.: Princeton University Press, 1973; originally published, 1949).

ADDITIONAL RESOURCES:

J. E. Knott, Mary Ribar, Betty Dusen, and Mary King, *Thanatopics: Activities and Exercises for Confronting Death* (Lexington, Mass: Lexington, 1989).

Elisabeth Kübler-Ross, *Working It Through: An Elisabeth Kübler-Ross Workshop on Life, Death and Transition* (New York: Macmillan, 1982). An account of a workshop in progress.

Irvin Yalom, *The Theory and Practice of Group Therapy*, 4th ed. (New York: Basic Books, 1995). A classic in the field.

CHAPTER 12: RIDING THE EMOTIONAL ROLLER COASTER

1. Harold Kushner, *When Bad Things Happen to Good People* (New York: Schocken, 1981).
2. American Psychiatric Association, *DSM-IV*, 4th ed. (Washington, D.C.: 1994): 326, 684.
3. Peter Kramer, *Listening to Prozac: A Psychiatrist Explores Antidepressant Drugs and the Remaking of the Self* (New York: Viking Press, 1993).

4. Peter Breggin, *Talking Back to Prozac* (New York: St. Martin's Press, 1994), p. 210.
5. Ibid., p. 212.
6. David Antonucci, cited in Breggin, *Talking Back*, p. 206.
7. M. Brewster Smith, personal communication, 1995.
8. Lydia Temoshok and Henry Dreher, *The Type C Connection*.
9. Jeremy Taylor, *Where People Fly and Water Runs Uphill: Using Dreams to Tap the Wisdom of the Unconscious* (New York: Warner Books, 1992). The best on dreams.
10. There are many fine books that help you cope with your emotions; most don't mention coping with impending death. I believe the best for this stage of life include greater philosophical and spiritual issues. I recommend:

    Susan Jeffers, *Feel the Fear and Do It Anyway* (New York: Harcourt Brace Jovanovich, 1987).

    Joann LeMaistre, *Beyond Rage: Mastering Unavoidable Health Changes*, revised and expanded (Oak Park, Ill. 1993).

    Merle Shain, *Hearts We Broke Long Ago* (Toronto, Canada: Bantam Books, 1983). Wise stories that illuminate our feelings.

    David Viscott, *The Viscott Method: A Revolutionary Program for Self-Analysis and Self-Understanding* (Boston: Houghton Mifflin, 1984).

    David Viscott, *Emotionally Free: Letting Go of the Past to Live in the Present* (Chicago: Contemporary Books, 1992).
11. Marc Ian Barasch, *The Healing Path*.

CHAPTER 13: AID-IN-DYING

1. Lisa Hobbes Birnie, *Uncommon Will: The Death and Life of Sue Rodriguez* (Toronto, Canada: Macmillan, 1994).
2. Timothy Quill, "Death and Dignity: A Case for Individualized Decision-Making," *New England Journal of Medicine* 324 (March 7, 1991): 691–694.
3. Donald W. Cox, *Hemlock's Cup: The Struggle for Death with Dignity* (Buffalo: Prometheus Books, 1993).

    Jack Kevorkian, *Prescription—Medicide: The Goodness of Planned Death* (Buffalo: Prometheus Books, 1991). Note: This book is filled with historical accounts of the grisly deaths we've inflicted on each other down through the ages—entirely unrelated to the book's topic. I include it only for reference.
4. "Bioethicists' Statement on the U.S. Supreme Court's Cruzan Decision," signed by thirty-seven bioethicists, *New England Journal of Medicine* 323 (September 6, 1990): 686–689.

5. Esther B. Fein, "Granting Father's Wish or Manslaughter?" *The New York Times,* October 18, 1994, A1.
   William Meyer III, personal communication, 1995.
6. Stephen A. Flanders, *Suicide* (New York: Facts on File, 1991).
7. For an excellent review of this subject, I recommend Dr. George Burnell's book *Final Choices: To Live or Die in an Age of Medical Technology* (New York: Insight, Plenum Press, 1993).
8. Ibid.
9. Judith Ahronheim and Doron Weber, *Final Passages.*
10. Rev. Ralph Mero, executive director of Compassion in Dying, P.O. Box 75295, Seattle, WA 98125-0295, personal communication, 1995.
11. Derek Humphrey, *Final Exit: The Practicalities of Self-Deliverance and Assisted Suicide for the Dying* (Eugene, Ore.: Hemlock Society, 1991).
12. Kathleen Foley, "The Relationship of Pain and Symptom Management to Patient Requests for Physician-Assisted Suicide," *Journal of Pain and Symptom Management* 6 (July 1991): 289.
    Kathleen Foley, "Doctoring the Doctor," review of *Death and Dignity,* by Timothy Quill, *Hastings Center Report* (May-June 1994): 45.
13. Kathleen Foley, "The Relationship of Pain and Symptom Management to Patient Requests."
14. Sherwin Nuland, *How We Die.*
    Rebecca Brown, *The Gifts of the Body* (New York: HarperCollins, 1994).
15. Jody Heymann, *Equal Partners.*
16. Lonny Shavelson, *A Chosen Death: The Dying Confront Assisted Suicide* (New York: Simon & Schuster, 1995). A wonderfully gentle and compassionate book.
17. L. R. Derogatis et al., "The Prevalence of Psychiatric Disorders Among Cancer Patients," *Journal of the American Medical Association* 249 (February 11, 1983): 751–757.
18. John Kilner, *Who Lives? Who Dies? Ethical Criteria in Patient Selection* (New Haven, Conn.: Yale University Press, 1990).
19. Pope John Paul II's encyclical, "Evangelium Vitae," *National Catholic Reporter* 31 (April 7, 1995): 4.
20. There seem to be as many versions of the Hippocratic Oath as there are translators. This one is from Lynne Ann DeSpelder and Albert Lee Strickland, *The Last Dance,* 3rd. ed. (Palo Alto: Mayfield Publishing Company, 1993). However, my favorite is ". . . To please no one will I prescribe a deadly drug, nor give advice which may cause his death . . ." At least, *women* are exempt!
21. Compassion in Dying (see note 10 above).
22. Brian Clark, *Whose Life Is It Anyway?* (New York: Avon, 1978).
23. George Burnell, *Final Choices* (see note 7 above).

24. Francis D. Moore, "Prolonging Life, Permitting Life to End," *Harvard Magazine* (July-August 1995): 46.

ADDITIONAL RESOURCES

Daniel Callahan, *Setting Limits: Medical Goals in an Aging Society* (New York: Simon & Schuster, 1987); Daniel Callahan, *What Kind of Life: The Limits of Medical Progress* (New York: Simon & Schuster, 1990). Both books propose reasoned arguments on extending the lives of the elderly.

Choice in Dying, Inc., The National Council for the Right to Die, 200 Varick Street, New York, NY 10014. Their legal services department supplies information about your state laws regarding advance directives and the like. Publishes the *Choice in Dying Newsletter*.

Hastings Center Report, 255 Elm Road, Briarcliff, NY 10510. A bioethical publication.

Elaine Landau, *The Right to Die* (New York: Franklin Watts, 1993). A primer on the main issues and their recent history.

Timothy Quill, *Death and Dignity: Making Choices and Taking Charge* (New York: Norton, 1993).

Betty Rollins, *Last Wish* (New York: Warner Books, 1986). Rollins faced the decision of whether to help her mother die.

David Thomason and Glenn Graber, *Euthanasia: Toward an Ethical Social Policy* (New York: Continuum, 1991). A serious exploration of many issues, including fifty-six court cases.

CHAPTER 14: WHERE WILL YOU DIE?

1. The National Hospice Organization, personal communication, 1995, citing a 1992 Gallup poll.
2. Ezekiel J. Emanuel and Linda L. Emanuel, "The Economics of Dying: The Illusion of Cost Savings at the End of Life," *New England Journal of Medicine* 330 (February 24, 1994): 540.
3. Larry Beresford, *The Hospice Handbook* (Boston: Little Brown, 1993).
4. Trudy Lieberman, "Nursing Homes: A Special Investigative Report," *Consumer Reports* 60 (August 1995): 518–528.
5. Larry Beresford, *The Hospice Handbook*.
6. Lawrence LeShan, *Cancer as a Turning Point*, p. 166.
7. Vicki Brower, "The Right Way to Die," *Health* (June 1991): 39.
8. Marilyn Webb, "The Art of Dying," 25 *New York* (November, 23, 1992).
9. Ernest Becker, *The Denial of Death* (New York: Free Press, 1973): 12.

ADDITIONAL RESOURCES

AARP, "Nursing Home Life: A Guide for Residents and Families." Available from the American Association of Retired Persons, 601 E Street,

N.W., Washington, DC 20049. Very helpful on assessing your needs, admission policies, selection, adjusting to a nursing home, evaluating care, patients' rights, and the like.

Deborah Duda, *Coming Home: A Guide to Dying at Home with Dignity* (New York: Aurora Press, 1987).

Mary Brumby Forrest, Christopher Forrest, and Richard Forrest, *Nursing Homes: The Complete Guide* (New York: Facts on File, 1990).

National Citizens' Coalition for Nursing Home Reform, 1424 16th Street N.W., Suite 202, Washington, DC 20036-2211. Many publications, focused on assessment of nursing homes and quality care. Phone (202) 332-2275.

National Hospice Organization, 1901 North Moore Street, Suite 901, Arlington, VA 22209. Lists of hospices in your area. Hospice helpline, (800) 658-8898.

CHAPTER 15: CONTROLLING THE UNCONTROLLABLE

1. Anne Munley, *The Hospice Alternative: A New Context for Death and Dying* (New York: Basic Books, 1986), p. 127.
2. Jane Brophy, "Doctors Admit Ignoring Patients' Wishes," *The New York Times*, January 14, 1993, A18.

   The SUPPORT Principal Investigators, "A Controlled Trial to Improve Care for Seriously Ill Hospitalized Patients." Also reported by Doug Levy, *USA Today*, November 22, 1995, pp. 1A and 12D.

   In the first phase of this study of 9,105 patients at five medical centers, physicians either misunderstood or disregarded patients' requests for non-resuscitation in approximately 80 percent of the cases.
3. Reported in *American Medical News* 37 (December 5, 1994): 6.
4. Anne Munley, *The Hospice Alternative.*
5. Herbert and Kay Kramer, *Conversations at Midnight: Coming to Terms with Dying and Death* (New York: William Morrow, 1993). Highly recommended.
6. Ibid.
7. *Conversations at Midnight* by Herb and Kay Kramer has a number I recommend. Also, *Rituals of Healing* by Jeanne Achterberg, Barbara Dossey and Leslie Kolkmeier; Shakti Gawain, *Visualization* (New York: Bantam Books, 1985, originally published 1979)—a justifiably long-lived book; and Stephen Levine's *Who Dies?*

CHAPTER 16: RETAINING YOUR IDENTITY

1. Arthur Frank, *At the Will of the Body.*
2. Jody Heymann, *Equal Partners*, p. 34.
3. Lon Nungesser with William D. Bullock, *Notes on Living.*

4. Lawrence LeShan, *Cancer as a Turning Point*. *Do* read the chapter "How to Survive in a Hospital."

CHAPTER 17: WHEN YOU DON'T WANT TO FORGIVE

1. Harriet Webster, *Family Secrets: How Telling and Not Telling Affect Our Children, Our Relationships, and Our Lives* (Reading, Mass.: Addison-Wesley, 1991).
2. Elaine Scarry, *The Body in Pain*.
3. Beverly Flanigan, *Forgiving the Unforgivable: Overcoming the Bitter Legacy of Intimate Wounds* (New York: Macmillan, 1992).
4. Lewis Smedes, *Forgive and Forget: Healing the Hurts We Don't Deserve* (New York: Harper & Row, 1984).
5. Beverly Flanigan, *Forgiving*.
6. Lee Atwater with Todd Brewster, "Lee Atwater's Last Campaign: Battling an Inoperable Brain Tumor, the Bad Boy of Republican Politics Discovers the Power of Love and a Dream for America," *Life* (February 14, 1991): 58.
7. Joan Borysenko, *Guilt Is the Teacher, Love Is the Answer* (New York: Warner Books, 1990).
8. Lewis Smedes, *Forgive and Forget*.
9. Harold Kushner, *When Bad Things Happen to Good People*.

ADDITIONAL RESOURCE
Patrick D. Miller, *A Little Book of Forgiveness* (New York: Viking, 1994).

CHAPTER 18: TRANSCENDING THE LOSS OF ALL YOU LOVE

1. Patricia Weenolsen, *Transcendence of Loss Over the Life Span*, Series in Death Education, Aging and Health Care (Washington, D.C.: Taylor & Francis/Hemisphere, 1988).

CHAPTER 20: WHAT'S LEFT UNDONE

1. Carlos Castaneda, *The Teachings of Don Juan*.

CHAPTER 21: CREATING LIFE MEANING FROM DESPAIR

1. Della's and Gwen's full stories appear in my book, *Transcendence of Loss over the Life Span*. I interviewed Luke, Marty, Sam, and Nina for another project on life dreams.
2. Jean Paul Sartre, *Nausea* (New York: New Directions, 1964).
3. Lawrence LeShan, *Cancer as a Turning Point*.

CHAPTER 22: OUR GREAT VALUE AS DYING PEOPLE

1. Larry Dossey, *Healing Words: The Power of Prayer and the Practice of Medicine* (San Francisco: HarperSanFrancisco, 1993).

2. Elisabeth Kübler-Ross, *On Death and Dying*.
3. David Veale, personal communication, 1994.

CHAPTER 23: RITUALS AND MYTHS FOR THE END OF LIFE

1. A number of books will be helpful in creating your own rituals, especially Jeanne Achterberg, Barbara Dossey, and Leslie Kolkmeier, *Rituals of Healing*. Highly recommended.
2. Frank Lawlis, "Shamanic Approaches in a Hospital Clinic," in *Shaman's Path: Healing, Personal Growth and Empowerment*, ed. Gary Doore (Boston: Shambala, 1988). Highly recommended.
3. Jeanne Achterberg et al., *Rituals of Healing*.
4. Patricia Weenolsen, *Transcendence of Loss*.
5. Larry Dossey, *Healing Words*.
6. Joseph Campbell, *The Hero with a Thousand Faces*, p. 30.
7. Paul Rebillot, "The Hero's Journey: Ritualizing the Mystery," in *Spiritual Emergency*, by Stanislav Grof and Christina Grof (Los Angeles: J. P. Tarcher, 1989).

ADDITIONAL RESOURCES

Clarissa Pinkola Estés, *Women Who Run with the Wolves: Myths and Stories of the Wild Woman Archetype* (New York: Ballantine, 1992).

David Feinstein and Peg E. Mayo, *Rituals for Living and Dying* (New York: HarperCollins, 1990).

Evan Imber-Black and Janine Roberts, *Rituals for Our Times: Celebrating Healing and Changing Our Lives and Our Relationships* (New York: HarperCollins, 1992). Although there are no rituals for the dying specifically (only the bereaving), this book is excellent on issues affecting rituals such as broken and strained relationships, as well as on the creation of new ones.

Sam Keen and Anne Valley-Fox, *Your Mythic Journey* (Los Angeles: Jeremy P. Tarcher, 1973, 1989).

Stephen Larsen, *The Mythic Imagination: Your Quest for Meaning Through Personal Mythology* (New York: Bantam Books, 1990). This book becomes very helpful, I think, as it progresses from intellectual to experiential. The exercises in Chapter 12 are valuable.

National Funeral Directors Association, 11121 W. Oklahoma Avenue, Milwaukee, WI 53227. Information on funeral preplanning and other options.

CHAPTER 24: BELIEF IN AFTERLIFE IS A CHOICE

1. Raymond Moody, *Life After Death* (New York: Bantam Books, 1975).
2. Sherwin Nuland, *How We Die*.
3. Nancy Gibbs and Howard G. Chua-Eoan, "Angels Among Us," *Time* 142 (December 27, 1993): 56.

4. George Gallup, Jr., and Jim Castelli, *The People's Religion: American Faith in the '90s* (New York: Macmillan, 1989).
5. Raymond Moody, *Life After Death*.
6. Kenneth Ring, *Heading Toward Omega: In Search of the Meaning of Near-Death Experiences* (New York: William Morrow, 1984).
Bruce Greyson and Charles P. Flynn, *The Near-Death Experience: Problems, Prospects, Perspectives* (Springfield, Ill.: Charles C. Thomas, 1984).
Karlis Osis and Erlendur Haraldsson, *At the Hour of Death: The Results of Research on over 1,000 Afterlife Experiences* (New York: Avon, 1977).
Melvin Morse, *Closer to the Light* (New York: Villard, 1990).
7. Tom Harpur, *Life After Death* (Toronto, Canada: McClelland & Stewart, 1991).
8. In case this story seems familiar, I originally published it as "Epitaph" in *Pulpsmith* (summer 1982) under the pseudonym Patricia Otway-Ward.
9. Susan Blackmore, *Dying to Live: Near-Death Experiences* (Buffalo: Prometheus Books, 1993).
10. *The Fantastic Voyage*, film, 1966.
11. Kenneth Ring, *The Omega Project: Near-Death Experiences, UFO Encounters, and Mind at Large* (New York: William Morrow, 1992).
12. Ibid.
13. Bernie Siegel, *Peace, Love and Healing*: 239.
14. Kenneth Ring, *The Omega Project*, p. 11.
15. Michael Murphy, *The Future of the Body: Explorations into the Further Evolution of Human Nature* (Los Angeles: Jeremy P. Tarcher, 1992). Superb book by a founder of Esalen.
16. Joan Townsend, "Neo-Shamanism and the Modern Mystical Movement," in *Shaman's Path*, ed. Gary Doore.
17. Gary Doore, *Shaman's Path*.
18. Benjamin Franklin: Epitaph for Himself. In *Dictionary of Quotations*, collected and arranged by Bergen Evans (New York: Delacorte Press, 1968).

ADDITIONAL RESOURCES
Ian Currie, *You Cannot Die: The Incredible Findings of a Century of Research on Death* (New York: Methuen, 1978).
Arnold Mindell, *The Shaman's Body: A New Shamanism for Transforming Health, Relationships, and the Community* (San Francisco: HarperSanFrancisco, 1993). Includes valuable exercises for helping the reader attain wisdom.
Soygal Rinpoche, *The Tibetan Book of Living and Dying* (San Francisco: HarperSanFrancisco, 1992).

Carol Zaleski, *Otherworld Journeys: Accounts of Near-Death Experience in Medieval and Modern Times* (New York: Oxford University Press, 1987). Fascinating scholarly work.

CHAPTER 25: PLANNING YOUR ETERNAL FUTURE
1. George Gallup, Jr., *The People's Faith*.
2. Susan Blackmore, *Dying to Live*.

CHAPTER 26: ENHANCING YOUR SPIRITUAL DEVELOPMENT
1. Eugene Taylor, "Desperately Seeking Spirituality," *Psychology Today*, (November-December 1994): 54.
2. Douglas Groothuis, "To Heaven and Back? Near-Death Experiences," *Christianity Today* 39 (April 3, 1995): 39.
3. Thomas Kuhn, *The Structure of Scientific Revolutions* (Chicago: University of Chicago Press, 1970).
4. Michael Murphy, *The Future of the Body*.
5. Larry Dossey, *Healing Words*.
6. Randolph Byrd, "Positive Therapeutic Effects of Intercessory Prayer in a Coronary Care Unit Population," *Southern Medical Journal* 81 (July 1988): 826–829.
7. Larry Dossey, *Healing Words*.
8. Richard Foster, *Prayer: Finding the Heart's True Home* (San Francisco: HarperSanFrancisco, 1992).
9. Harold Kushner, *When Good Things Happen to Bad People*.
10. Bernie Siegel, *Peace, Love and Healing*.
11. Patricia Weenolsen, "Transcending the Many Deaths of Life: Clinical Implications for Cure versus Healing," *Death Studies* (January-February 1991): 59–80.

ADDITIONAL RESOURCES

Joan Borysenko, *Pocketful of Miracles* (New York, Warner Books, 1994). Wonderfully interfaith, weaving Christian, Jewish, Islamic, Native American, and other religions in both Eastern and Western traditions into an inspiring "calendar" of thoughts and prayers for each day of the year. I love this book.

Kahlil Gibran, *The Prophet* (New York: Alfred A. Knopf, 1923).

Stanislav and Christina Grof, *Spiritual Emergency: When Personal Transformation Becomes a Crisis* (Los Angeles: Jeremy P. Tarcher, 1989).

Marianne Williamson, *Illuminata* (New York: Random House, 1994). A book of prayers for many different occasions, with ways of personalizing them to your own situation. Powerful and beautiful.

CHAPTER 27: WHAT IS IT LIKE TO DIE?
1. Robert Browning, *Prospice*.
2. Philippe Aries, *The Hour of Our Death*.
3. Anne Munley, *The Hospice Alternative*.
4. Reynolds Price, *A Whole New Life*.
5. Tom Harpur, *Life After Death*.
6. Herbert and Kay Kramer, *Conversations at Midnight*.
7. Jeremy Taylor, *Where People Fly and Water Runs Uphill*.
8. Rosalind Cartwright and Lynne Lamberg, *Crisis Dreaming: Using Your Dreams to Solve Your Problems* (New York: HarperCollins, 1992).
9. Malcolm Godwin, *The Lucid Dreamer: A Waking Guide to Conscious Dreaming* (New York: Simon & Schuster, 1994). Stunningly beautiful book with two hundred illustrations of great artworks, many surreal, conveying the mysticism of dreams. I love it!
10. Stephen Larsen, *The Mythic Imagination*.
11. Herbert and Kay Kramer, *Conversations at Midnight*.
12. Shakti Gawain, *Creative Visualization*.
13. Maggie Callanan and Patricia Kelly, *Final Gifts: Understanding the Special Awareness, Needs, and Communications of the Dying* (New York: Poseidon Press, 1992). Highly recommended.
14. Karlis Osis and Erlandur Haraldsson, *At the Hour of Death*.

ADDITIONAL RESOURCES
Gayle Delaney, *Breakthrough Dreaming: How to Tap the Power of Your 24-Hour Mind* (New York: Bantam Books, 1991).
Anya Foos-Graber, *Deathing* (Boston: Addison-Wesley, 1984).
Stephen Levine, *Meetings at the Edge* (New York: Anchor, 1980). Individual accounts of the dying process.
Henry Reed, *Getting Help from Your Dreams* (New York: Ballantine, 1985).
Alan Siegel, *Dreams That Can Change Your Life* (Los Angeles: Jeremy P. Tarcher, 1990).
Linda Sheppard, *Wake Up to Your Dreams* (London: Blandford, 1994).

EPIGRAPH
1. Paramahansa Yogananda, *Sayings of Paramahansa Yogananda* (Los Angeles: Self-Realization Fellowship, 1968).

SELECTED FICTION
James Agee, *A Death in the Family* (New York: Bantam Books, 1981; originally published in 1938). A classic!
Elizabeth Berg, *Talk Before Sleep* (New York: Random House, 1994). While this is not a memoir, it reads like one. Two friends, one dying of breast cancer, help themselves, each other, and their families to grow.

Rebecca Brown, *The Gifts of the Body* (New York: HarperCollins, 1994). A gritty, superb novel about a health-care worker who takes us into the homes of the AIDS patients she tends.

Margaret Craven, *I Heard the Owl Call My Name* (New York: Doubleday, 1973). A beautiful, beautiful book. Find the film if you can.

Michael Cristofer, *The Shadow Box* (New York: Avon, 1977). A gripping play.

Thomas Mann, *The Magic Mountain* (New York: Vintage Books, 1992). This book was my companion during a serious illness at age twenty. I lived it.

Gail Perry and Jill Perry, *A Rumor of Angels: Quotations for Living, Dying and Letting Go* (New York: Ballantine, 1989). Includes inspirational excerpts from fiction, essays, and poetry.

Leo Tolstoy, *The Death of Ivan Ilych* (New York: NAL, 1960). A classic on life meaning.